FOOD LOVERS'
GUIDE TO
WASHINGTON, D.C.

Help Us Keep This Guide Up to Date

We would love to hear from you concerning your experiences with this guide and how you feel it could be improved and kept up to date. Please send your comments and suggestions to:

editorial@GlobePequot.com

Thanks for your input, and happy travels!

FOOD LOVERS' SERIES

FOOD LOVERS'
GUIDE TO
WASHINGTON, D.C.

The Best Restaurants, Markets & Local Culinary Offerings

1st Edition

Beth Kanter

Guilford, Connecticut

Editor: Amy Lyons
Project Editor: Lynn Zelem
Layout Artist: Mary Ballachino
Text Design: Sheryl Kober
Illustrations © Jill Butler with additional art by Carleen Moira Powell and MaryAnn Dubé
Maps: Daniel Lloyd © Morris Book Publishing, LLC

ISBN 978-0-7627-7317-6

Printed in the United States of America
10 9 8 7 6 5 4 3 2 1

All the information in this guidebook is subject to change. We recommend that you call ahead to obtain current information before traveling.

Contents

Introduction, 1

How to Use This Book, 6

Getting Started, 7

Keeping Up with Food News, 7

Food Festivals & Events, 8

Curbside Kitchens: D.C.'s Food Truck Fleet, 23

**The Return of the Milkman:
Delectable Home Deliveries, 39**

To Market, To Market, 54

Brick & Mortar Shops, 56

Farmers' Markets, 67

Pick-Your-Own Produce (Overalls Optional), 73

Cultural Cuisine:
Where Food, Art & History Meet . . . to Eat, 81

Coffee, Tea & Cafes, 92

Yum's the Word:
Underground Restaurants & Speakeasies, 102

The Most Important Meal of the Day:
Breakfast, Brunch & Other Happy Thoughts, 112

    Breakfast Served All Day, 112

    Brunch & Other Morning Meals, 118

Lunch, 130

    Power Lunch, 130

    Casual Lunch, 138

Pizza, Burgers & Falafel, 146

    Pizza, 146

Burgers, 154

Falafel, 156

Dinner, 159

Tasting Tables, 160

Hotel Hot Spots, 164

Nights Out, 172

Fun & Funky, 176

Neighborhood Feel, 182

Casual Eats, 188

Oh, Sweetie:
Cupcakes, Chocolate, Ice Cream & More, 190

Bakeries, 191

Frozen Treats, 200

Feeding Your Soul: Making a Difference with Food, 210

Cooking Classes, 220

Foodie Getaways, 230

    Frederick for Foodies: Frederick, Maryland, 233

    Eat, Stroll, Shop: Leesburg, Virginia, 245

    Almost Heaven: Berkeley Springs, West Virginia, 254

    Seaside Capital: Annapolis, Maryland, 264

    Subtly Southern: Culpeper, Virginia, 275

    Horse & Hunt Country: Middleburg, Virginia, 286

Recipes, 293

    Grassroots Gourmet's Peanut Butter Buttercream (Sara Fatell and Jamilyah Smith-Kanze of Grassroots Gourmet), 295

    Empanada de Pollos Ensapados (Chef José Andrés for the National Gallery of Art, Garden Cafe), 297

Louisiana Crawfish Etouffée with Mahatma Rice (Chef de Cuisine Chris Clime and Executive Chef Jeff Tunks of Acadiana), 300

Grilled Red Wine Braised Octopus with Smoked Avocado, Roasted Olive Gremolata & Olive Aioli (Executive Chef and General Manager Daniel Bortnick of Firefly), 302

Roasted Beet Salad (Executive Chef Brian McBride and Chef de Cuisine Eric Fleischer of Blue Duck Tavern), 305

Geeta's Chai (Chef Geeta of Hush Supper Club), 306

Shellfish Stew with Coconut & Lime (Executive Chef John Critchley of Urbana Restaurant and Wine Bar), 307

Wild Rice Salad from the National Museum of the American Indian's Mitsitam Cafe (Smithsonian's National Museum of the American Indian, Restaurant Associates, and Fulcrum Books), 309

Miriam's Kitchen Venison Pot Pie (Miriam's Kitchen), 311

"Cream" of Asparagus Soup (Sara Polon of Soupergirl), 313

Scallop Margarita with Tequila Ice (Ris Lacoste of RIS), 314

Zola Strawberry Basil Smash (Zola), 317

Gluten-Free Pecan Butterscotch Cake (Executive Pastry Chef Chris Kujala of RIS, in honor of the 90th Anniversary of the Phillips Collection), 318

CapMac Bolognese (Chef Brian Arnoff of the CapMac food truck), 321

Grandma Goodell's Famous Chocolate Chip Cookies (Or, The "Be Well and Happy" Cookie), 323

Estadio Spice-Grilled Chicken (Estadio Executive Chef Haidar Karoum), 325

Appendices, 327

Appendix A: Eateries by Type, 328

Appendix B: Cooking Classes, Shopping, Food-Related Services, and Agriculture, 338

Index, 341

About the Author

Beth Kanter's books and articles help visitors and locals alike experience the tastes, sights, and sounds that make up Washington, D.C. Beth reviews hotels for the *Fodor's Washington, D.C.* series and has authored the most recent *Michelin Green Guide Washington, D.C.* Her essays and articles have appeared in a variety of publications, including *Wondertime, Parents, Kiwi, American Baby, Shape,* and the *Chicago Tribune*. Beth teaches writing workshops and has an MSJ from Northwestern's Medill School of Journalism. She is also the author of *Day Trips from Washington, D.C. (*Globe Pequot Press). You can visit her online at www.bethkanter.com.

Acknowledgments

The experience of food, really good food, rarely happens alone. Carefully choreographed meals are meant to be shared with others—friends, family, coworkers and loved ones. I am beyond lucky to have so many who have helped me on the food-fueled journey of writing this book. Thank you to Amy Lyons for approaching me for this feast of a task and for once again being so lovely to work with on this project. Thanks to Lynn Zelem and the entire team at Globe Pequot Press for the editing and other magic that turns a manuscript file into a book. Thank you to those who generously shared recipes for the book: Brian Arnoff, Brian McBride, Daniel Bortnick, John Critchley, Sara Fatel, Eric Fleischer, Geeta, Haidar Karoum, Chris Kujala, Ris Lacoste, Miriam's Kitchen, the National Gallery of Art, Sara Polon, Jamilyah Smith-Kanze, the Smithsonian's National Museum of the American Indian, Jeff Tunks, and Zola.

Thank you to those who cheered me on, made suggestions, recommendations, introductions, lent me power cords, and broke bread (and cupcakes, cocktails, and curry, too) with me along the way, including Melissa Hecht, Alyson Weinberg, Sharon Samber, Gayle Neufeld, Steve Neufeld, Laurie Moskowitz, Jackie Eyl, Jenna Schnuer, Jessica Nemeth, and Elissa Froman.

Gabriel and Miriam, my sushi-loving son and frozen-yogurt-adoring daughter, put up with the many hours I spent in front of my computer and away from the house. I'll try to remember this next time you ask me to go to Yogiberry after school or order Meiwah for dinner—just not every time. Jeff, thanks for feeding my soul to say nothing of feeding our family with your cooking and caring ways. Any meal with you is good one.

Introduction

When I first moved to Washington, D.C. in 1991 it was a city filled with cherrywood reproductions, navy pinstripe suits, and heavy steak dinners. At that time that city offered little in the way of creative culture, counter or otherwise. Many, including myself, spent considerable time lamenting the fact that a (fill in the blank: good piece of pizza, good ice cream cone, good bagel, good deli sandwich, good take out . . .) was hard to find. Restaurants seemed to be clustered in a few office-heavy areas, many of which closed up shop not long after quitting time. A few exceptions existed here and there along with the promise that D.C. one day might find its identity beyond its monuments. Fast-forward 20-plus years and I am pleased to say that this town has skyrocketed beyond what most of us could have ever hoped for in 1991. Today Washington not only has its own vibe, it proudly owns it, and this is perhaps best seen through its food. One part East Coast city, one part Chesapeake Bay, and one part Southern with a dash of Capital pride for seasoning, the D.C. food scene takes bits and pieces from elsewhere and, like a good recipe, combines them to make something new.

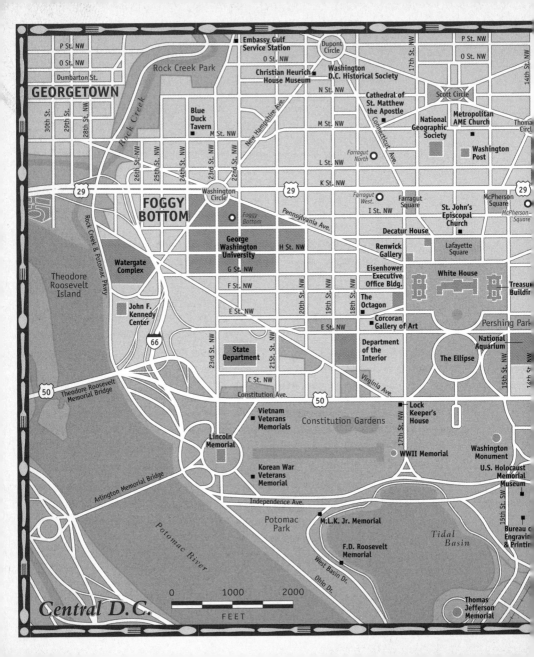

Washington's food scene offers locals and visitors choices that go far beyond a grilled meat with a potato and two sides. D.C. boasts destination restaurants, creative cuisine, underground supper clubs, and holes-in-the-wall. Chefs come here to experiment with new concepts and new dishes. The farm-to-table movement continues to soar here no doubt in large part due to the city's close proximity to a host of independent farms in nearby Maryland, Virginia, Pennsylvania, and West Virginia. Restaurant kitchens and markets tap into the bounty of locally sourced fresh ingredients so easily available in our corner of the world. Experimental, ethnic, trendy, and neighborhood restaurants fill the city with choices like Komi, Estadio, and the Blue Duck Tavern leading the pack. Smaller off-the-beaten-path spots like Thai X-ing, Amsterdam Falafel, or the Greek Deli keep the tradition of neighborhood favorites alive and well. The dessert heaven that is Baked & Wired is either a reminder of a higher power or, at the very least, the power of butter mixed with eggs and sugar. Markets from the picturesque Dupont Circle FRESHFARM Market on Sunday mornings to the grittier wholesale treasure hunt that is the Florida Market provide enough variety that you might never look at a supermarket in the same way again. If you don't find what you are looking for in a traditional form, look for it on four wheels in the shape of a food truck with CapMac, Fojol Bros. of Merlindia, and Red Hook Lobster Pound leading the fleet. Washingtonians have become so enamored with the food truck trend that on any given day D.C.'s food truck chatter on Twitter comes second to only California's, where the rolling restaurants began. If the trucks, restaurants, and markets aren't enough for you, consider taking your search underground, where secret supper clubs like Hush bubble up below the surface.

Food Lovers' Guide to Washington, D.C. is designed to help you experience them all. Think of it as a guide to Washington steered by the sense of taste. Countless wonderful (to say nothing of flavorful) hours were spent browsing farm stands, tasting small plates, sipping creative concoctions, and chatting with chefs to uncover the best. As a result, this book is not just a collection of restaurant reviews or a list of products to buy but rather a blueprint for experiencing this fabulous city through food. I focused primarily on the indie spots within city limits for the texture and taste they bring to the city, and I hope you will continue to add to the list with your own discoveries.

Food connects us in a way little else does. Celebrations often center on a specific dish or meal while special recipes or tastes can bring us back to a time and place otherwise forgotten. Often more reliable than memory and more alive than a snapshot, food helps define time and place. And the food and experiences listed in this book help define this great city that I love calling home. I have tasted my way through the town and have included the restaurants, shops, and markets that together make up a kind of edible tapestry of the city. From well-established historic spots to the new crop of underground restaurants, D.C.'s food scene defines an important part of the city and the people who live here. I hope that this book helps connect you, as it has me, to Washington, be it your first meal here or your thousandth.

How to Use This Book

This book focuses on how to experience the city through its food and flavors. Each market, restaurant, and cafe helps paint a whole picture of the city. As a result many of the listings found among these pages reflect the neighborhood where they are found. The eateries along 14th Street tend to be the most urban, with a vibe that at times feels light years away from the 24-hour news cycles and other political trappings. Many of the restaurants along this strip of the city tend not to take reservations, giving the people who live around the corner the same access to the tables as those who drive in from the suburbs. A similarly urban vibe can also be found among the restaurants along the expanding H Street Corridor in Northeast. Many new foodie favorites can be found in the area surrounding Eastern Market and in particular along the ever-growing Barracks Row. Look for other clusters of restaurants and cafes of all shapes and sizes in busy Penn Quarter and Dupont Circle, while the ones on Capitol Hill and in Georgetown cater to more formal crowds and business meals.

Restaurants that demonstrate a strong commitment to the local food movement have been identified as such. Kitchens and staff who do a particularly good job in offering gluten-free choices—or have special gluten-free menus or offerings—are noted. Eateries that stand out as vegan and vegetarian friendly have also been noted.

Price Code

Restaurants at all price points can be found in most of these neighborhoods. Prices are based on dinner entrees for two before tax.

$	**Inexpensive ($20 or less)**
$$	**Moderate ($20 to $40)**
$$$	**Expensive ($40 to $60)**
$$$$	**Splurge ($60 and up)**

Getting Started

In order to help you navigate the actual scene, try out the virtual one first. **Destination DC** (www.washington.org) is a good first stop.

Keeping Up with Food News

Consider signing up for the regular emails from **Tasting Table** (www.tastingtable.com) and **Daily Candy** (www.dailycandy.com/

washington-dc/) for a once-a-day dose of what's new and notable in the world of D.C. food. *Washington City Paper*'s **Young and Hungry** is a must-check (www.washingtoncitypaper.com) as are *Washingtonian* magazine's food blogs, such as **Best Bites** (www.washingtonian .com). Other bookmark-worthy bloggers include **Metrocurean** (www .metrocurean.com), **Eat Washington** (www.eatwashington.com), the **Arugula Files** (http://arugulafiles.typepad.com), **D.C. Foodies** (www.dcfoodies.com), **Capital Spice** (www.capitalspiceblog.com), **The District Domestic** (http://sarahmeyerwalsh.wordpress.com), and the delightful **Wild and Crazy Pearl** (www.wildandcrazypearl .com).

Food Festivals & Events

January

Annual Seed Exchange at Brookside Gardens, Wheaton, MD; (301) 962-1400; www.montgomeryparks.org/brookside. Chase away the winter blues by beginning to plan for this year's kitchen garden.

Capital Wine Festival, www.capitalwinefestival.com. A series of dinners hosted by either featured winemakers or proprietors is the focus of this prestigious event.

Sugar & Champagne Affair, http://support.washhumane.org. An elegant evening of sweets and drinks for foodies and their four-legged friends that benefits the Washington Humane Society.

Winter Restaurant Week, www.restaurant wkmetrodc.org. For one week many of the city's top restaurants offer special multicourse menus at special prices. Restaurant Week has quickly become a favorite week for foodies and bargain hunters alike, so make your reservations early so you don't get shut out.

February

Berkeley Springs International Water Tasting and Competition, Berkeley Springs, WV; www.berkeleysprings.com/water. Sparkling, still, and municipal waters from around the globe compete for the honor of being named the best during the annual competition.

International Wine and Food Festival, www.wineandfooddc .com. A yearly weeklong festival celebrating cuisine and culture, filled with special events, tastings, new products, and exhibits. A 2-day tasting is held at the Ronald Reagan Building and International Trade Center and is a must for any foodie.

St. Jude Gourmet Gala, www.stjude.org. The best local chefs and restaurants provide the food for this elegant evening that raises money for children with life-threatening illnesses.

March

Chocolate Lovers Festival, Fairfax, VA; http://chocolatefestival
.net. Chocolate tastings, art created from chocolate, and a Kiwanis
pancake breakfast featuring chocolate chip pancakes, are some of
the highlights of this annual event held in Fairfax's Old Town.

**Cunningham Falls State Park Annual Maple Syrup
Demonstration,** Thurmont, MD; (301) 271-7574; www.dnr.state
.md.us/publiclands/western/cunninghamfalls.html. Held during
two weekends in March, a look into how the sweet stuff gets from
tree to pancake.

The Great Latke vs. Hamentasch Debate, http://jewishstudy
center.org. Sponsored by the Jewish Studies Center, the age-old
debate about which is tastier, Hanukkah's potato pancake or Purim's
triangular cookies.

April

ARTINI Cocktail Celebration, www.corcoran.org. At the
Corcoran Gallery of Art, mixologists from the best restaurants and
lounges in town are shown specific works from the museum before
being challenged to use them as the inspiration to create an artistic
martini that captures the spirit of the artwork. In addition to the
competing "artinis," the event also features music, art viewings,
and a dessert buffet.

The Food Safety Summit Conference and Exhibition, www
.foodsafetysummit.com. Food safety products, solutions, and information fill the exhibit hall during this meeting, which also includes
educational seminars.

The Heart of America Foundation's Sweet Charity, www
.heartofamerica.org. Dozens of award-winning chefs come together
to create tasting stations at this annual event that raises money to
purchase books for children in need.

Leesburg Flower and Garden Festival, Leesburg, VA; www
.leesburgva.gov. A celebration and sale of everything garden.

Open-Air French Market. It's Georgetown meets Paris
every spring at this annual event where you can
nibble on French treats as you
browse and shop along the
cobblestone sidewalks of
Book Hill.

**Share Our Strength's
Taste of the Nation,**
www.strength.org. The country's premier chefs and mixologists donate their time, talent,
and creations to raise money to end hunger.

Songkran Festival, Silver Spring, MD; www.watthaidc.org/ watdc10. Thai New Year Festival in Silver Spring with lots of authentic and unusual dishes.

Southern Maryland Celtic Festival and Highland Gathering, Prince Frederick, MD; (443) 404-7319; www.cssm.org. Held on the grounds of the Jefferson Patterson Park and Museum, the festival is the state's oldest Celtic celebration.

May

Delaplane Strawberry Festival, Delaplane, VA; www.delaplanestrawberryfestival.com. A celebration of all things strawberry.

The Food and Wine Festival at National Harbor, National Harbor, MD; www.wineand foodnh.com. Food and wine with a waterside views.

Food Festival of the Americas, www.oas.org. A flavorful afternoon held in the Aztec Gardens of the Main Building of the Organization of American States.

Frederick Beer Week, Frederick, MD; www.frederickbeer.com. A celebration of the growing craft beer in and around the charming town of Frederick.

Hearts Delight Wine Tasting and Auction, www.hearts delightwineauction.org. Exclusive tastings, dinners and receptions benefiting the American Heart Association.

Lamb Jam, www.fansoflambdc.com. All lamb, all the time as top restaurants and chefs prepare and experiment with the meat to make an array of gastronomic creations to pair with specially selected wines.

Mount Vernon's Spring Wine Festival and Sunset Tour, www.mountvernon.org. Virginia wine, live blues, and sunset tours are served up at this festival held at historic Mt. Vernon. Held again in Oct.

National Asian Heritage Festival, www.asiaheritagefoundation .org. An array of pan-Asian food is part of this street festival that in the past has even featured a flash mob.

The Phillips Collection's Annual Gala, www.phillipscollection .org. Dine among the museum's masterpieces at this annual black-tie gala.

Richmond Greek Festival, Richmond, VA; (804) 358-5996; www .greekfestival.com. A celebration of Greek culture with food, music, dance, crafts, and cathedral tours.

ZooFari, www.nationalzoo.si.edu. Sample food from more than 100 of the area's best restaurants at this night of fun, animals, wine, and food at the Smithsonian's National Zoo.

June

Lavender Farm Festival, Catlett, VA; (540) 788-4352; www .sevenoakslavenderfarm.com. A celebration bathed in soft fragrant purple including lavender-infused eatables.

Manassas Wine and Jazz Festival, Manassas, VA; www.visit manassas.org. A popular annual event held on Father's Day at the Harris Pavilion in Old Town Manassas.

Park Hyatt Masters of Food & Wine Tour of the World, http://parkwashington.hyatt.com. Award-winning chefs pair their best creations with exquisite wines. The Park Hyatt Washington is one of four hotels worldwide that sponsor the exclusive event.

Safeway National Capital Barbecue Battle, www.bbqdc.com. Watch and taste as teams and restaurants battle it out for the title of National Pork Barbecue Champion. Tens of thousands gather on Pennsylvania Avenue near the Mall for the charred extrava- ganza, and all proceeds benefit the Boys & Girls Club of Greater Washington.

SAVOR: An American Craft Beer & Food Experience, www .savorcraftbeer.com. A weeklong celebration of craft beer.

Tilghman Island Seafood Festival, Tilghman Island, MD. On the fourth Saturday in June, island dwellers and visitors gather in Kronsberg Park to celebrate the food from the sea, with music, crab races, a parade, and lots of seafood.

July

Asia Festival, Fairfax, VA; www.asianfestivaldc.com. The rich heritage and diversity of Asian culture and nations are the focus of this annual festival held on the campus of George Mason University.

Brew at the Zoo, www.nationalzoo.si.edu. The National Zoo's annual beer-tasting fundraiser.

Fauquier County Fair, Warrenton, VA; (540) 351-6086 or visit www.fauquierfair.org. A more than 50-year-old county fair.

Montgomery County Farm Tour and Harvest Sale, Various locations in MD; (301) 590-2823; www.montgomerycountymd.gov/farmtour. A chance to tour some the county's farms including many not usually open to the public. Held the fourth weekend in July.

Reggae Festival, Mt. Airy, MD; (301) 831-5889; www.linganore-wine .com. Music and red, red wine at the event held at the Linganore Winecellers Vineyard and Winery.

Smithsonian Folklife Festival, www.festival.si.edu. For 2 weeks every summer the Smithsonian Folklife Festival celebrates international cultures past and present. The festival is free to the public, takes place on the National Mall, and features authentic and diverse foods, available for purchase, from the different cultures and countries highlighted that year.

Summer Fancy Food Show, www.specialtyfood.com. Trade show and exhibition sponsored by the National Association for the Specialty Food Trade.

August

Homestead Farm Corn Roast, Poolesville, MD; (301) 977-3761; www.homestead-farm.net. A beloved tradition at a beloved pick-your-own farm.

Maryland State Fair at the Timonium Fairground, www.chocolatefestival.net. Everything from funnel cakes to corn dogs.

Summer Restaurant Week, www.restaurantweekmetrodc .org. The same as the winter week, but with hotter outside temperatures. Book your favorite table early as the in-demand eateries in town roll out special menus and special prices for lunch and dinner.

September

Adams Morgan Day Festival, www.adamsmorgandayfestival.com. A favorite of the many D.C. neighborhood days.

Barrack's Row Festival, www.barracksrow.org. A military chef cook off is one of the fun events that takes place during this annual fall event celebrating the Capitol Hill corridor and its revitalization.

Brainfood Grill-Off, www.brain-food.org. A grilling competition where both amateurs and professionals compete.

DC VegFest, www.dcvegfest.com. A day of meat-free merriment.

Fiesta Washington, DC, www.fiestadc.org. Parades, performances, and lots of authentic cuisine help define this colorful celebration of D.C.'s Latino community that began in 1971.

Germantown Oktoberfest, Germantown, MD; www.germantownoktoberfest.org. The Biergarten is one of the most popular tents at the almost 30-year-old celebration.

Grapes with the Apes, www.nationalzoo.si.edu. Sip wine and toast the great apes at this annual wine-tasting fundraiser.

H Street Festival, http://hstreet.org. One of D.C.'s most up-and-coming neighborhoods celebrates itself and all its hip glory during this event which even includes a pie eating contest by one of the local bakeries.

Maryland Irish Festival, Timonium, MD; www.irishfestival.com. Dart, Fleadh, and Men In Kilts, competitions are held during this celebration of the culture and flavors of the Emerald Isle.

Maryland Renaissance Festival, Annapolis, MD; www.rennfest .com. Mead, steak on a stake, and smoked turkey legs as far as the eye can see.

Maryland Seafood Festival, Annapolis, MD; www.mdseafood festival.com. A crab soup cook-off and a children's mermaid parade are among the many highlights at this annual Annapolis event.

Maryland Wine Festival, Westminster, MD; www.marylandwine festival.org. Local wine and local food are the order of the day at this decades old festival.

The Mid-Atlantic Red Fruit Festival , http://redfruitfestival .wordpress.com. An annual reception celebrating all things and all dishes tomato. Expert chefs create tomato-inspired meals and wine pairings. Home chefs and enthusiastic gardeners also help present tomato tastings and sessions at the Ronald Reagan Building and International Trade Center.

Washington Ukrainian Festival, www.standrewuoc.org. Handmade borsch, pierogi, and halusky are some of the delicacies found at this annual cultural celebration.

Wine Entrepreneur Conference, Wheaton, MD; www.gira ventures.com. A meeting of wine entrepreneurs and hospitality professionals from across the nation who come together for targeted seminars and programs.

October

Berkeley Springs Apple Butter Festival, Berkeley Springs, WV; (800) 447-8797, www.berkeleysprings.com/apple. Annual apple butter–making contest celebrated with a parade, sidewalk sales, music, and lots of other fun small-town activities including a beard and mustache contest.

Bowie International Festival, Bowie, MD; (301) 262-6200. Art, food, song, and dance from around the globe held the first Saturday of October at Allen Pond Park.

Butler's Orchard Annual Pumpkin Festival, Germantown, MD; www.butlersorchard.com. Hay rides, cider, caramel apples, a rubber duckie derby and a straw maze are a few of the highlights at this fun-filled festival at the pick-your-own farm.

Dine Out for Farms, http://action.farmland.org. Participating restaurants raise money for the American Farmland Trust during the weeklong event.

La Festa Italiana, www.festaitalianadc.com. Italian food, wine, and culture.

Leesburg Kiwanis Halloween Parade, www.leesburgkiwanis .org. Candy, kids, costumes, and lots of Halloween fun for all ages.

Mount Vernon Wine Festival, www.mountvernon.org. Virginia wine, live blues, and sunset tours are served up at this festival held at historic Mt. Vernon. Also held in May.

Taste of Bethesda, Bethesda, MD; www.bethesda.org. More than 50 restaurants participate every year offering samples and other nibbles to the crowds.

Taste of Georgetown, www.tasteofgeorgetown.com. A chance to taste the best Georgetown has to offer.

Taste of Success, www.swpevents.org. Eat, sip, and schmooze to raise money for the mentoring program sponsored by StreetWise Partners.

Turkish Festival, www.turkishfestival.org. Turkish food, coffee, music, dance, and even a fortune-teller at this colorful and fun festival.

Virginia Wine Month, Various VA locations; www.virginiawine festival.org. A month devoted to Virginia's fruit of the vine.

Waterford Homes Tour and Crafts Exhibit, Waterford, MD; www.waterfordfoundation.org/fair. A juried crafts show of artisans from across the country and tours of the historic homes not often open to the public.

World Fare: A Street Food Festival, Arlington, VA, www .womenchefs.org. A gourmet street food festival put on by the local members and leadership of the Women Chefs & Restaurateurs (WCR).

November

FreshFarm Farmland Feast, www.fresh farmmarket.org. An elegant opportunity to celebrate the bounty of the season and the bay with a 5-course meal prepared by expert local chefs.

The Metropolitan Cooking and Entertaining Show, www .metrocooking.com. Celebrity chefs, party planners, personal chefs, kitchen designers, cookbook signings and caterers are some of the exhibitors at this massive consumer food show.

Oyamel Annual Day of the Dead "Dia de los Muertos" Festival, www.oyamel.com. Each year the Penn Quarter restaurant marks the ancient Mexican holiday with festivities and special dishes created by Owner José Andrés and Head Chef JohnPaul Damato.

December

Butler's Orchard Holiday Open House, Germanton, MD; www.butlersorchard.com. Hot chocolate, a marshmallow roast, and a hayride through a Christmas tree field take the chill out of winter at this family friendly event.

The National Building Museum Gingerbread Workshop, http://nbm.org. Learn to craft a tasty house using icing, gingerbread, and the architectural know-how of the experts at the National Building Museum.

National Harbor Outdoor Holiday Market, National Harbor, MD; www.nationalharbor.com. Do your holiday shopping while getting into the spirit of the season at this annual market.

Curbside Kitchens:
D.C.'s Food Truck Fleet

Before I started writing this book I must admit that I just didn't really get the food truck trend. Sure, it seemed a bit cute and I could get behind the camp of it all, but the thought of tracking down a truck and then waiting in line on the sidewalk for a meal just didn't appeal to me. If I wanted to go out then I wanted to have the option of being seated and served. Not to mention that the cynical side of me thought that the whole waiting-in-line-for-something-not-everyone-had brought to life a bad D.C. stereotype. And really, how good could food be from a truck? But after spending many hours in line and tasting the product of quality mobile kitchens, my mind has been changed. Bite by bite, I began to get it.

So today I stand before you as a food truck evangelical singing from the rafters about the mobile food craze and the many niche cuisines and creations it brings to the city. I now understand that these tricked-out, souped-up food wagons offer the chance to sample a range of cooking styles and recipes that otherwise might not make it onto the menu of a brick-and-mortar restaurant. Food trucks tend to have short, relatively inexpensive targeted menus that allow the owners to hyper-focus and perfect a recipe without worrying about achieving the balance you need at a sit-down establishment. The relatively low overhead allows owners and chefs to take more chances, offer good deals, and maybe even have more fun while doing it. But most important, so much of what is being served curbside is quite good.

Many of the folks who have taken the trend to the streets were inspired by the California scene, where the food truck trend initially exploded. I am now told that D.C. currently ranks not far behind the Golden State in Twitter activity about food trucks. Twitter stands as the single best way to become part of the food truck community. The trucks also post regular updates on Facebook and on their own sites, but Twitter will give you the up-to-the-minute reports on traffic delays, the day's menu, and what's sold out. Individual sites also state if the trucks accept credit cards or if it's a cash-only operation, as is the case for some of the wheeled vendors. In addition to following your favorite trucks individually, it's worth bookmarking http://Foodtruckfiesta.com, a real-time automated D.C. food truck tracker. The site also has updates on which new trucks are about to launch and keeps track of those trucks that have gone to the great

Top Five Things Not to Do While Waiting in Line at a Food Truck

(Sadly, I have seen all these transgressions committed.)

Do NOT wait until you get to the front of the line to start deciding what you want to order. (After waiting almost 2 hours on opening day of a new truck, the man in front of me didn't know what he wanted when it was his turn and only then started verbally debating the options for all of us behind him to hear. Sir, you had 2 hours to ponder the 6-item menu. I beg of you, don't tempt karma, or the line of hungry Washingtonians behind you, in this awful way.)

Do NOT mention people you know to a friend by first and last names and then speak ill of them or reveal intimate secrets they would not like shared with the lunchtime rush. Let's just say, I know who you were talking about.

Do NOT chat on speakerphone.

Do NOT repeatedly complain about the length of the line or how it's so important for you to get back to work. You doth protest too much, methinks.

Do NOT let a large group of your friends cut you in line. It makes the rest of us feel like we are in 7th grade and nobody wants to go back to 7th grade.

parking lot in the sky. If you can't decide what to try first, check out the monthly Truckeroo (www.truckeroodc.com) festival where dozens of trucks roll in together to serve the masses. The event is held June through Oct from 11 a.m. to 9 p.m. across the street from the Navy Yard Metro stop in Southeast. On Thursday from 6:30 to 8 p.m. the urban hip Chinatown Coffee Co. sponsors Food Truck Thursdays, a kind of food truck happy hour with about a half dozen of the more popular vendors.

This chapter offers a snapshot of the current world of D.C. food trucks. It talks about some of the fan favorites as well as some of the trucks that still cruise right below the radar. So go chase your poison, be it a lobster roll, a Korean taco, or a corned beef sandwich. Look both ways before you cross the street, bring small bills, and enjoy every bite.

Big Cheese, www.bigcheesetruck.com; @bigcheesetruck; Comfort Food; $. Big Cheese grows up the quintessential childhood comfort meal of grilled cheese and tomato soup. The cheese comes from the wonderful Cowgirl Creamery and the bread from the delicious Lyon Bakery in Southwest. Five grilled creations make up the core of the menu and are rotated in and out depending on the day. Purists will want to stick with the classic version made with cheddar and sourdough. More adventurous types might want to try the chipotle goat cheese and roasted red peppers on sun-dried tomato bread or the grilled brie, Fuji apple, and honey on multigrain. Sandwiches are around $6.50 and the tomato soup is $2 for a small and $4 for a large.

CapMac, www.capmacdc.com; @CapMacDC; Comfort Food; $. I wouldn't be surprised if someone somewhere right now is writing an epic poem devoted to CapMac's CapMac'n Cheese. The cheddar cheese, elbow macaroni, and pimiento mix topped with crumbled Cheez-Its is divinely inspired stuff worthy of volumes. And this coming from a person who didn't think she liked half the ingredients in it. The warm cheesy creation with the slight crunch has made me a CapMac believer. You can even add a couple of meatballs to it. The truck has other warm gooey takes on the favorite childhood combo like a goat cheese mac with a broccoli pesto and spicy bread crumbs, and a Reuben version where the macaroni is smothered in a swiss and fontina cheese sauce, sauerkraut, house-made pastrami, and rye bread crumbs. Choices other than the classic version tend to change with the season. Most of the offerings cost either $6 or $8. Afternoon food coma at no additional charge. Cash only. See the recipe for **CapMac's Bolognese** on p. 321.

Carnivore BBQ, www.carnbbq.com; @carnbbq; Barbecue; $$. The soul of Carnivore BBQ is Ol' Smoky, a smoker that looks like a steam engine that was lovingly hand-pieced together by a disabled Vietnam veteran in Florida. The current owner and Pit Master Stephen Adelson strives to donate a portion of his profits to Ol' Smoky's creator. After years on the farmers' market scene, Ol' Smoky's pulled pork and brisket now are sold to the masses via the Carnivore BBQ truck, a converted '88 Chevy pick-up. Meat is locally

A Driving Force:
Food Trucks That Give Back

The food truck community as a whole does not have a blind spot when it comes to supporting local causes. Many of D.C.'s mobile eateries donate a percentage of their profits to worthy causes and groups right here in the town. Here is a list of some of the trucks that do a particularly good job at giving back:

TaKorean

Pleasant Pops

Eat Wonky

Fojol Brothers of Merlindia

Sweetflow Mobile

Pi Truck DC

sourced and all the sauces and rubs are made from scratch. A pulled pork sandwich will run you $8, beef brisket $9, and the combo $10. Supports the local food movement.

Cupcake Buggy, www.cupcakebuggy.com; @cupcakebuggy; Cupcakes; $. One of the newer players in the crowded cupcake field, Cupcake Buggy offers fun flavors like PB&J, coconut red velvet, and green tea and honey. The buggy also dabbles in fun seasonal creations. Keep an eye out for orange Creamsicle, sweet potato marshmallow, and cherry blossom as the year marches on. Gluten-free options and vegan/vegetarian friendly.

Curbside Cupcakes, www.curbsidecupcakes.com; @Curbside Cupcake; Cupcakes; $. Curbside Cupcakes and its fleet of pink trucks earned the distinction of being the first local food truck to bring the cupcake craze to the streets of Washington. Starting at around 10:30 a.m. on weekday mornings, Pinky I, Pinky II, and Pinky III hit the road loaded with the day's selection of flavors and continue on their routes until around 4 p.m. Red velvet is the truck's bestseller, with carrot cake, vanilla, and the intensely chocolate black cupcake as close seconds. In the summer the seasonal tequila cupcake, an orange cake with a tequila and butter cream icing, sells quickly, while in the winter seasonal favorites trend toward eggnog and gingerbread. Cupcakes off the truck cost $3 for one, $15 for 6, and $27 for a dozen. The trucks also do special events and can be hired to pull up to your front door, office party, or wedding reception. The pink cupcake mobile even made a behind-the-scenes cameo when the *Transformers* movie was filming in town.

DC Empanadas, www.dcempanadas.com; @DCEmpanadas; Latin/Caribbean; $. All empanadas, all the time. DC empanadas breaks down its offerings into four categories—beef, pork, chicken, and vegetarian. The website lists all the possible choices in each categories, but as with most food trucks the menu changes daily and is a small sampling of what's on the comprehensive list. (Hey, it's a small food truck not an 18-wheeler.) Many of DC Empanadas' stuffed pastries boast fabulous names. Cases in point: The Weapons of Max Deliciousness (chili, beans, and cheddar cheese), the Mr. Miyagi (chicken with fresh veggies tossed in a spicy ginger teriyaki sauce) and the Ménage à Trois (brie, figs, and Marcona almonds).

DC Slices, www.dcslices.com; @dcslices; Pizza; $. DC Slices is helping to fill D.C.'s pizza-by-the-slice void one stop at a time. The popular truck bakes the pies on board and offers a bunch of different toppings and combos like pepperoni, Hawaiian, and Italian sausage. Fresh basil, Parmesan cheese, oregano, and crushed red pepper are available upon request. The basil is a fan favorite for good reason. Tater tots and mozzarella sticks are also sold. The large thin-crust slices cost $4.

Eat Wonky, www.eatwonky.com; @eatwonky; Comfort Food; $. One of the first successful food trucks to drive on to the D.C. scene, Eat Wonky serves a simple yet delicious menu revolving around Wonky Fries. Known to our neighbors in the great white north as *poutine,* Wonky fries combine french fries, gravy, and cheese curds to create a dish that resides on the border between sinful and spiritual. The truck's most popular sell is the Wonky Dog, which is a hot dog in a bun topped with Wonky Fries. It sells for $6. You can also

Good to Go

Several brick and mortar restaurants here in town have taken to the streets to bring truth, justice, and lunch to the hungry people of our fair city. Here are some popular ones along with their Twitter handles.

DC Pie Truck from Dangerously Delicious Pies, @dcpietruck. Sweet and savory pies from the folks at Dangerously Delicious.

District of Pi's Pi on Wheels, @PiTruckDC. You don't have to be a math geek to appreciate the anything-but-formulaic deep-dish cornmeal-crust pizza made by the 3.14-loving folks at District of Pi. Gluten-free crusts and vegan cheese can be ordered at the restaurant.

Sweetgreen's Sweetflow Mobile, @SweetflowMobile. Sky-high salads and tart frozen yogurt are the order of the day on this healthy traveling arm of the popular local Sweetgreen chain.

buy grilled cheese, the dog without the fries, fries minus the wonk, and whoopie pies for dessert.

Fojol Brothers of Merlindia, www.fojol.com; @fojolbros; Indian; Ethiopian; $. The Fojol truck serves up curry with a side of shtick. Clad in brightly colored turbans and bad fake mustaches, the five "brothers" (only two of whom are technically related) serve popular Indian and Ethiopian street food from the far-out but fully fictional lands of Merlindia and Benethiopia. The truck usually offers two veggie options and two meat options. Choices include buttered chicken, *palak paneer,* cauliflower and potatoes, *saag paaner,* chicken masala, berbere lentils, *shiro* with beef, and split peas. You can order a small portion of one dish for $2, two larger portions for $6, or three "feast-size" portions for $9. The Indian-inspired dishes come served over fluffy basmati rice while the Ethiopian ones can be scooped up with the flatbread provided. The self-proclaimed traveling food circus of Fojol embraces a pretty strict green approach toward food trucking. Food comes on biodegradable trays and with equally planet-friendly, junior-high-school-cafeteria-reminiscent sporks. Refreshing frozen Lossipops in flavors like ginger and mango coolly complement the spicy food. In addition to the lunch run, the truck also hits the downtown club scene when the sun goes down.

Halal Gyro Plus, @Halalgyroplus; Halal; $. Halal Gyro Plus lacks the fancy logo, funny tag lines, and other gimmicky approaches employed by so many of the other food trucks that take over downtown at lunch hour. The truck doesn't even have a website right now—just a Twitter account and a Facebook page. What it does have is simple, good food that is helping it to amass a steady following. The truck sells six choices—three gyro sandwiches (one lamb, one chicken, and one combo) and three different combo platters that come with rice and salad or veggies. The combo platters cost $6.99 and the gyros are $5.99. Cash only.

Hula Girl Truck, www.hulagirltruck.com; @hulagirltruck; Hawaiian; $. Mikala Brennan brings the aloha spirit to the streets of D.C. in the truck she tricked out to look like a 1950s surfboard-carrying station wagon. An Oahu native, Brennan's menu centers around her Hawaiian teriyaki recipe. Choose from steak, chicken, or tofu in either a sandwich or salad or on a plate with two sides. Spam musabi, mac salad, and sticky rice can be added to any order. Wash it down with a Hawaiian Punch or a Waialua soda in flavors like pineapple, lilikoi, or vanilla.

Pleasant Pops, www.pleasantpops.com; @pleasantpops; Ices; $. Let's start by saying this. Pleasant is an understatement. Inspired by traditional Mexican fresh-fruit ice pops called *paletas,* Pleasant Pops are a nothing short of fabulous, particularly on a hot and humid D.C. summer day. The frozen treats come in a variety of flavors, with the best ones combining flavors not typically paired in the world of desserts, like pineapple basil, sweet cream 'n corn, coconut curry, cucumber chile, and watermelon and black pepper. The ginger peach, Guac Pop (avocado and lime) and Chongos (Mexican sweet cream and cinnamon) also are not to be missed. The two 20-somethings behind the effort only use locally sourced dairy products, fruit, vegetables, and other ingredients. The company's truck, nicknamed Big Poppa, takes the pops to the streets every day. Priced at $2.50 per pop, the frozen delicacies are also sold at local farm markets, Chinatown Coffee Co., and Campus Fresh at George Washington University.

PORC, www.porcmobile.com; @porcmobile; Barbecue; $. Not surprisingly PORC (Purveyors Of Rolling Cuisine) specializes in, wait for it, pork. Cooked for 16 hours, the pulled pork sandwich tops the menu. The truck, a former US Postal service vehicle, changes its offerings daily and often rotates in other favorites like its green chile chicken sausages topped with pico de gallo and *queso fresco*. A veggie sandwich is almost always on the menu, too. Cookies on a stick, baked beans, and a vegetable of the day round out the choices found on this biodiesel-powered mobile kitchen. BBQ sandwiches are $7 and the vegetarian ones are a dollar less.

Red Hook Lobster Pound, www.redhooklobsterdc.com; @lobstertruckDC; Seafood; $$. A spontaneous crowd lining a downtown sidewalk during lunchtime means one of two things: either the president's motorcade is passing by or the Red Hook Lobster Truck is pulling up. The Red Hook Truck boasts some 20,000 Twitter followers and stands as the fan favorite of the D.C. food truck world. Lines can be hours long, but after the first bite of the sweet Maine lobster the wait is forgiven. Red Hook packs the truck with two kinds of lobster rolls. The Maine roll has big chunks of fresh lobster meat mixed with Red Hook's own lemon-based mayo and sliced celery, sea salt, and white pepper. The more straightforward Connecticut roll is just sweet lobster chunks gently sautéed in butter. All sandwiches come on buttered rolls toasted to perfection and come with a pickle spear. The truck also sells shrimp rolls (another fan favorite), Cape Cod potato chips, chocolate whoopie pies, Maine soda, homemade lemonade, and iced tea. During the winter indulge in a cup of hot New England clam chowder. Lobster rolls run $15 apiece. Shrimp rolls are $8. For an additional $3 you can make either a "meal" with chips and a soda.

Sixth & Rye, www.sixthandi.org/sixthandryefood truck.aspx; @sixthandrye; Kosher/Deli; $$. Your bubbe wouldn't know from a food truck but she would kvell over the corned beef on rye with house mustard served every Friday from the city's first kosher food truck. Created in conjunction with Top Chef and Member of the Tribe Spike Mendelsohn, Sixth and Rye is sponsored by the Sixth and I Historic Synagogue and finally brings good deli to the streets of D.C. The signature corned beef sandwich is the star of this truck. There also is a good grilled vegetable wrap and some exceptional homemade sides. The fresh-cut Yukon gold potato strips fried in peanut oil have the potential to be addictive and the Israeli couscous salad filled with chopped olives, sun-dried tomatoes, and shredded vegetables could almost stand as a light lunch on its own. For $12 you can get a sandwich, side, and drink. Not a bad deal, especially for

Top Five Suggestions for Keeping Busy While You're Waiting in Line for a Food Truck.

Tweet. Give the hungry masses some intel on the wait and what's available today.

Decide what to order. (See Number 1 on the What Not to Do List.)

Read a book. Hey, better yet, read this book.

Clean out your inbox.

Compose an original piece or music or a sonnet. But, please, do it in your head.

kosher food. The truck also sells whole loaves of braided challah to take home and black and white cookies for dessert.

Stix, www.eatstixnow.com; @eatstix; Shish Kabob; $. If you want to embrace the food truck experience without having the food truck experience embrace your waistline, Stix is the truck for you. The entire menu revolves around healthy choices that can be served on a stick. No forks or knives needed here. Flavorful, grilled lean meats, chicken, vegetables, and fruits are the basis for all of the offerings. The truck lists the Weight Watchers points for each menu item and even offers a bite-size dessert pop that is only 2 points and carries a $2 price tag. Meal sticks cost between $3.50 and $4.50 each.

Sweetbites Mobile Cafe, www.sweetbitesdesserts.com; @Sweetbitestruck; Bakery; $. Sandra Panetta understands the art and the science of baking, and the biochemist brings both to the delicious array of pastries she creates every day for her dessert truck. Loaded on board is a sweet mix of cupcakes, bars, cookies, scones, and muffins. All 11 of Panetta's cupcake flavors go out on the truck every day so you don't have to worry that it's not chocolate peanut butter day when you spot the truck in your hood. Other daily staples include the chocolate chip banana bar and cheesecake bites topped with the fruit-of-the-day. The rest of the menu is a rotation of the rest of the sweet offerings. Cupcakes are $3 and most of the other goodies are $2.50. Gluten-free options.

TaKorean, Korean BBQ Tacos, www.takorean.com; @taKorean; Tacos; Fusion; $. Taken with the Korean tacos he sampled on the west coast but unable to find a good substitute here in D.C., Mike Lenard perfected his own recipe and took it on the road. The response has been overwhelming. TaKorean is one of the most followed mobile food stations in the city with the long lines to prove it. Three fillings are always on board—bulgogi steak, tangy chicken, and caramelized tofu. Mike swears even the most devoted of carnivores like his tofu. You first get your choice of either a napa-romaine slaw done with rice vinegar, lime, and a sesame oil vinaigrette, or a spicy kimchee-style slaw made with fresh tossed, rather than brined, cabbage. Then you pick all or some of the four toppings of cilantro, sesame seeds, lime crema, and spicy *sriracha* sauce. Your choices are wrapped up in warm corn tortillas and make for a filling lunch that is not so heavy that you have to stumble back to the office with your belt loosened. You can also take a pass on the tortilla and have your choices served in a bowl. Vegan/ vegetarian friendly.

The Return of the Milkman:
Delectable Home Deliveries

The sun shines on a tidy pastel house surrounded by a white picket fence, a cheery yard with perfectly cut grass and several pots of pink geraniums. A knock comes at the door and a woman in a pressed apron and a non-medicated smile answers it but not before unconsciously patting her Aqua Net hairstyle in place. She answers the door to find the milkman dressed in spotless white and with a smile that matches hers and also seems too unnatural for the hour. He hands her today's delivery of a half-dozen glass bottles filled with the full-fat white stuff that she will pour for her family with everything from eggs over easy to meatloaf. They make small talk before he drives away and she goes back to the kitchen to contemplate laundry, dishes, and a Valium.

Milk delivered to your doorstep harkens back to simpler times, or at least back to the way those times were portrayed on those old sitcoms that run in the middle of the night. Even if the milkman wasn't always as affable as he appears on the tube or in my imagination, the part about not having to go to a supermarket or farm to buy fresh milk is indeed something that happened back in those black-and-white days, I am told. Add eggs, meat, and, in the case of my Brooklyn-born grandparents, seltzer to that list of fresh items that had a delivery route once upon a time. (Although I can't tell you what he wore because I don't recall ever seeing a seltzer man on TV Land.)

Thankfully home delivery of farm-fresh milk, eggs, and other goodies is no longer just for women with the last name Cleaver. The growing locavore movement has resulted in a new generation of milkmen and milkwomen. Many houses, apartments, and condos in the area now get regular deliveries of organic produce, meat, soup, cookies, and, of course, dairy products. The new crop of delivery-driven businesses tends to take orders online, giving participants a list of currently available products to peruse much like an online farmers' market. Some like Arganica Farm Club work on a subscription basis while others like Washington Green Grocer, a personal favorite, allow you to order every week or just once in a while. A deep commitment to seasonal locally sourced and sustainable ingredients drive many of these new world/small planet services—the fabulous Souper Girl and Grassroots Gourmet are perfect examples of environmental and social commitment driving a business model.

So pull a June Cleaver and give milk (or egg, bison meat, brownie, coffee, soup, or cheese) delivery a shot. I promise you won't get a sudden urge to press shirts or get behind the wheel of a Studebaker. Although after your first taste of Trickling Springs Creamery chocolate milk you might find yourself obsessively peeking out the window waiting for your next delivery.

Arganica Farm Club, 8287-A #110 Seminole Trail, Ruckersville, VA 22968; (434) 979-0480; www.arganica.com. Arganica acts as your personal link to the food chain. The food club makes eating locally easy by offering weekly deliveries of artisan and organic foods to its subscribers. All the food comes from local, family-run farms and organic growers. Arganica's products change every week to reflect what is in season and available, and they are always scouting new products to add to the lineup. The offerings can be as diverse as eggs, bison meat, live blue crabs, seltzer in glass bottles, forest mushrooms, and mill-ground flour. An order form with the long list of products is e-mailed to subscribers each week. In addition to ordering individual items from the weekly listing, you can also get a weekly Arganica Produce Crate, a rustic wooden box filled with a bounty of fruits and vegetables that represent what is fresh and good that week. The all-local option costs $35 and a smaller organic and local version is $25. There are some membership fees and minimum delivery charges based on how much and how often you order. D.C. residents get their crates on Thursday while subscribers outside of the city have a Sunday delivery date. The service will even pick up and take away member's compostables on delivery days. Arganica also maintains a nice blog on its website filled with recipes and fun information about the farms and finds of the week.

Bon Vivant, (703) 459-8458; www.bonvivantcompany.com. When Bon Vivant Founder Jawad Laouaouda was diagnosed with diabetes, it inspired him to commit himself to eating whole foods. Soon after his online farmers' market delivery service was born. Fine local food is the focus of Bon Vivant, which sells grass-fed beef,  free-range eggs, fresh dairy products, pure wildflower honey, free-range chickens, fair-trade organic coffee that is packaged locally, and even cocktail mixes made of local ingredients. The vast majority of the items come from seven farms throughout Virginia. Bon Vivant makes deliveries on Tuesday during two time windows—one in the late afternoon and one in the evening. Orders that total $100 or more carry no delivery charge and orders that total less than $100 have a $12.50 delivery fee tacked on to the total.

Field to City, www.fieldtocity.com. Field to City makes eating—and shopping—locally a click away. The web-based service delivers to your door organic food with an emphasis on items like produce, dairy products, meats, poultry, pork, and eggs that come from the Mid-Atlantic region. A host of organic and seasonal products ranging from brown basmati rice to cereal to unbleached coffee filters to fair trade French roast can also be added to your order. The milk comes from Pennsylvania's Trickling Springs Creamery and the eggs from Polyface, Inc., nestled in Virginia's Shenandoah Valley. It's like shopping at every great farm stand in Virginia, Maryland, and Pennsylvania without having to change out of your jammies.

First Vine, www.firstvine.com; Wine. If your fruit-of-the-vine fantasy involves traveling to off-the-beaten path European wineries to collect new bottles, but your wallet and schedule have other ideas, then a First Vine subscription can help make your dream come true. The Virginia-based wine importer and retailer delivers a carefully edited selection of wines predominantly from small producers in France, Italy, and Spain. Most bottles cost less than $15 and cannot otherwise be found in the area. Owners Tom Natan and Dare Wenzler regularly hit Europe's grapevine trail in search of new wineries and vintages. Recent finds include a 2008 Domaine Chaume-Arnaud La Cadène Côtes du Rhône Blanc, a 2005 Cave La Romaine Côtes du Ventoux Rouge, a 2006 Bodegas Fusión Lara O Crianza Ribera del

Duero, and a 2006 Cuvée des Templiers Côtes du Rhône Rosé. Each listing includes suggestions for food pairings. The wines' ability to be enjoyed with a variety of meals is one of the criteria the owners look for when on the hunt for new wines to add to the service. First Vine delivers to D.C., Virginia, California, and some parts of Alaska. Washington delivery is free when you order a half-dozen or more bottles and just $5 if you order fewer than six. You can also purchase a First Vine Wine Club membership, where you get two bottles every month for six months—you can choose all reds, whites, and rosés or opt for a mix of the three. Club and regular deliveries are made Monday through Saturday and must be received by a real, live sober person (really, the driver will not hand the wine over to someone who is visibly drunk). No porch or mailbox drop-offs.

Grassroots Gourmet, (202) 596-5448; www.grassrootsgourmet .org. Grassroots Gourmet is the Washington, D.C. equivalent of running away and joining the circus. Foodie Sara Fatell started her baking business while still working her day job in the nonprofit and progressive political worlds. Once she made her baking business her day job she began providing delicious cupcakes, cookies, and cakes—all made locally and consciously—to the many important causes she worked with on staff. Her cousin Jamilyah Smith-Kanze then joined the team and now Grassroots Gourmet is more than a passion project for the two. The cousins now bring sweet goodness to organizations and individuals around the city while holding on strong to their ethical and environmental business practices. Further keeping it in the family, most of the recipes come from their grandma. Red velvet anything is the pair's hands-down best seller and the Grassroots Gourmet's triple chocolate chip cookies packed with milk, dark, and white chocolate chips have a cult following. Lately Sara has been experimenting a lot with Nutella-based recipes (yum, you had me at Nutella, Sara) the result of which is delicacies like Nutella rugelach and vanilla Nutella whoopie pies. Vegan/vegetarian friendly. See the recipe for **Grassroots Gourmet's Peanut Butter Buttercream** on p. 295.

Harvest Delivered, 727 6th St. SE, Washington, DC 20003; (202) 544-4960; www.harvestdelivered.com. Harvest Delivered prides itself on only selling produce within 72 hours of being picked and only doing business with farms in the Chesapeake Bay region that embrace sustainable agricultural practices. The two owners scour local farms to find the best of what is fresh that week and then offer it to their subscribers. Harvest Delivered brings customers a weekly, every-other-week, monthly, or occasional box of locally grown, pesticide-free fruits and vegetables. You can also add organic eggs and farm-baked flatbread to any box. The smallest box costs $28 and the largest one $46.

Milk Moo-vers, 7548 East Howard Rd., Glen Burnie, MD 21061; (410) 320-0840; http://milkmoo-vers.com. The milkman cometh.

CSAs

The popularity of community-supported agriculture, or CSAs, continues to grow as city dwellers and suburbanites alike take more of an interest in eating locally. CSAs are a way for community members and farmers to enter into a mutually supportive relationship. Members pay a fee at the beginning of the year to the farm and then the farm pays out with a share of the crops produced over the course of the growing season. During good years members receive more and in bad years less. Sometimes members volunteer in the fields and often have the choice of either coming to the farm to harvest their share or pick up their share box at a designated location. Here are a few local CSAs:

Claggett Farm, 11904 Old Marlboro Pike, Upper Marlboro, MD 20772; (301) 627-4662; www.cbf.org. Claggett Farm has both pick-up sites and work shares where you pick your own veggies.

Great Country Farms, 18780 Foggy Bottom Rd., Bluemont, VA 20135; (540) 554-2073; www.greatcountryfarms.com. Great Country Farms offers pick-your-own and delivery shares.

The Lamb's Quarter, 8111 Bourne Rd., Owings, MD 20736; (443) 624-3365; www.thelambsquarter.com. In addition to vegetable shares, The Lamb's Quarter sells pastured meat shares and fresh egg shares. You can either pick up or have your shares dropped off at a predetermined site.

Norman's Farm Market, 8028 Inverness Ridge Rd., Potomac, MD 20854; www.normansfarmmarket.com. Pick-up sites are in Bethesda, Chevy Chase, Rockville, and Potomac. The brothers and owners operate farm stands and have a small farm in Woodbine, Maryland.

Sligo Creek Farm, 19715 Zion Rd., Brookeville, MD 20833; (240) 328-8180; www.sligocreekfarm.com. You can pick up your produce at locations in Rockville, Silver Spring, Olney, and Langley Park.

Milk Moo-vers brings fresh, organic, hormone-free dairy products straight from local family-owned farms to your home. The service prides itself on only working with farmers who treat their animals humanely and embrace ethical and environmental farming practices. Milk comes from Trickling Springs Creamery in Chambersburg in Pennsylvania, where the cows are grass-fed and the milk is pasteurized with a High Temp Short Time process. Aficionados can even order creamline milk, non-homogenized but still pasteurized milk where the cream naturally separates and rises to the top of the bottle. When milk that goes through a homogenization process, the cream stays suspended in the milk. Milk Movers currently deliveries to Anne Arundel County, Prince George's County, Baltimore County, Howard County, and some parts of Baltimore City. Yogurts, breads, butters, eggs, meats, cheeses, jams, honeys, and coffee can also be added to your order. You can also get organic Trickling Springs Creamery ice cream in flavors like chocolate marshmallow, peppermint, and blueberry delivered to your front door.

Soupergirl, (202) 609-7177; www.thesoupergirl.com. Think of Sara Polon as the anti-Soup Nazi. Polon ladles out her broths and stews with a smile and includes "love" as one of the regular healthy, vegetarian, organic, locally and ethically sourced ingredients she uses in her soups.

Polon got the idea for a soup subscription business after reading Michael Pollan's *The Omnivore's Dilemma* several years ago. The book inspired her to join the local food movement and soon thereafter her new alter ego, Soupergirl, was born. Soups need to be ordered a week in advance. Polon always offers a smooth or pureed choice and a heartier "chunky" selection. You can also order a grain salad of the week—usually some type of couscous, quinoa, or whole-grain pasta—and vegan corn bread or pita chips. The items are either delivered straight to your home or you can pick your order up at one of the dozen or so pre-designated delivery sites around D.C., Maryland, and Virginia. Sara's Soupermom, Marilyn Polon, is responsible for recipe development and the dynamic mother-daughter duo spend every Monday and Tuesday together cooking up pot after pot of delicious, healthy vegan soup. The West African Safari Soup, a peanut stew created from homemade peanut butter, is the current customer favorite. Sara points to the Maple Syrup Roasted Butternut Squash soup as her favorite, although she doesn't like being asked to choose between her children. And Soupermom loves anything and everything lentil.

The secret to deciding the soup menu is simple, she tells. It's always based on what the farmers have for her that week. And the secret for the super pair's close relationship in and out of the kitchen also is simple. "She is allowed to say whatever she wants," Sara tells. "She's allowed to say I need a haircut or that she hates what I am wearing because I brought her out of retirement to do this," she tells. "And, besides, she's Soupermom." Sara just opened a soup shop in Takoma Park, DC (314 Carroll St. NW). Kosher and vegan/vegetarian friendly. See the recipe for Soupergirl's **"Cream" of Asparagus Soup** on p. 313.

South Mountain Creamery, 8305 Bolivar Rd., Middletown, MD 21769; (301) 371-8565 or 877-COW-2-YOU (877-269-2968); www.southmountaincreamery.com. The milk from South Mountain Creamery and the kind that comes in a cardboard carton from the supermarket are both white and share a name, but the similarities stop there. The creamy, sweet milk that South Mountain Creamery delivers to its loyal Washington area subscribers is days, not weeks, old. You can taste the difference. The delivery service offers chocolate milk, strawberry milk, whole milk, skim milk, butter, cream, and heavy cream. (The chocolate milk is rich and divine.) A quart runs about $2.75 and a half-gallon, $3.75. There is also a $1.50 refundable deposit per bottle, so relax if one slips out of your hand while you are on a chocolate milk–induced high. You can also add cage-free eggs, cheese, meat, veal, butter, and yogurt to your order most weeks. You don't need to be at home when the delivery arrives but you do need to leave a cooler out. Orders can be made up until 2 days before your delivery day. If you want to see where the milk comes from, the farm is always open to visitors. The cows are milked—even the chocolate ones—between 1:30 and 5 p.m. The baby calves eat every day at 4 p.m. and you are welcome to help fed them.

Sunflower Bakery, (240) 361-3698; www.sunflowerbakery.org. Most cookies taste good. The ones from the Sunflower Bakery also make you feel good. The nonprofit Gaithersburg-based bakery serves as an on-the-job training program for adults with developmental and other cognitive disabilities. French macaroons, cream puffs, brownie pops, mandel bread, jam bars, cakes, and many varieties of yummy cookies come from Sunflower's busy kosher dairy-free kitchen. I especially recommend the ginger spice cookies and the frosted mini carrot cupcakes (you will swear there is butter in there). Individual orders can be submitted online and then picked up at one of several locations around town. Sunflower also runs a Sweets of the Month program through various local schools. Kosher and vegan/vegetarian friendly.

Urban Tastes, (202) 277-7251; www.urbantastes.com. Urban Tastes is fast food for the farmers' market set. The family-style meal delivery service allows anyone inside the Beltway to order home-cooked meals built around fresh local produce and healthy, tasty recipes. The process is relatively simple. You place your order by noon on Sunday and your meal will be delivered in an ice-filled cooler the following Tuesday afternoon along with instructions on how to reheat the food. Unlike many other meal services, you don't have to commit to regular deliveries. You can order once, every week, or every once in a while—your call. Some choices include Thai curry chicken, Thai curry tofu, lentil and summer squash salad, and tilapia with rice noodles. You can also choose from a few different side dishes like black-bean salad, edamame, and a mixed green salad with toasted pumpkin seeds, cranberries, and a miso

Urban Compost Dilemma

It's a modern problem. You want to compost but don't have the time or space. A few new businesses can help. These services will pick up your organics and deliver them to local farms where they will be transformed into fertile soil:

Compost Cab, www.compostcab.com.

The Compost Crew, www.compostcrew.com.

Envirelation, www.envirelation.com.

Fat Worm Compost, www.fatwormcompost.com.

dressing. For dessert choose from several kinds of cookies including chocolate chip oatmeal and ginger roll cookies. There is a flat delivery fee of $5.

Washington's Green Grocer, 8741 Ashwood Dr., Unit O, Capitol Heights, MD 20743; (301) 333-3696; www.washingtonsgreengrocer .com. Every Thursday afternoon my kids fly through the front door to find out what surprises came in our Green Grocer box. When it's a mango week you would think that I just gave in to their campaign for a new puppy. If you could taste the mangoes you'd understand why.

Washington's Green Grocer is a produce delivery service that operates a bit like a CSA but gives you far more control over what you get and how often you get it. The week's list is e-mailed every Monday and typically includes 12 to 14 fresh, in-season, and when possible, local fruits and vegetables, all of which are the caliber of the mangoes my kids love. You not only get to choose if you want that week's offerings but you also get to substitute anything on the list for anything else on the list. So if you want all peaches and asparagus one week, no problem. You can sign up for weekly, biweekly or whenever-you-feel-like-it deliveries—no obligations, no contracts to sign, and no free set of Ginsu knives if you act now.

A long list of other fruits and vegetables beyond what is on the weekly list also can be added to any box, as can a host of other farm-fresh items including organic eggs, dairy products, herbs, honey and even meats. Boxes come in two sizes—small (a good choice for an individual or couple) or large (more family friendly). You can also pick a fully organic list or a mixed list that has some organic items and some conventional ones. There's also an all-fruit option. No matter which list you choose from, everything is flavorful, beautiful, and as a rule, far better than anything at your local supermarket. Small boxes start at $31.25 and large boxes at $37.75. If you break down your box and leave it by your door on delivery day, it will be picked up and reused or recycled. Washington's Green Grocer also keeps a great blog filled with recipes based on the week's list and runs a free lending library for cookbooks, books, and movies related to whole food, local produce, and farming.

White House Meats, (202) 320-4829; www.whitehousemeats .com. White House Meats only sells meat from animals that were naturally raised, killed under humane conditions, and inspected by the USDA. Additionally, the local meat seller only does business with farms that are within 100 miles of Washington, D.C. and that practice sustainable agriculture. There are three ways to purchase from White House Meats. The first is to purchase a box of assorted cuts from a specific kind of animal like a cow or lamb. Another choice is to buy a share of an animal and then purchase the meat during a draft. You pay about $20 to participate in the draft and then attend a "meat up" where you draw a number and pick a package of steaks, roasts and the like when it's your turn. Finally, you can buy an entire, quarter, or half of an animal like a cow, hog, or lamb and then have it cut to your specifications.

To Market, To Market

By day it sautés and by night it fights crime. The seemingly ordinary frying pan that sits on the counter at Hill's Kitchen boasts these superpowers and a storied past. A tale Leah Daniels, the owner of this friendly neighborhood store, happily shares with her customers. After an intense chase with police one night, a suspected armed robber found his way into the home of a local man through a basement door. Just as he was making his way up the stairs into the kitchen the owner of the house clocked the crook over the head with this heavy pan, Bugs Bunny–style. The cookware and the enthusiasm with which Daniels shares the story are a good reminder that indie shops offer more than great inventory.

On these pages are some my favorite indie food-related shops around town. In this chapter you will find everything from the all-but-the-kitchen-sink discount gourmet supermarket Rodman's to the authentic Italian market A Litteri, Inc., which carries more kinds of extra-virgin olive oil than Washingtonians carry political opinions. After you finish shopping for treasures on its packed shelves, search for hidden treasures at bargain prices at the gritty but great Florida Avenue Market.

Other more picturesque community shopping experiences can be found in almost every neighborhood of the city. Washington's proximity to agriculturally rich Virginia, Pennsylvania, and West Virginia has translated into a literal harvest of farmers' markets selling fresh, seasonal, and local goods. FRESHFARM, an independent nonprofit organization committed to forging an urban-rural partnership, sponsors the granddaddy of D.C. farmers' markets, the Dupont Circle FRESHFARM Market. The outdoor sale happens every Sunday morning rain or shine. The group also stands as the energetic force behind growing markets in formerly food-dead zones where residents and employees don't have easy access to healthy, fresh food. FRESHFARM at Health and Human Services, H Street NE, and at the White House, which First Lady Michelle Obama attended on opening day, all fall under this important heading. Organizers at all of the FRESHFARM markets strive to make it easier for shoppers to use EBT/Food Stamps and WIC/Senior coupons by providing portable ATM-style swipe machines and running incentive programs.

More than just offering beautiful produce, the farmers' market experience allows you to shop with your neighbors and get to know the people selling you your food. At my own neighborhood market every Tuesday afternoon in the summer, my kids are encouraged to sample more than their fair share of blackberries and get to examine garlic scapes that have just been pulled from the ground. I always savor the opportunity not just to get the sweetest corn around but also to read the latest corny joke handwritten by the good-natured folks who run the sale. (Case in point: What does the ear of corn say when it is embarrassed? Answer: Oh, shucks. Thank you, I'll be here all week . . .) This chapter lists some of the markets found around D.C. Enjoy my favorites and have fun finding your own.

Brick & Mortar Shops

A Litteri, Inc., 517 Morse St. NE, Washington, DC 20002; (202) 544-0183; www.litteris.com. This under-the-radar shop reminds me of the Italian groceries in Queens where I grew up. The aisles are packed high with almost every kind of Italian olive oil, pesto, tomato sauce, and balsamic vinegar imaginable. Not far from Gallaudet University, the shop also has a good wine selection and makes overstuffed subs at its popular deli counter, where you can buy salami, dried sausages, prosciutto, cheeses, and stuffed cherry peppers.

A Mano, 1677 Wisconsin Ave. NW, Washington, DC 20007; (202) 298-7200; www.amano.bz. A Mano's owner regularly travels to Europe to bring back handmade treasures to adorn your table. The exquisite linens and hand-painted dishes from Italy and France found here look as though they should be gracing a table in Provence.

All African Food Store, 325 5th St. NE, Washington, DC 20002; (202) 547-5300. The New York Avenue African grocer sells a variety of authentic African spices and products. There is even a butcher who sells free-range chicken and smokes goat on the premises.

And Beige, 1781 Florida Ave. NW, Washington, DC 20009; (202) 234-1557; www.andbeige.com. The upscale home furnishings store proves neutrals are anything but boring. In addition to the furniture and art, the store sells unusual serving and tabletop pieces, all of which embrace the color palette advertised in its name. A tray made from a buffalo horn, candlesticks crafted from bone, rounded serving platters crafted from brass-brazed nails, and an iron and gold-leaf bowl made to look like a sea urchin are a few of the items sold here that give new meaning to the expression "conversation piece."

Biagio Fine Chocolate, 1904 18th St. NW, Washington, DC 20009; (202) 328-1506; www.biagiochocolate.com. Biagio Fine Chocolate is a must-visit (and then a must-taste) for any self-respecting chocoholic. Biagio showcases an array of Certified Fair-Trade and Organic chocolate bars, truffles, caramels, bonbons, drinking chocolates, and other cacao delicacies, which are the foundation of this Dupont Circle shop. The owner and staff are extremely knowledgeable and helpful and take great pride in the products.

BlackSalt Fish Market, 4883 MacArthur Blvd. NW, Washington, DC 20007; (202) 342-9101; www .blacksaltrestaurant.com. The same superb seafood Chef Jeff Black selects for his kitchen can be purchased from the small market  in the front of the house. Freshness and sustainability are the two major criteria Black uses to guide his selections and it comes through in all he serves and sells at this gem of a neighborhood restaurant. You can call a day ahead to place special orders and you can also browse the market's sampling of oils, seasonings, and condiments.

Broad Branch Market, 5608 Broad Branch Rd. NW, Washington, DC 20015; (202) 249-8551; www.broadbranchmarket.com. If you called in set designers to create the perfect neighborhood store, I'm pretty sure the end product would be the Broad Branch Market. From the marble-topped ice cream counter in the candy room to the glass canister filled with homemade dog biscuits on the counter, the corner store is rich with charming touches along with a nice mix of groceries, fresh food, baked goods, and dry goods. You can order sandwiches, fish, deli, premade dishes, and cakes from the glass counters that run along the side of the store. In the back, browse the beer, wine, soaps, and organic bulk grains, popcorn, nuts, and loose teas. Most of the products throughout the market lean toward the organic, independent, natural, or international. Picnic tables out front are painted to look like the charming nearby residential streets, and the market regularly sponsors book readings, tastings, musicians, and in the summer, bring-your-own-mat outdoor yoga.

Calvert Woodley Wines & Spirits, 4339 Connecticut Ave. NW, Washington, DC 20008; (202) 966-4400; www.calvertwoodley.com. In Cleveland Park, the first sign that the weekend truly is near is when the traffic starts to form around Calvert Woodley. Crowds getting ready to entertain flood the store, attracted to its broad selection of domestic and international wines, beers, spirits, and the gourmet cheese counter. The staff, some of whom have been with the shop since it opened in 1982, know the merchandise extremely well and have built up reputations for making educated recommendations based on region, taste, occasion, and price. The bargain bin is one of the store's most popular destinations (a great place to score a good bottle for under $12).

Canon's Fish Market, 1065 31st St. NW, Washington, DC 20007; (202) 337-8366; www.cannonsfishmarket.com. The Canon family has been selling seafood for the past 70 years and continues to provide area individuals and businesses with some of the freshest fish around. The Georgetown market sells everything from sushi-grade tuna to live lobsters to caviar. Canon's delivers to homes and businesses within a 20-mile radius of its Georgetown store.

Chez Hareg Gourmet Bakery, 2312 Fourth St. NE, Washington, DC 20002; (202) 832-2253; www.chezharegpastries.com. Growing up, Haregewine Messert learned to cook in Ethiopia. After moving to the United States as a young woman, she rediscovered her passion for baking and cooking and soon thereafter Chez Hareg Gourmet Bakery was born. Messert focuses on classic European desserts and creates everything from cakes to pies to cookies. She also sells a full line of vegan baked goods.

Cork Market and Tasting Room, 1805 14th St. NW, Washington, DC 20009; (202) 265-2674; www.corkdc.com. The first thing most notice when you walk into Cork is the 14th Street store's varied selection of European and New World wines. And while the store gets high marks for its wine, it shouldn't be overlooked for its gourmet market items. Cheese, charcuterie, sandwiches, and some of the city's best baked goods are also sold here. Wine tastings are held every evening except Sun (Mon through Thurs from 5 to 7 p.m., Fri from 6 to 8 p.m. and on Sat from 3 to 6 p.m.). Cork also hosts other more formal tastings and events. The shop makes a great cup of coffee that many locals swear by as their go-to afternoon pick-me-up.

Cowgirl Creamery, 919 F St. NW, Washington, DC 20004; (202) 393-6880; www.cowgirlcreamery.com. If you get the feeling that you have just stepped into cheese heaven, you are not alone. The clean, white look of this sun-dappled store, coupled with the fine selection of hand-crafted artisan cheeses, makes many a cheese-loving customer feel they are walking on a full-fat milk cloud. Cowgirl Creamery, originally started outside San Francisco, sells its own seven independent cheeses along with carefully selected samples from about 60 other American and European producers. In addition to the cheese, the Penn Quarter shop carries yummy premade sandwiches, wine, cheese boards, chocolate, olive oil, and a great $2 cup of coffee.

Hana Japanese Market, 2004 17th St. NW, Washington, DC 20009; (202) 939-8853. Hana is a tiny store that packs a dizzying number of high-quality and hard-to-find Japanese food products into a small space. Gems found here include miso paste, sushi-grade mackerel, tuna, and salmon in the freezer case, and mochi ice cream in not-often-seen flavors like strawberry.

Hill's Kitchen, 713 D St. SE, Washington, DC 20003; (202) 543-1997; www.hillskitchen .com. Hill's Kitchen is the neighborhood kitchen store where everyone knows your name. Owner Leah Daniels, who grew up just blocks from the Eastern Market store, laughs with customers, asks them about their recent purchases, and chats with them about local goings on. But the personal atten-tion is just the beginning of this store's charm. Daniels stocks fabulous cooking items like gorgeous LamsonSharp knives with red bowling ball–style handles, Brooklyn Slate cheese boards and The Spice Lab's gourmet salts in flavors like Italian black truffle. State cookie cutters, one for each of the union's fifty nifty plus a custom-made D.C. cookie cutter, rank as best sellers, and she even has a collection of aprons to fit young cooks who love to help mom and dad in the kitchen.

Home Rule, 1807 14th St. NW, Washington, DC 20009; (202) 797-5544; www.homerule.com. Home Rule stocks everything from the funky to the practical and many items that fall somewhere in between. On any given shopping trip to the neighborhood house-wares shop, you might walk away with onion goggles, an All-Clad saucepan, or a Virgin Mary bread stamp. Home Rule holds two sales during the year: The Lost Love sale the week after Valentine's Day and the Dog Days of August sale the first weekend of August.

Le Petit Corner Store, 1643 34th St. NW, Washington, DC 20007; (202) 338-7555. Another tiny gem of a shop here in D.C.

 This one sells a host of Turkish delicacies like rose jam, black olive spread and, of course, Turkish delight. Delicious made-to-order sand-wiches and house-made spinach pies can be taken to go.

P&C Market, 1023 East Capitol St. SE, Washington, DC 20003; (202) 391-3509. Milk in glass bottles, organic meats, and farm-fresh eggs are staples at the P&C Market on Capitol Hill. The milk, dairy, and eggs come straight from the popular Trickling Springs Creamery. Coffee, sandwiches, locally made gelato, wine, and other grocery items also are sold at this neighborhood store.

Palena Market, 3529 Connecticut Ave. NW, Washington, DC 20008; (202) 537-9250; www.palenarestaurant.com. Chef Frank A. Ruta sells many of his favorite imported and artisanal products that he uses in the kitchen of **Palena** (see p. 174) in the tiny, charming market attached to the cafe portion of the restaurant. Pretty bottles of locally made honey, small-batch pickles from Brooklyn, and pasta from Naples sit on the shelves here. Each day the market also sells a small selection of sweet and savory treats like potato frittata, asparagus focaccia, honey ricotta cake, banana bread, and the restaurant's much-loved lemon-glazed and orange-zested doughnuts. The shop has no seating, so plan on taking your goodies to go.

Periwinkle, 3815 Livingston St. NW, Washington, DC 20015; (202) 364-3076; www.periwinklegiftsdc.com. It's hard not to feel happy when you walk into Periwinkle, a small but charming gift shop on a Chevy Chase side street. The light-filled neighborhood boutique carries a colorful mix of items, including cute finds for the foodie shopper like Bridgewater pottery, Stonewall Kitchens sauces, and Tea Forte samplers. Don't leave without visiting the glass chocolate case and candy counter in the back left part of the store. Locally made artisanal chocolates, truffles, and other gourmet goodies fill the space, and the section overflows with pretty treats during Easter, Christmas, Halloween, Valentine's Day, and other candy-fueled holidays.

Rodman's Discount Gourmet, 5100 Wisconsin Ave. NW, Washington, DC 20016; (202) 363-3466; www.rodmans.com. I don't know of anyplace in town other than Rodman's where you can pick up a bottle of shiraz, Belgian chocolates, a one-egg fry pan, unbleached wax paper, Portuguese sardines, cardamom pods, olive oil–based soap and a box of Arborio rice all at the same time while also getting a prescription refilled. Upstairs you'll find shelves of international and ethnic gourmet foods, the wine and beer, and perishables. Downstairs is kind of an old-time small department store stocked with kitchenware, candles, cleaning products, paper goods, cooking gadgets, small appliances, seasonal items, and other eclectic items. There is also a full pharmacy downstairs. Many of the brands of merchandise found on both levels are organic, independent, international, or just plain out of the mainstream.

Schneider's of Capitol Hill, 300 Massachusetts Ave. NE, Washington, DC 20002; (202) 543-9300; www.cellar.com. For almost 60 years Schneider's has been a D.C. institution selling wine and spirits from its corner location on Capitol Hill. The family-owned liquor store is crowded with its varied selection. Knowledgeable staff work the floor and are known for pointing out hard-to-find bottles and vintages.

Seasonal Pantry, 1314½ 9th St. NW, Washington, DC 20001; www.seasonalpantry.com. The shelves at this tiny gourmet paradise are lined with affordable homemade everything—sauces, rolls, jams, rubs, sausages, vinegars, bacon, pasta. The selection changes from moment to moment based on what the chefs create and what ingredients are available to them. The interesting shop transforms itself into supper club from time to time, where a limited number of guests sit down together at a communal table to share a multicourse dinner cooked before them. Classes are also held in the space.

Shemali's, 3301 New Mexico Ave. NW, Washington, DC 20016; (202) 686-7070. The retail level of a medical building is not where you would expect to find a little Middle Eastern market, but that is exactly where Shemali's hides itself. The unusually placed gem stocks a host of authentic fresh and packaged products including several kinds of olives, feta, halvah, imported spices, and the same Syrian dried apricot paste my grandfather used to have to take several subways to find when I was a kid. Check out the small case by the counter for the day's freshly made items, which typically include spinach pies, meat pies, baklava, kibbeh, and stuffed grape leaves. The shop also does catering and is opening a cafe across the hall.

Tabletop, 1608 20th St. NW, Washington, DC 20009; (202) 387-7117. Tabletop bills itself as the place to find functional objects for every service. Most of the objects in the Dupont Circle store embrace a midcentury aesthetic with a contemporary twist, like the set of sleek glass schnapps glasses. Many others like the collapsible cheese grater, udder-shaped creamer, or whale butter dish are functional and fun. Tabletop also sponsors cookbook signings and other food-related events.

Taylor Gourmet, 1116 H St. NE, Washington, DC 20002; (202) 684-7001; www.taylorgourmet.com. The Atlas District sub shop sells overstuffed sandwiches and a selection of packaged Italian deli goods. Popular items include the cold-cut-filled Ninth Street Italian deli hoagie and the meatball sub. Taylor Gourmet works with a green firm to maintain an eco-friendly business. The store also has a location at 485 K St. NW, Washington, DC 20001; (202) 289-8001.

The Tea and Spice Exchange, 1069 Wisconsin Ave. NW, Washington, DC 20007; (202) 333-4540. The Tea and Spice Exchange looks like it belongs in Harry Potter's Diagon Alley rather than Georgetown's Blues Alley. The rows of large glass jars filled with different spices against the exposed brick wall gives something of a magical-potion feel to this little shop that sells its own blends of spices, herbs, blends, and rubs. Teas, mortars and pestles, spice racks, mills, and grinders can also be found here.

Trohv, 232 Carroll St. NW, Washington, DC 20012; (202) 829-2941; http://trohvshop.com. The funky Baltimore store recently opened a second location on the D.C. side of the Takoma Park Historic District. Selling a blend of vintage, repurposed and new items for the home, this is the place to find the perfect housewarming present—or the perfect present to warm your own home. Trohv really is an artfully mismatched urban shopping treasure chest.

Wagshal's, 4855 Massachusetts Ave. NW, Washington, DC 20016; (202) 363-5698; www.wagshals.com. Butcher Pam Ginsberg knows her stuff and knows it extraordinarily well. And as a result, the Spring Valley shop is known for its high-quality cuts and service. Pam can even order you a host of exotic meats like alligator, rattlesnake, yak, Kobe beef, and ostrich. Wagshal's also sells more conventional but still tasty deli meats, cheeses, and sandwiches, in addition to offering catering.

Farmers' Markets

Shopping with your neighbors does not have to be limited to the brick-and-mortar stores lining D.C.'s streets. A farmers' market allows you to squeeze melons alongside the person who lives upstairs or around the corner from you. Once a hard-to-find throwback to quieter times, farmers' markets have bloomed across the country and D.C. is no exception.

Capital City Market/Florida Avenue Market, 500 Neal Place NE (between N. 5th St. & N. 6th St.), Washington, DC 20002; (202) 547-3142. Erase the images of pretty urban farmers' markets with decorative signs, hand-tied cut flowers, and artfully displayed produce and you'll do just fine at the Capital City Market. The wholesale market, which also goes by the name the Florida Avenue Market, is a gritty series of warehouses where suppliers sell a huge range of wares. If you can suspend your need for creative displays there are some great finds here at great prices. Everything from organic chicken breasts to fresh seafood to ethnic foods can be bought here for a fraction of the cost they sell for at Whole Foods or Giant. There is also an old-school flea market section where you can buy everything from tennis shoes to snow mittens to diabetic socks all at deep discount. The market closes on Sunday and most vendors only take cash. Log onto the Capital City Market (aka Florida Avenue Market) blog, http://capitalcitymarket.blogspot.com, kept by a loyal market fan for news, tips, and a printable map and directory.

Dupont Circle FRESHFARM Market, 20th St. NW between Massachusetts Ave. and Connecticut Ave., Washington, DC 20009; www.FRESHFARMmarket.org. For many Washingtonians, Sunday morning means a cup of coffee, a thick newspaper, and a trip to the Dupont Circle farmers' market. The market attracts a nice mix of people from the urban hipsters to the stroller-pushing shopper. Many of the chefs at nearby restaurants also come here to pick up fresh vegetables and herbs. Only regional growers can sell at the market resulting in a good mix of locally sourced fresh fruits, vegetables, eggs, dairy products, seafood, meat, flowers, and baked goods. There's a full stand devoted solely to mushrooms and even an artisan wool seller.

Eastern Market, 1 7th St. & North Carolina Ave. SE; Washington, DC 20003; (703) 534-7612. Eastern Market holds the distinction as the city's oldest continually operating fresh food public market. The almost 140-year-old institution houses a variety of stalls that sell produce, flowers, meat, baked goods, seafood, pasta, and the like during the week inside South Hall Market. On the weekends the nearby outdoor Farmer's Line explodes with table after table of vendors showcasing their farm-fresh produce. At yet another outdoor section, local artisans sell crafts, art, and other original creations on Sat and Sun.

14th and U Farmers Market, Corner of 14th and U St. NW, Washington, DC 20001, in front of to the Reeves Center; Sat morning; www.marketsandmore.net. Shopping with your neighbors is the main focus of the growing 14th and U Farmers' Market, which stands not far from many of the city's in-demand urban eateries.

Like its sister market, the Bloomingdale Farmer's Market on Sunday at 102 R St. NW, 14th and U prides itself on being a producers-only market that only allows local vendors who sell locally grown and locally produced items. Baked goods from Whisked, plants from Reid's Orchard, and loaves from Panorama Bakery are some of the favorite new products at this open-air market, which also sells a variety of beautiful fruits, vegetables, and herbs. The Bloomingdale Farmer's Market hosts many of the same sellers.

FRESHFARM Market by the White House, 810 Vermont Ave. NW (between H St. NW and I St. NW), Washington, DC 20571; Thurs 3 to 7 p.m., May through Oct; www.FRESHFARMmarket.org. Thomas Jefferson shopped here. And, for the first time in 200 years, Washingtonians can, too. The weekly FRESHFARM Market, by the White House, stands practically in the shadow of historic Jefferson market on a wide downtown street and helps fill a healthy shopping void for the many government employees, commuters, and visitors who pass through this area during the workweek. In addition to a cornucopia of fresh produce, vendors also sell bison meat, baked goods, and organic eggs. Capital Kettle Corn, Soupergirl, and Pleasant Pops are among some of the local vendors who now sell at the open-air sale. Michelle Obama came to the very first market and White House chefs and kitchen staff still come by from time to time to shop and browse.

Glover Park—Burleith Farmers' Market, 819 35th St. NW, Washington, DC 20007; May–Oct, Sat 9 a.m. to 1 p.m.; http://dcgreens .org/at-market. DC Green, a nonprofit organization, runs this Saturday haunt and uses the proceeds from the market to support local food education and access in the schools. A popular spot in Glover Park to bring dogs and kids, Burleith Farmers' Market prides itself on being a producer-only market showcasing local produce, meat, cheese, bread, eggs, plants, flowers, handmade soap, and pasta, among other items. Live bluegrass music plays during market hours and fresh coffee can be purchased to sip as you shop and people-watch.

Maine Avenue Fish Market, 1100 Maine Ave. SW, Washington, DC 20024; (202) 484-2722. A morning at the Maine Avenue Fish Market should be on every good Washingtonian's D.C. bucket list. The open-air seafood market buzzes with customers on the prowl for fresh fish and seafood. Just browsing the commotion and catch is an experience on its own. Vendors sell fish to take home as well as cooked items to eat on the go as you take in the scene. Oysters, lobster, shrimp, bluefish, snapper, and lots and lots of crabs from the Bay are among the catches regularly spotted here. The market opens at 7 a.m. and tends to get very crowded, especially on Fri and Sat, so prepare to be a bit aggressive about your strategy.

Mt. Pleasant Farmers Market, Lamont Park, 17th St. NW and Lamont St. NW, Washington, DC 20010; (410) 303-0864; Sat from May–Oct from 9 a.m. to 1 p.m.; www.mtpfm.org. Pleasant is the operative word at this very neighborhoody market held beneath the trees of Lamont Park. Everything from the kale to the early-season strawberries to the rhubarb is fresh and beautiful and the customers and sellers all seem genuinely happy to be there. The Pleasant Pops cart and the free bicycle fix-up clinic are among the more popular stands.

New Morning Farm Market, held at the Sheridan School, 36th St. and Alton Place NW, Washington, DC 20008; www.newmorning farm.net/html/markets.html. I happily call this small outdoor market my own. On Tues from June to Sept from 4 to 8 p.m. and on Sat morning year round, the friendly crew from New Morning Farm sets up shop in front of the school selling fresh produce that makes my heart and kitchen sing. The farmers refer to the outrageously sweet Sun Gold cherry tomatoes as farmer's crack but they are so addictive I am not so sure that description is all that far off. Other summer favorites include the garlic scapes, blackberries, and peaches. You can pre-order a flat of strawberries during the height of the season and they will be held for you on the truck so you don't face a sad sold-out scenario when you arrive.

Petworth Community Market, 9th St. between Georgia Ave. and Upshur St. NW, Washington, DC 20011; www.petworthmarket.org. The Petworth Community Market opened to big cheers in 2010 as it brought a welcome source of local and fresh food to the evolving Georgia Avenue Corridor. Local produce, egg, baked goods, flower, and craft vendors sell their wares every Fri from mid-May until the end of Sept at this open-air neighborhood sale. On the last Fri of the month local bands come and jam as neighbors shop and schmooze.

Pick-Your-Own Produce (Overalls Optional)

Some of my favorite childhood memories revolve around my family's yearly apple-picking trip in upstate New York. Something magical seemed to happen when we hopped on the tractor that drove us out to the tall trees. Climbing to a high branch to find apples to toss into the bushels below felt like pure bliss. When I moved to Washington I was thrilled to learn that I could still go apple picking in the fall, even if the more southern locale means leaving coats at home and that most of the leaves on the ride up will still be green. The Maryland trees look smaller than the ones I remember through the lens of childhood but I suppose that is always the case. What hasn't changed is the fun of twisting ripe apples off the branches and biting into the first Red Delicious of the season while standing among the rows of fruit trees. And I still think it's pretty funny to bite an apple while it's still on the tree, but now I know better than to leave it hanging there for someone else to discover.

Today with the popularity of pick-your-own produce farms, apples are just one fruit on a long list of crops that can be picked locally. Within an hour of the city you can collect everything from berries to snap peas to pumpkins. Many farms now even let you select and cut down your own Christmas tree.

So if you want to take the farm-to-table experience a step beyond the farmers' market than you might want to try picking your own berries, apples, or green beans. Picking your own produce is a great way to put a little sweat equity into your salad to say nothing of a lot fun, especially for us city slickers. Here are a few of my favorite pick-your-own spots.

Butler's Orchard, 22200 Davis Mill Rd., Germantown, MD 20876; (301) 972-3299; www .butlersorchard.com. The first time I headed up to Butler's Orchard some twenty years ago I drove past farmland and empty fields pretty much the entire way between the highway exit and the orchard. I remember one gas station and maybe a church along the way, but other than that it pretty much seemed like the middle of nowhere to a city kid like me. I made a point of coming back to the pick-your-own farm every year or two to collect apples or berries out in the country. With each trip I spied more and more box stores, garden apartments, and strip malls cropping up along the landscape. On my last trip almost the entire route between the highway and the Germantown orchard had been developed. But even with a Target and a Best Buy along the way, Butler's still feels like a little farmland oasis. Once you turn onto the narrow road leading to the farm, the tree canopy and fields make all the city-slicker stuff disappear. Even though the farm can be crowded at the peak of season, it still beats a crowded Metro platform during Monday morning rush hour.

The Butlers opened their farm to the public some 50 years ago with a crop of pick-your-own strawberries. At the time the PYO concept was brand new, but the Butlers watched it catch on quickly and expanded their PYO offerings. Today the farm plans an almost year-round PYO calendar that starts in May with strawberries and ends in December with cut-your-own Christmas trees. In between, crops from blueberries to tart cherries to pumpkins can be picked at the massive Germantown farm.

I think over the years I have picked just about everything Butler's will let me. While everything they grow is fresh and delicious, the enormous thornless blackberries are my favorite. (The Butlers first planted the crop in the 1970s, for which I am seasonally grateful.) I must admit I'm not sure how many blackberries my family has smuggled out in their stomachs over the years but I have a feeling it's significant. Really, you have never seen such a big berry or tasted such a sweet one. The farm also runs evening hayrides from May to December and holds a popular pumpkin festival in the fall.

While you are in the neighborhood check out the **Lancaster County Dutch Market** (12613 Wisteria Dr., Germantown, MD 20874; 301-916-4039; www.lcdutchmarket.com). The Lancaster

County Dutch Market brings a little bit of Amish Country to Germantown 3 days a week. About a dozen vendors share the indoor market space and sell everything from fresh meat to cheese to Amish soft pretzels. People line up for the fried chicken and ribs. The ice cream also tends to be a big hit. The market holds limited hours and is only open on Thurs, Fri, and Sat, so check the website (yes, the Amish market really has a website) before you head over. The vendors have a reputation for polite, friendly service and some only accept cash so stop at the ATM before you arrive.

FarmAtHome Produce, 15350 Partnership Rd., Poolesville, MD 20837; (240) 372-0674; www.farmathome.com. It's a very exciting day in my house when blueberries come back in season. And if you have as much trouble keeping the supermarket pints of the blues around for more than 10 minutes then you might find yourself wanting to spend a significant amount of time at FarmAtHome. The pick-your-own Poolesville farm only grows blueberries and during June and July visitors can come and pick to their hearts' content. Blueberries are not native to D.C. so they are not always found at PYO farms in the region, which is precisely the reason why FarmAtHome was started. There is a 1-pound minimum per adult, which will probably last you at least half of the drive home.

Frog Eye Farm, 19600 Frog Eye Rd., Knoxville, MD 21758; (571) 484-1149; www.frogeyefarm.com. Blue is the operative word at Frog Eye Farm, where you can pick 20 different varieties of blueberries in

It's (a whole lot of) Great Pumpkins, Charlie Brown

Comus Market, 23830 Old Hundred Rd., Dickerson, MD 20842 (near the intersection of Comus and Old Hundred Roads); (301) 349-5100; www.comusmd .com. Before I stopped at the Comus Market I thought pumpkins came in two varieties: big and small. How wrong I was. Farmer, beekeeper, and local son David Heisler sells some of the more than 30 different varieties of pumpkins and squashes he grows on his nearby farm here at his picturesque roadside stand. There are striped pumpkins, bumpy pumpkins, white pumpkins, green pumpkins, and blue-gray pumpkins. He even grows a flat, round pumpkin that looks remarkably like the before picture of Cinderella's coach.

In addition to the rainbow of heirloom and unusual pumpkins, Heisler also sells locally harvested apples, fresh cider, and honey from the beehives he keeps out back. (You can see some of his bees buzz by on the way to the hives while you shop.) The market is only open in the fall. The hours tend to be from 10 a.m. until dusk and the last day of the season is Dec 24.

the shadow of the magnificent Blue Ridge Mountains under a crisp blue sky. Look closely for a touch of green in all that beautiful blue. The 30-acre farm is a pesticide-free operation.

Homestead Farm, 15604 Sugarland Rd., Poolesville, MD 20837; (301) 977-3761; www.homestead-farm.net. Homestead is a pretty pick-your-own farm that glows under a blue sky on crisp autumn days. The farm offers several PYO crops  including strawberries, peaches, and tart cherries, but it's the apples that seem to be the biggest draw here. Homestead grows row upon row upon row of apple trees. At last count, varieties at the farm included Jonathan, Empire, Golden Delicious, Red Delicious, Jonagold, Stayman, Winesap, Braeburn, Rome Beauty, Cameo, Pink Lady, and Sun Fuji. Tractor-pulled wagons take visitors out to the orchard and the farm even provides wheelbarrows for your haul—or for hauling your kids when they are too tired or too full to walk. Although Homestead is certainly not just for families, it does offer a lot in the way of kid-friendly activities like said wheelbarrows. Hay-bale jumping takes place all around the farm and a grouping of friendly animals live in and near the barn. Many of the chicks found here came from school hatching projects. Goats, ducks, sheep, and pigs can also be visited at Homestead.

On your way home from Homestead stop at the **Poole's General Store** (16315 Old River Rd., Poolesville, MD 20837; 301-948-5372). Poole's General Store is a step back in time. The small white shop with the green shutters and awning sells a little bit of everything including homemade pulled pork sandwiches, birdseed, and horse treats. The store is still run by the Poole family and is Montgomery

County's oldest general store in continuous operation. Right across the street is a public entrance to the C&O Canal and Towpath, a 187-mile-long towpath that starts in Georgetown.

If you are at the farm during the summer, take a detour to **McKee-Beshers Wildlife Management Area** (Poolesville, MD 20837; 410-356-9272; www.dnr.state.md.us/publiclands/central/mckeebeshers.asp). During the summer a field of happiness, in the form of sunflowers, blooms at the McKee-Beshers Wildlife Management Area. Every year the state plants hundreds of the tall yellow blooms. Photographers, painters, birdwatchers, and anyone who needs a dose of yellow love the spot but the reason the flowers are planted can be a buzzkill for some. Maryland plants the sunflowers to attract doves for the fall hunting season. On River Road about 2 miles from the intersection of River Road and Seneca Road.

Kingsbury's Orchard, 19415 Peach Tree Rd., Dickerson, MD 20842; (301) 972-8755; www.kingsburysorchard.com. More than 50 different varieties of peaches grow at Kingsbury's Orchard and they can be yours for the picking. Owned by the same family for more than 100 years, the orchard grows several different kinds of fruits but specializes in white peaches. Among the juicy varieties that can be picked here are Peach Tree Road, White Lady, Saturn, Summer Pearl, Lady Nancy, and Scarlet Snow.

Lewis Orchard Fresh Farm Produce, 18901 Peach Tree Rd., Dickerson, MD 20842; (301) 349-4101; www.lewisorchardfarm market.com. The Lewis family has been farming in the county for more than a hundred years. Located at the intersection of Darnestown and Peach Tree Roads, the family's shop sells a rainbow of seasonal fruits and vegetables along with milk, cheeses, jellies, jams, flowers, dressings, and other country products. The store is open from mid-June to Thanksgiving.

Seven Oaks Lavender Farm, 8769 Old Dumfries Rd., Catlett, VA 20119; (540) 788-4257; www.sevenoakslavenderfarm.com. Get lost in a gentle sea of purple at the Seven Oaks Lavender Farm, where acres upon acres of fragrant lavender soothe the soul. Every spring when the pastel crop is in season, the mother and daughter farmers who make magic bloom from the ground let visitors pick their own lavender. Edith and Deborah Williamson also host a few open houses and parties during the off seasons and products like sachets, lotions, and culinary lavender made from their harvest.

Cultural Cuisine:
Where Food, Art & History Meet . . . to Eat

The polished marble of the monuments. The gleaming dome atop the Capitol. The grand façades of the museums. The National Mall is far from lacking when it comes to majestic landmarks and stately sites. Where it does fall a bit short is in the food department. Most of the museum cafes downtown serve some variation of overpriced and under-inspired fast food. Thankfully there are exceptions. The National Museum of the American Indian's Mitsitam Native Foods Cafe dishes remains one of the best and most original museum cafes in the country. Nearby, the restaurants at the National Gallery of Art also impress with their art-inspired menus crafted with the help of some heavy-hitting guest chefs.

Elsewhere in town, other cultural institutions seize the opportunity to marry culture and cuisine. Elegance is always the special of the day when you dine at the National Museum of Women in the

Arts. Good food has also caught on at some of this town's newer museums. Wolfgang Puck's The Source at the Newseum ranks as one of the city's best restaurants and the International Spy Museum's Zola brings the museum's sexy spy vibe to upscale American cuisine.

The Washington National Cathedral and Hillwood Estate, Museum, and Garden tie for best off-the-beaten-path tea experiences while brunch at the Kennedy Center will leave you anything but hungry. Finally, no gastronomic tour of D.C. would be complete without sampling the astronaut ice cream. So don't forget to grab a pouch of the oddly addictive freeze-dried stuff at the National Air and Space Museum gift shop next time you are on the Mall.

Bohemian Caverns, 2001 11th St. NW, Washington, DC 20001; (202) 299-0800; www.bohemiancaverns.com; Soul Food; $$. The smooth sounds of jazz will nurture your soul at this historic and intimate jazz club where Billie, Duke, and Ella once took the stage while the southern and soul food–steeped menu will feed the rest of you. The subterranean club made to look like an actual cavern (think Luray with a beat) serves dishes such as catfish fingers, lobster mac & cheese, jerk chicken pasta, spicy crab cakes, and a much-loved shrimp and grits. Fried Oreos with raspberry sauce hit a high note for dessert.

The Garden Cafe and the Cascade Cafe, National Gallery of Art, 4th St. NW, Washington, DC 20565; (202) 737-4215; www.nga .gov/ginfo/cafes.shtm; $$. The art on the walls inspires the food on the plates at the eateries housed among the masterpieces at the

National Gallery of Art. The Garden Cafe, located on the ground floor of the West Building, regularly changes its offerings to reflect the current installations. The cafe teams up with chefs who specialize in the cuisine from the region the art represents and then design a menu based on the paintings, sculptures, and other priceless pieces. Chef Fabio Trabocchi recently teamed up with the talent in the kitchen to create a special Italian menu, a kind of culinary homage to two exhibits showcasing Italian Renaissance art. Trabocchi, who is responsible for bringing **Fiola** (see p. 173) to Penn Quarter, has created such dishes as prosciutto San Daniele and marinated eggplant served with Parmigiano-Reggiano cheese and aged balsamic vinegar, and *tortellini al basilico e mozzarella* (basil tortellini with buffalo mozzarella). Desserts include a classic tiramisu with chocolate sauce, hazelnut-chocolate ice cream, and lemon sorbet with berry compote. Trabocchi also helped craft a buffet of classic Italian dishes like Venetian seafood stew, macaroni with tomato-braised beef oxtail and Pecorino Romano cheese, and lattarolo, a vanilla and honey flavored custard. The cafe has collaborated with many other well-known guest chefs including José Andrés and Michel Richard.

The salads, soups, and sandwiches at the Cascade Cafe are a nice change from the typical food court–type offerings at most of the other Smithsonian cafeterias. And, personally, I could stare at the cooling—and cool—fountain wall for hours. I recommend doing said staring while nursing a cup of the surprisingly good house-made gelato sold at the espresso bar. See the recipe for the **Garden Cafe's Empanada de Pollos Ensapados** on p. 297.

Hillwood Estate, Museum, and Gardens, 4155 Linnean Ave. NW, Washington, DC 20008; (202) 686-5807; http://hillwood museum.org; Russian; Afternoon Tea; $$$. Far from the camera phone–carrying crowds on the Mall stands the Hillwood Estate, Museum, and Gardens, the former home of Post cereal heiress and collector Marjorie Merriweather Post. Tucked away on a tree-lined street in Northwest D.C., Hillwood and its beautiful gardens are nothing short of fabulous. (If you don't believe me just consult your museum admission pin, which simply reads "fabulous.") And with your admission to this off-the-beaten-path gem you get access to the site's cafe.

The cafe and its simple decor are far less opulent than the house, home to Post's extensive collection of Fabergé eggs and Russian treasures. A 3-course Sunday afternoon tea is the most in-demand meal at the cafe and reservations tend to go quickly, particularly in the spring when the gardens bloom. The three tea courses are brought out at once, and for an extra $5 you can add a glass of wine or champagne to your service. The tea selection comes from Harney & Sons and includes Russian Country, Sencha Green, and Lemon Verbena. A sun-dried cranberry-walnut chicken salad, roasted pear sandwich, and Roquefort blue cheese blini are among the finger sandwiches presented, and mini éclairs, cinnamon maca-roons, and cheesecake lollipops are part of the pastry selection.

The cafe also serves a seated lunch with a nice menu sprinkled with offerings—like a chilled borscht served with a hard-cooked egg and lemon dill cream—that pay homage to the Russian imperial art collection next door. And the Grape Nuts atop the warm apple and cranberry cobbler with cinnamon whipped cream are a fun nod to the Post family business.

You cannot enter the cafe without paying the Hillwood entrance fee first so go see the fabulous collection before your Grape Nuts cobbler. You won't regret it.

The Mezzanine Cafe, National Museum of Women in the Arts, 1250 New York Ave. NW, Washington, DC 20005; (202) 783-5000; www.nmwa.org; Brunch, Sandwiches; $$. It's almost a literal interpretation of the word "picturesque," and a delightful one at that. The first Sunday of the month brunch at the National Museum of Women in the Arts gives art and food lovers the chance to sip mimosas and nibble on made-to-order crepes while surrounded by priceless paintings. The grand building serves as the perfect backdrop to the lovely brunch, which also features waffles, smoked salmon, and an omelet station. Brunch is priced at $25 per person, which includes free admission to the museum (usually $10 per person) and the chance to participate in a docent-led tour of the impressive collection. The National Museum of Women in the Arts' better-than-most gift shop also offers a 10 percent discount with a brunch receipt.

Worshiping at the Altar of Butter: Julia Child's Kitchen at the Smithsonian

Through the television set, Julia Child showed the world how to beat an egg with chopsticks, debone a duck, and slip a live lobster head-first into a pot of boiling water. But perhaps more than anything else the iconic chef showed us that you can cook seriously good food without taking yourself too seriously. Child's actual kitchen from her Cambridge home, which served as the backdrop for several of her popular television cooking programs, is now housed at the Smithsonian's National Museum of American History and is a necessary pilgrimage for anyone who owns a dog-eared copy of Child's best-selling *Mastering the Art of French Cooking.*

"It feels like home," declared a then 90-year-old Child when she attended the opening of the exhibit in 2002. "It makes me want to turn something on and cook."

Kitchen highlights include the mortar and pestle she purchased in Paris while studying at the Cordon Bleu, the straight razor she used to slash the tops of French bread and her beloved "Big Garland," the six-burner Model 182 Garland commercial stove she purchased secondhand in 1956. (Child's used an electric wall oven, which also is part of the kitchen exhibit, when she cooked on TV but always preferred her Garland.)

If you stand very still you can almost hear the onions browning in butter and smell the beef bourguignon simmering on top of the big Garland.

Bon Appétit!

Mitsitam Native Foods Cafe, National Museum of the American Indian, 300 Maryland Ave. SW, Washington, DC 20024; www.nmai .si.edu; Native American; $$. The cafe at the National Museum of the American Indian almost qualifies as an exhibit in its own right. The tasty entrees, side dishes, desserts, snacks, and drinks served at Mitsitam embrace the rich and varied Native culinary traditions of the Americas and help bring alive the Native experience through the sense of taste. Four times a year the menu at Mitsitam, which means "let's eat" in the Native language of the Delaware and Piscataway peoples, changes to reflect the current season. The dishes represent Native cooking from five distinct regions in the Western Hemisphere—South America, Northern Woodlands, Northwest Coast, Meso America, and the Great Plains. Information about the recipes' origins and significance can often be found displayed in the light-filled cafeteria-style eatery overlooking the museum's atrium. Standouts include the fry bread, buffalo chili, and chicken *mole verde* tacos. Gluten-free options are available and the cafe is vegan/vegetarian friendly. Many of the authentic Native ingredients used in the kitchen are purchased directly from tribal companies or co-ops. If technique intrigues you, take a few minutes to check out the fire pit in the kitchen where the cedar-planked juniper salmon is grilled. And, if you still can't get enough of authentic Native cuisine, pop into the gift shop and treat yourself to a copy of the new *Mitsitam Cafe Cookbook: Recipes from the Smithsonian National*

Museum of the American Indian. See the recipe for **Wild Rice Salad** from the National Museum of the American Indian's Mitsitam Cafe (Smithsonian's National Museum of the American Indian, Restaurant Associates and Fulcrum Books) on p. 309.

Roof Top Restaurant and KC Cafe, John F. Kennedy Center for the Performing Arts, 2700 F St. NW, Washington, DC 20566; (202) 416-8555; www.kennedy-center.org/visitor/restaurants; Brunch, Seafood; $$$. Sunday brunch steals the show at the landmark Kennedy Center's Roof Top Restaurant, and the restaurant's kitchen serves as the stage for the extensive spread. The huge raw bar featuring oysters on the half shell, crab claws, shrimp, and other gifts from the sea wins for best featured performance, with the cheese and antipasto selection getting the nod for supporting roles. Bravo to the made-to-order omelet station in the main dining room and the musicians whose melodies fill the large room. The separate dessert room provides the sweet finale. And, if you can stand one last theater metaphor, the majestic view of the monuments from the outdoor terrace is worthy of your standing ovation, so don't forget to leave yourself some extra time before your curtain to stroll along the terrace.

The Source by Wolfgang Puck, The Newseum, 575 Pennsylvania Ave. NW, Washington, DC 20001; (202) 637-6100; www.wolfgang puck.com/restaurants/fine-dining/3941; Asian Fusion; $$$$. Left-coast chef extraordinaire has housed his D.C. take on Asian fusion on three levels of the Newseum, the massive Pennsylvania Avenue museum dedicated to the Fourth Estate. On the ground floor near the entrance you'll find Source's more casual bar and lounge where you can order from a traditional Japanese *izakaya* menu featuring sushi, sashimi, noodles, dumplings, and wine and sake by the glass. Upstairs is all modern with floor-to-ceiling glass windows and Puck's contemporary Asian fusion selections. Here you can order creations like crispy suckling pig with black plum puree or sautéed turbot with spicy Szechuan garlic sauce, and lobster fried rice. A dim sum brunch is served every Saturday. You can either pick five plates for $30 or eight for $40. Bao buns, spring rolls and, of course, dumplings filled with everything from wild field mushrooms in ginger broth to king crab and Chinese mustard are on this special menu. And I really wouldn't sleep well at night if I did not mention the triple chocolate plate for dessert, complete with chocolate soufflé, chocolate sorbet, and the chef's 10-year chocolate sauce named as such because of the number of years it took him to perfect the perfect sweet stuff. And while I'm at it, here are a few more words to the wise from the dessert menu: molten chocolate purse with peanut butter ice cream.

Tour and Tea at the Washington National Cathedral, 3101 Wisconsin Ave. NW, Washington, DC 20016; http://nationalcathedral .org/visit/tourAndTea.shtml; Afternoon Tea; $$$. Every Tuesday and Wednesday afternoon, the Washington National Cathedral offers the chance to sip high tea with a bunch of gargoyles during its popular Tour and Tea program. Poured on high in the Pilgrim Observation Gallery, the freshly brewed tea is served at tables adorned with crisp white linens and fresh flowers from the cathedral's magnificent gardens. Tea tends to include raisin scones, clotted cream, fruit preserves, tea cookies, and finger sandwiches filled with choices like smoked salmon, egg salad, and curried chicken salad. There is also a menu of almost a dozen different tours to choose from throughout the year. During the patriot tour, docents point out the various American symbols and art found in the cathedral while on the painting with yarn tour, the 1,500 pieces of needlework become the focus. Other Tour and Tea choices include an angels tour, a women in glass and stone tour, and an early-spring cherry blossom tea. Bring your high-powered binoculars along for the popular gargoyle tour, given Apr through Oct, so you can get a good look at the Darth Vader gargoyle and his grotesque brethren. Tours begin at 1:30 p.m. and tea is served at 2:45 p.m.

Zola, 800 F St. NW, Washington, DC 20004; (202) 654-0999; zoladc.com; New American; $$$. Connected to the wonderfully fun International Spy Museum, Penn Quarter's Zola gives a sleek nod to the world of covert operations without crossing over into Hard Rock Cafe territory. Subtle details like the floor-to-ceiling red velvet booths, the wall of declassified documents, and the chrome peepholes into the kitchen help create a restaurant that looks as put together as James Bond himself. And Zola would do Bond proud. Zola's famous $5 martini, shaken or stirred, tops the popular cocktail menu. The restaurant holds two nightly happy hours every weeknight with an extensive list of creative mixed drinks and wines. The first happy hours runs from 4 to 6 p.m. and the second from 9:30 to 11 p.m. Both offer several $5 drink specials beyond the martini and a menu of reimagined bar food including miso crab sticks, lobster rolls with a wasabi mango sauce, and beef sliders topped with chile spice, guacamole, and blue cheese.

Zola also offers a full dinner and lunch menus. The business lunch lets you pick a main, starch, and side dish, which then is served in a white porcelain TV-dinner-style tray that even has a compartment for the chef's dessert of the day. A 3-course pre-event special from 5 to 7 p.m. at dinnertime caters to those who are Verizon Center bound. Small plates, artfully composed salads, and a nice mix of main dishes round out the rest of the choices at dinner and lunch. The lobster mac and cheese was recently brought back by popular demand.

Around the corner, the light and airy **Zola Wine & Kitchen** (see p. 229) also offers an increasingly popular weekday lunch served with a view of its state-of-the-art test kitchen. A long chalkboard announces the day's choices. The best seats in the house are alongside the counter of the kitchen where you can watch as your lunch is prepped, diced, sliced, grilled, and sautéed. Communal tables along with some cozier seating options dot both the kitchen and the market portions of ZWK. It's also the perfect place to pick up a premade picnic to enjoy on the nearby Mall. See Zola's recipe for **Strawberry Basil Smash** on p. 317.

Coffee, Tea & Cafes

The mismatched furniture. The communal *New York Times*. The smell of fresh coffee being carefully brewed by someone who isn't required to use the word *grande*. It may not be home, Dorothy, but on days when you need to chill out with a cup of something warm, delicious, and caffeinated, there's no place better than a good indie coffeehouse. Thankfully, D.C. has several.

Really good, expertly prepared coffee is the focus at most of these spots. The cafes listed in this chapter employ baristas steeped (pun intended) in coffee culture and well versed in techniques like the hand pour. The beans tend to come from high-quality independent roasters like Intelligentsia and Counter Culture that produce a high-quality product while embracing fair-trade practices at the same time. Qualia Coffee, much to the delight of its customers, even goes so far as to roast its coffee beans on site in the back of the coffeehouse.

But what's in the cup tells only part of the story. It's the atmosphere—the laptop warriors, the local art displays on exposed brick walls, and the counter culture clientele—that creates the backdrop to the coffee-drinking experience. It's what turns that coffeehouse into *your* coffeehouse and makes you want to linger long after the last drop.

Azi's Cafe, 1336 9th St. NW #1, Washington, DC 20001; (202) 232-0001; www.aziscafe.com. Azi's corner location and big windows make it a light and bright spot to sip a good cup of coffee or have a light meal. Coffee is by Illy, and in addition to the hot offerings, Azi's serves a nice selection of iced drinks including an Iced Chocolate Biscotti made from milk, double espresso, chocolate syrup, hazelnut syrup, and whipped cream. The actual biscotti sold at the counter are worth the splurge, too. Salads, bagels, paninis, sandwiches, and a soup of the day round out the menu.

Baked & Wired, 1052 Thomas Jefferson St. NW, Washington, DC 20007; (202) 333-2500; www.bakedandwired.com. If you can find a better strawberry cupcake than the one served at Baked & Wired, please let me know immediately. Better yet, send me a dozen, *stat*. This fabulous Georgetown coffee shop hits it out of the park with both its baked good and its coffee drinks. Other than its large and in charge cupcakes, Baked & Wired also serves up sweet treats like its soft ginger cookie sandwich filled with a lemon-honey buttercream, a muffin-donut hybrid served only on Friday and Tuesday mornings, and a caramel s'more named the O.M.G. because those are the three words you utter when you take the first bite. (True story, btw. I totally and unknowingly said it after biting into the homemade graham cracker, caramel, marshmallow, chocolate glaze creation for the first time.) The coffee here gets the same love given to the sweets. The artistic baristas at the charming shop chat with customers about the products and brew up amazing concoctions from independent fair-trade coffee brewers Stumptown Coffee Roasters and Intelligentsia. All the milk and cream is organic and comes from Trickling Springs Creamery in Chambersburg, Pennsylvania. Tea drinkers will not feel slighted by the impressive hot and cold tea menu. Check out the chalkboard wall and the "this be the verse" collection in the back for a dose of daily wisdom to go with your latte. Gluten-free options.

Big Bear Cafe, 1700 1st St. NW, Washington, DC 20001; www .bigbearcafe-dc.com. Welcome to the neighborhood coffeehouse where everyone knows your name. Or at least your regular order. French press is the star of the menu here and is done exceptionally well. Behind the coffee bar, the sugar is raw and the milk is whole (the cafe only buys Trickling Springs organic whole milk and none of its lower-fat cousins, but does stock soy milk for the lactose intolerant among us). Tables at the urban hipster haunt tend to fill up with locals who come in for the coffee, music, and atmosphere. Seating on the patio out front is at a premium when the weather cooperates and the cafe's garden is in bloom. Free Wi-Fi further helps draw in the laptop crowd. Big Bear serves pastries throughout the day and the lunch and dinner menus feature salads and other items made with lots of fresh veggies. In the evening, you can even enjoy your smoky chipotle chili with a bottle of beer. Every third Thursday (well, almost every third Thursday, so check before you head out) at 8 p.m., Big Bear plays host to a free poetry reading and music performance series.

Busboys and Poets, 2021 14th St., Washington, DC; (202) 387-7638; www.busboysandpoets.com. Busboys and Poets bills itself as a community. Artists, writers, activists, and free thinkers gravitate toward the neighborhood hangout that at once serves as a coffee shop, bookstore, and salon. Readings, poetry slams, community rallies, film screenings, and progressive gatherings are held just about every night of the week. The cafe's long menu of soups, salads, pizzas, burgers, brunch items, and coffee drinks feeds the body as the atmosphere feeds the soul. Vegan/vegetarian friendly.

Chinatown Coffee Co., 475 H St., Washington, DC, 20001; (202) 559-7656; http://chinatowncoffee.com. A favorite spot in the East End, Chinatown Coffee Co. bills itself as the third wave in the coffee experiment. After spending some time in the urban shop, you'll want to ride out that wave with them. The friendly baristas serve hand pour, French press, espresso, and drip coffee. All of it exceptionally good. The lattes get a lot of attention and for good reason. But the drink menu is not limited to great coffee. Chinatown Coffee Co. also has a bar that serves up a good selection of indie wines and beers and even absinthe. Chinatown Coffee Co.'s atmosphere is as good as its beverage selection. Many regulars spend hours hanging out enjoying the baked goods, free wireless, great location, and good music. The shop even sponsors a kind of food truck happy hour every Thurs beginning at 6:30 p.m., when you can buy dinner and enjoy it inside the shop with a hot or cold drink.

Filter Coffeehouse and Espresso Bar, 1726 20th St. NW, Washington, DC 20009; (202) 234-5837; www.filtercoffeehouse .com. Tucked behind an orange door and away from the hubbub of Dupont Circle, this little indie shop has earned its reputation for good strong coffee and friendly staff. The pour-over coffees are the main attraction here. The slow and deliberate process punctuates the flavors, subtle and otherwise, that can otherwise be lost during more conventional brewing processes. Filter's pour-over listings read a bit like a wine primer and include not only the name and origin of the bean but also the notes, aromas, and acidity level associated with the particular coffee. For example, when you sip the Guatemala Finca La Soledad expect to be tickled by caramel, vanilla, and floral aromatics, notes of chocolate, and orange-like acidity, while the medium-bodied Brasil Carrado Gold is defined by rich cocoa aromatics, caramel sweetness, and a mellow acidity.

Mid City Caffé, 1626 14th St. NW, #2, Washington, DC 20009; (202) 234-1515; www.midcitycaffe.com. Perched atop a slightly whimsical (and very pink) antique furnishings shop, Mid City Cafe is a solid independent neighborhood coffee shop with a loyal following. Mid City serves good coffee drinks and a nice selection of baked goods from local D.C. outfits like Pollystyle, Delectable Cakery, and Georgetown Bagelry. The coffee comes from Counter Culture and Caffee Pronto and the milk is the good sweet stuff from Trickling Springs Creamery. The second-floor cafe embraces a kind of vintage auto theme, a nod to when 14th Street housed many an auto body shop.

Modern Times Coffeehouse at Politics & Prose Bookstore, 5015 Connecticut Ave. NW, Washington, DC 20008; (202) 362-2408; www.moderntimescoffeehouse.com. Tucked away in the basement level of the city's best-loved independent bookstore, this neighborhood coffeehouse serves up good coffee, good music and good people-watching. At any given moment during the day you might spy writers working on laptops, students debating social issues, and moms wiping cookie crumbs from the mouths of their little ones. Most of them will have a cup of something warm and home-brewed in hand. Espresso is the star attraction of the coffee here and the staff is well trained on the traditional lever machine behind the counter that is responsible for keeping the cafe's loyal following well caffeinated. Other hot drinks include cafe mocha, from-scratch hot chocolate, chai with ginger, and a personal favorite, the London Fog, a soothing mix of Earl Grey tea, honey, and soy milk. A series of hanging blackboards list the revolving selection of salads, hot and cold sandwiches, and the soup of the day, which is always vegetarian and is often very good. Fresh croissants, bagels, and other baked goods are in the display case and some packaged baked goods, like Pollystyle's amazing honey graham crackers, sit on the counter. The cafe sponsors an open mic night every Friday and local artists display their creations throughout the cozy space. Vegan/vegetarian friendly.

Peregrine Espresso, 660 Pennsylvania Ave. SE, Washington, DC 20003; (202) 629-4381; http://peregrineespresso.com. Although Peregrine serves only one size of coffee, the brew here is anything but one size fits all. The baristas prepare each espresso drink individually and artistically, often adding museum-quality latte art to the finished product. And, even without the pretty designs on top, Peregrine lattes are gallery-worthy based on taste alone. In addition to the six-item espresso menu (espresso, espresso macchiato, cappuccino, Americano, latte, and mocha), you can also order from a selection of fresh filter drip coffees (a revolving selection of a macro-brew and several micro-brews). All the coffee comes from Counter Culture. Teas, cold drinks, baked goods, and snacks are also sold. The

shop also runs a coffee bean delivery service for true devotees. You can sign up for either a monthly or every-other-week subscription. Each selection comes with a page-long biography about that week's beans and a list of tasting notes designed to help enhance the coffee experience. And to tread lightly on the planet, the delivery people ride bicycles.

Pound, 621 Pennsylvania Ave. SE, Washington, DC 20003; (202) 621-6765; www.poundthehill.com. I am going to tell you the two must important words you need to know about Pound coffee shop: Nutella Latte. And, really, you had me at Nutella. What's even better is that this drink does not disappoint. All the coffee, including what is used in the lattes, comes from the micro-roaster Kickapoo and the tea is from Mighty Leaf. Limited but satisfying breakfast, lunch, and dinner menus list the origins of many of local fresh ingredients. Pound started its life as one of the very first indie businesses in NoMa when the area still was more coming than up. The owners recently shut that store down and now solely operate the current one near Eastern Market.

Qualia Coffee, 3917 Georgia Ave. NW, Washington, DC 20011; (202) 248-6423; www.qualiacoffee.com. They take coffee seriously here and you'll be seriously happy that they do. The final product has a loyal and happy following. Only the fair trade, single-sourced stuff is ever served at the cozy Petworth cafe. The beans are roasted on-site in small batches and each cup is brewed individually via a careful hand pour technique that includes the use of a special filter designed by the owner. Varieties include Kenya French Mission, Rwanda Rwabisindu, Costa Rica Cariblanco, Peru Norte, Brazil Pocos de Caldas, Yemen Mocha Sanani, and Zimbabwe Salimba Estate. Whichever you choose, you can either snag a seat by the coffee bar or take your cup of joe outside on the patio. You can also head upstairs to the larger seating area, a quiet space perfect for plugging in or zoning out. The shop also accepts Potomacs, a local currency. Check out www.ecolocity.org/group/communityexchange to find out more about it.

SOVA, 1359 H St. NE, Washington, DC 20002; (202) 397-3080; www.sovadc.com. SOVA is like two cafes in one. An inviting coffeehouse downstairs complete with the requisite chalkboard coffee list and rotating art display on the walls, and upstairs, a loungelike refuge with muted red walls and mismatched velvet ottomans. Live music often fills the second floor or, in good weather, out on the back patio. The coffee is well made and from Intelligentsia and all the teas are from Rishi. The affordable wine list features some nice selections from some smaller vineyards.

Tryst, 2459 18th St. NW, Washington, DC 20009; (202) 232-5500; www.trystdc.com. Tryst is kind of like Adams Morgan's living room. People come to sit and sip the day and night away at this part coffeehouse, part bar and part cafe. Baristas are well trained in crafting the perfect cup before they serve up their first macchiato, cafe au lait, or cortado. Counter Culture Coffee is Tryst's roaster and each cup is served with couple of animal crackers beside it.

Loose-leaf teas, hot mulled orange juice, and a frozen chai are just a few of the non-coffee drink options. An on-staff pastry chef bakes up new goodies every day and you can also order off the small plate, sandwich, and all-day brunch menus complete with Belgium-style waffles, homemade granola and a Lebneh Baguette. Coffee-based cocktails (think Irish coffee and an espresso drink made from Bailey's, vanilla vodka and Tryst espresso) round out the alcoholic selections at the bar.

Yum's the Word:
Underground Restaurants & Speakeasies

Forget about secret ingredients. At D.C.'s new crop of underground eateries it's everything from the location to the menu that's on the down low. Veiled in layers of mystery, these occasional or one-night-only food-centered events take place in private homes or other off-the-beaten-path venues and provide a lucky few with a dining experience that goes beyond the confines of a conventional restaurant.

The expertly curated dinner party–style meals are limited to the lucky few who are both in the know and manage to reserve a coveted space in time. Some, like the Hush Supper Club, maintain websites that list upcoming dates. Others, like the more elusive Orange Arrow, require an actual invitation along with a promise that you are not a buzzkill, crybaby, or whiner. Prices are often listed as donations as a way of bypassing licensing regulations.

The underground food experiences also tap into the up-and-coming trend of communal dining. Meals are more often than not served family style at a large table, where you likely will be seated next to someone you did not walk in with. (Couples and friends who come together often are not seated next to one another.)

The speakeasies in town are more relaxed about whom you sit with but have plenty of rules and regulations about when you can actually be seated. If you are able to snag a reservation at one of the intimate underground bars, come prepared to wait and to wait somewhere away from the front door. Many speakeasies prohibit guests, even those with reservations, from standing around the outside of the club. You will get a text or phone call letting you know when—and only when—your table is ready. Your contact will also give you a secret password (I kid you not), which you need to utter to get through the door. Hopefully all the creative mixology going on inside these establishments will be worth all the James Bond–style antics and will leave you feeling stirred rather than shaken at the end of the night.

Since mum's the word with many of the underground operations, organizers rarely list phone numbers and only reveal actual locations several hours before the event. I have provided enough contact information to get you started—the chase is part of the fun. Besides, if I revealed any more, this book would self-destruct and I am pretty sure neither of us would want that to happen. And, remember, trust no one; taste everything.

Columbia Room, 1021 7th St. NW, Washington, DC 20001; (202) 393-0336; www.passengerdc.com/Columbia; $$$$. Master Mixologist Derek Brown has turned cocktails into an art form. At his exclusive 10-seat bar within a bar, Brown expertly blends flavors to create what have earned the reputation as the best cocktails in town. There is no menu at the Columbia Room, a secret warm-yet-elegant room behind the bar Passenger. Here Brown does everything from start to finish including chopping his own ice. For $64 per person, guests are served a 3-course progression of cocktails that are paired with a selection of small plates. The first two drinks are Brown's choosing and often reflect the season. The final one is your choice. Walk-ins are not allowed and you must cancel at least 48 hours in advance in order not to lose the $30 per person deposit needed to hold your space. You may order additional cocktails after the tasting or request an a la carte reservation if you want to bypass the recommended tasting menu.

DC Grey Farmers' Market, www.greydc.com. Maya Robinson is a grocery store junkie. When she travels, she makes a point of checking out the local food haunts. And here in town, Robinson is always on the prowl for independent places and vendors, especially ones that that sell fresh and affordable local food, like the ones she fell in love with in her native Puerto Rico.

Frustrated by D.C.'s somewhat limited options, Robinson began Grey DC and DC Grey Farmers' Market, an underground food market that does not require vendors to be licensed. By avoiding the licensing requirement, Grey Market taps into a whole world of

independent vendors who can't yet afford the price tag attached to the certification process. As a result, Grey Market serves as a kind of incubator for new, small, food-centered businesses.
A self-proclaimed accountant by day and food activist by night, Robinson uses her skills from her day job to help many of her vendors develop business plans and secure start-up funding. Grey DC also gives grants directly to some of its vendors to use toward licensing costs.

The revolving list of vendors at DC Grey Farmers' Market show-cases much of the community's local emerging food talent. Regulars include White House Meats, where you can buy and order locally raised beef and Crunkcakes, which allows you to indulge your sweet tooth and forget your troubles at the same time with a spiked cupcake. The baker has figured out how to keep the alcohol from burning off to create such inebriated wonders as the Rattler, a peanut butter cupcake with whiskey buttercream, and the Fat Elvis, a rum-soaked banana cake topped with peanut butter.

After you have had your fill of drunken cakes, stumble over to The Pickle, a fan favorite that quickly sells out of such delicacies as kiwi chutney pickles, pickled oranges (file them under gross sounding but delicious tasting), and chimichurri.

Dining Under the Table, Location: Private home in Silver Spring; www.diningunderthetable.net; $50 donation. Dining Under the Table's tag line just about says it all: one table, two cooks, six guests. The two anonymous cooking enthusiasts who run this intimate underground restaurant are drawn to Mediterranean flavors and local ingredients. Meals almost always include home-made breads and pastas like the cooking pair's homemade ravioli stuffed with ricotta, mozzarella, and shrimp. The club is held about once a month and the menu changes to reflect the season. Recent Dining Under the Table dishes have included cornmeal-crusted pork loin with a red-wine reduction; herb-stuffed leg of lamb; homemade tagliatelle in a Maine lobster cream sauce topped with shrimp and leeks; fresh tomato gazpacho with avo-cado; and a strawberry mascarpone tart. Supports the local food movement.

The Gibson, 2009 14th St. NW, Washington, DC 20009; (202) 232-2156; http://thegibsondc.com; $$$. It's easy to walk right by The Gibson. No sign hangs out front and there are no windows offering glimpses into the small, dark, candlelit bar housed beyond this deliberately unassuming exterior. It's what's inside that is meant to grab your attention. Mixologists at The Gibson work behind the scenes and behind the bar to create an array of carefully prepared and sometime complex cocktails. Prohibition-era mixes like the Sazerac are the specialty of the house. Regulars often tell the bartender what flavors or alcohol they are in the mood for and let the masters take it from there. But don't start ordering just yet. There are many hoops between that windowless front door and your barstool. The Gibson seats just under 40 people and has a strict no-standing-at-the-bar policy. About half of those seats may be reserved in advance. Whether you have a reservation or not, try turning the doorknob on the front door. If it's open go in and proceed to the host. If it's locked, ring the bell and someone will be with you shortly to take your cell phone number and instruct you not to wait outside, another Gibson no-no. When a table opens up, your contact will call and tell you the password. If you don't make it back in 10 minutes after the call, your password and reservation expire. You'll have to judge whether the game is worth it. But with all the *Spy Who Loves Me*–style antics, you'd be hard pressed to find a more appropriate place to order Bond, James Bond's dry martini of choice, the Vesper.

Hush Supper Club, www.hushsupperclub.com, hushreservations@ gmail.com; Indian; $75 donation. Geeta (she likes to keep her last name under wraps) doesn't just use her heirloom spice box or *masala dabba* to artfully flavor the 4-hour-long vegetarian Indian meal she creates for the underground supper club she runs out of her U Street home. The Hush Supper Club founder and hostess also uses her treasured *masala dabba* to paint a vivid picture of the region, religion, and food that help define her. "I'm a very good cook but I am not a chef," she tells. "I'm not someone who wakes up reading recipes. I'm in this for the story. The food is for the sake of the story."

Central to her story is her identity as a Jain, an Indian religion based on the principle of nonviolence to all living things. Jains are vegetarians who also do not eat potatoes, onions, and garlic in part because they do not regenerate once they are taken from the earth. Geeta claims that she can use the magic of her spice box to re-create these flavors and chemical reactions in her cooking. And most diners seem to not notice these three heavy hitters are missing from the majority of dishes she serves until she points out their absence. Between courses guests move between the living room and the dining room to listen to Geeta's talk. After a short while, the night begins to feel like a dinner party with those around the table laughing, talking, and sharing stories sparked by the food. Some will even be promoted to share jokes if they make the mistake of offering up the fact that they once performed stand-up. Significant others are asked not to sit together and Geeta swears many couples learn things they never knew about each other through the conversations that take place throughout the long meal.

Many of the recipes Geeta prepares for Hush have been handed down through generations and most reflect what you would find in Gujarat, a state in western India. While no meat is ever served at Hush, Geeta does cook with yogurt, milk, and ghee. Fresh and in-season ingredients drive the menu at the occasional supper club. During the summer months Geeta uses lots of mangoes, creating dishes like mango lassi or mango *rus*. In the winter, menus revolve more around rice and heavy bean dishes. Crowd favorites include her rainbow bell peppers with bean *makai*. Her personal favorite is her cilantro chutney, which Geeta's mother, whom she calls her teacher and guru, called better than her own. The 4-hour-long (and on some nights 5-hour-long) meal ends with her family's special chai. The suggested donation for the evening is $75, which includes one cocktail, but guests are encouraged to bring their own wine or beer to enjoy with dinner. Geeta places a small decorative box on the table and then leaves the room so diners can somewhat discretely leave the money for her. See the recipe for **Geeta's Chai** on p. 306.

Outstanding in the Field, Location: Rotating; http://outstandinginthefield.com; $$$$. Outstanding in the Field is a traveling restaurant without walls that sets its long communal tables at farms around the country, including farms in this area from time to time. The goal of the mobile feast that started in 1999 is to connect diners with the food they eat and the people who grow and raise it. Guest chefs come and prepare the multi-course meal with ingredients that are so local you can often see where they are grown from your seat at the table. The exquisite food coupled with the impossibly picturesque scenario of dining in a field make this a hard ticket to come by so plan accordingly. Supports the local food movement.

Patrón Social Club's Patrón Secret Dining Society, Location: Rotating; www.patronsocialclub.com; $$$$. Round and round the country this super-hip secret dining society goes and where it stops only you and a few connected others will know. A running countdown on Patron's Social Club's website keeps track of when and where this traveling underground dinner party will be held. Washington, D.C. recently joined the list of cities deemed hip enough to host this gathering sponsored by the Patrón Spirit Company. The 5-course D.C. extravaganza was held at the Finnish Embassy. Granville Moore Chef Teddy Folkman created the menu, which included a lobster and bison course, and famed New York mixologist Jason Littrell was the master behind the cocktail pairings, which of course all started out with Patrón spirits. Attendees not only had to "join" on the website but also had to solve a riddle in order to secure an invitation and receive the password needed to enter the soiree. Once you register online (it's free) you get e-mails updating you on the latest party. You never know when D.C. will get back in the line-up so keep an eye on your in-box for the club's latest news.

PX, 728 King St., Alexandria, VA 22314; (703) 299-8384; www .eamonnsdublinchipper.com/PX/px_home.html; $$$$. A blue light over an unmarked door lets you know you are in the right place. Ring the bell and eventually a hostess will come let you in and escort you to the dimly lit speakeasy that embraces a time gone by. Todd Thrasher, sommelier at Restaurant Eve, is the mix master here, crafting his "liquid art" for those who find him. Thrasher hand-squeezes all of his juices and makes all seven of the bitters (lemon, peach, mint, cherry, orange, kumquat, cranberry) found in his original creations. A limited selection of small plates can be ordered to go along with the cocktails.

Wok+Wine, Location: Rotating; www.woknwine.com; Seafood; Admission: $40. Forty is the magic number at Wok+Wine. Organizers of this "underground culinary concept" bring together 40 people, 40 bottles of wine, and 40 pounds of jumbo shrimp. The prawns are perfectly seasoned, cooked in a huge wok Venezuelan style, and then served on one long communal table. There are no forks, knives, plates, or chairs—just a bunch of people standing around eating great shrimp with their hands while they sip wine and chat. This occasional "underground culinary concept" pops up every now and again in cities all around the world, including Washington, and tends to be held in art galleries or funky office spaces.

The Most Important Meal of the Day:
Breakfast, Brunch & Other Happy Thoughts

Since we are told over and over again that breakfast is the most important meal of the day, why not make it one of the tastiest ones, too. Local greasy spoons, cafes, and elegant brunch spots alike provide many an option for getting your pancake on.

Breakfast Served All Day

Few things make me happier than a breakfast menu that doesn't go away when the clock strikes noon. When I first moved to D.C.

some 20 years ago, getting an omelet at 3 p.m. was almost as challenging as getting consensus on Capitol Hill. Fortunately, things have changed—at least on the omelet front. There are now a few solid places to order eggs over easy or a short stack no matter the time of day. These are a few favorites.

Brookland Grill, 3528 12th St. NE, Washington, DC 20017; (202) 526-7419; www.brooklandgrill.com; $. The menu here reminds me of my neighborhood diner growing up in Queens. It's broken down into categories like waffles, omelets, etc., has a ton of choices under each heading, and I have to admit those photos of loaded breakfast plates make me just a bit nostalgic for the Shalimar and my outer-borough days. The Big Breakfast is the first section of the menu, filled with about two dozen combo plates filled to capacity with things like eggs and ham, eggs and bacon, or eggs and hot half-smokes. Of course, they all come with home fries, toast, and your choice of another breakfast meat. The Big Grandpa breakfast has four hard-hitting choices: chicken-fried steak, chicken-fried chicken, cream chip beef, or sausage, biscuit and gravy. All come with two eggs, meat, and potatoes. Whoa, grandpa, don't forget to get your cholesterol checked. Brookland also serves several varieties of waffles, french toast, and breakfast sandwiches. The restaurant is not fancy but the food is good and the prices won't break the bank.

The Diner, 2453 18th St. NW; Washington, DC 20009; (202) 232-8800; www.dinerdc.com; $. The Diner puts it out there on its menu for all to see—everyone has the inalienable right to eat breakfast whenever they want even if it's 4 in the morning. And the people said Amen. The egg choices at the 24/7 Adams Morgan spot are long and varied. Omelets come in many choices, including an all-meat omelet, a corned beef hash omelet, and a bacon and blue cheese omelet. All come with toast and the choice of hash browns or grits. Buttermilk pancakes (including versions stuffed with bacon, sausage, chicken sausage, candied pecans, or blueberries), french toast, and salmon Benedict also go down nicely.

Highlands Cafe, 4706 14th St. NW, Washington, DC 20011; (202) 829-6200; www.thehighlandsdc.com; $$. The Highlands prides itself on being a neighborhood hangout committed to good coffee and an all-day brunch menu. The menu combines some Southern favorites with classic diner favorites to create choices that please most. The Highlands omelet is filled with ham, havarti, and spinach, while the Southern Breakfast comes with three eggs any style, sausage, a biscuit, and grits. Brioche french toast, Belgian waffles, and salmon cakes also appear on the menu. This Petworth cafe with the brightly colored mural also has a vegan menu. Vegan/vegetarian friendly.

Lincoln's Waffle Shop, 504 10th St. NW, Washington, DC 20004; (202) 638-4008; $. This greasy spoon near Ford's Theatre serves diner-style breakfast and even has the Southern breakfast favorite scrapple on its menu. The shop tends to be crowded and filled with many tourists heading to the Mall, but that doesn't scare away die-hards in search of a solid morning meal. Antacid sold separately.

Luna Grill and Diner, 1301 Connecticut Ave. NW, Washington, DC 20009; (202) 835-2280 www.lunagrillanddiner.com; $$. This Dupont Circle diner-style restaurant is a favorite haunt for many in the neighborhood looking for a place to read the paper while they eat breakfast. Eggs, omelets, and breakfast sandwiches make up the bulk of the choices. The Belgian waffles can be ordered up until 3 p.m.

Open City, 2331 Calvert St. NW, Washington, DC 20008; (202) 332-2331; www.opencitydc.com; $$. Part diner, part coffeehouse, and part bar, the Woodley Park hot spot serves breakfast all day inside and on its busy sidewalk patio. Open City puts a bit of a twist on its choices, offering about a half-dozen scrambles like chorizo, smoked salmon, or vegan tofu. Chai waffles and red velvet waffles satisfy sweet cravings while *croques* can be ordered at any meal. All can be topped with a choice of blueberry compote, warm straw-berry compote, banana walnut sauce, Nutella, or whipped cream. Open City pours many of the same Counter Culture Coffee drinks found at its sister restaurant, **Tryst** (see p. 100)—a great accompaniment to the popular restaurant's selection of fresh bagels and homemade baked goods. Gluten-free options.

Osman and Joe's Steak and Egg Kitchen, 4700 Wisconsin Ave. NW, Washington, DC 20016; (202) 686-1201; www.osmanandjoes .com; $. The hungover college student, night owl, and breakfast die-hard alike worship at the around-the-clock altar of Osman and Joe's Steak and Egg Kitchen. As you would expect, steak and eggs are the centerpiece of the operation. Country-fried steak and eggs, corned beef hash, and grilled pork chops and eggs can be ordered here at this small Tenleytown hole-in-the-wall anytime of the day or night. Orders come with the choice of fries, hash browns, home fries, or all three for a bit extra if you are feeling daring. French toast, pancakes, omelets, sandwiches, hot dogs, and burgers can also be ordered.

Pete's Diner, 212 2nd St. SE, Washington, DC 20003; (202) 544-7335; $. Pete's starts serving breakfast at 5 a.m., when most of the neighborhood restaurants are still locked up tight, and what Pete's lacks in ambience it makes up for in selection. All your typical diner-slash-country-style breakfast favorites are here including some great home fries, chocolate chip pancakes, and eggs scrambled, fried, and over easy. The food is inexpensive and filling.

Ted's Bulletin, 505 8th St. SE, Washington, DC 20003; (202) 544-8337; www.tedsbulletin.com; $$. Scrambled eggs, applewood

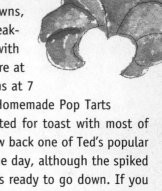

smoked bacon, sausage, hash browns, cheddar grits, pancakes, french toast, breakfast burrito, and even beer biscuits with sausage gravy are served all day long here at the popular Capitol Hill eatery that opens at 7 a.m. and closes long after dinnertime. Homemade Pop Tarts are a favorite here and can be substituted for toast with most of the breakfast combos. You can also throw back one of Ted's popular milk shakes or burgers at any point in the day, although the spiked shakes don't come out until the sun gets ready to go down. If you can't get enough of the Pop Tarts, you can purchase a few from the display case in the front room of this restaurant, with its decor that evokes an old-fashioned hangout suitable for newspaper men of days gone by.

Torrie's at Wilson, 700 V St. NW, Washington, DC 20001; (202) 462-3700; Soul; $. The chitterlings, collard greens, sweet tea, pigs feet, and macaroni and cheese at Torrie's have helped seal its status as a soul food institution. In fact, many have described the pork bacon as the best they have ever had. Across from Howard University Hospital, the walls of the no-frills dinerlike establishment are adorned with photos of the famous diners (Bill Clinton and Stevie Wonder, to name two) who have eaten here over the years.

Tunnicliff's Tavern, 222 7th St. SE, Washington, DC 20003; (202) 544-5680; $$. A neighborhood favorite that serves a popular brunch, Tunnicliff's Tavern is an especially nice choice during peak

Eastern Market hours. If the weather cooperates, opt for tables on the sidewalk patio where you can people-watch the market foot traffic as you nibble on a crab omelet and sip a Bloody Mary. Later in the day, the tavern embraces its other identity—local bar.

Brunch & Other Morning Meals

Elegant and indulgent, brunch separates us from the animals (unless you find yourself amid an aggressive buffet crowd, and then it's the wild beasts that want to be separated from us). Like a sunny, gentle weekend morning, brunch combines the promise of the day with beloved foods like french toast, pancakes, and eggs. Some of the city's best Sunday brunches, like the one at Seasons and Georgia Brown's, play with classic tastes to craft gourmet options, while others like the Slavic and Eastern European Domku are based on other breakfast traditions that feel at once familiar and foreign to most of us experiencing them for the first time.

Brasserie Beck, 1101 K St. NW, Washington, DC 20005; (202) 408-1717; www.beckdc.com. Nestled on the increasingly popular Barracks Row, Brasserie Beck offers a brunch menu with a decidedly Southern twist, with dishes like an oyster stew with applewood bacon and potatoes in bourbon cream, a fried green tomato crab stack, and a shrimp and grits with blue crab and tomato chow chow. Brunch is served on Sat and Sun from 10 a.m. to 3 p.m.

The Chesapeake Room, 501 8th St. SE, 20002; (202) 543-1445; www.thechesapeakeroom.com; Seafood; $$. The flavors of the sea are featured prominently on the brunch menu at The Chesapeake Room. Oyster stew, a fried green tomato crab stack and shrimp and grits can all be ordered during brunch served from 10 a.m. to 3 p.m. every Sat and Sun. The Barrack's Row restaurant incorporates fresh and in-season organic, sustainable, and free-range ingredients into its dishes.

Domku, 821 Upshur St. NW, Washington, DC 20011; (202) 722-7475; www.domkucafe.com; Eastern European; $$. And now for something entirely different—Domku, a Petworth restaurant specializing in Slavic and Eastern European fare. The slightly whimsical restaurant with its exposed brick, hanging chandeliers, and coffeehouse-style mix-and-match furniture serves a fabulous selection of brunch dishes. The traditional Norwegian pancakes here come with fresh fruit, powdered sugar, and lavender syrup but can also be ordered Dutch-style with a choice of bacon and fried egg, cinnamon apples and whipped cream, or kielbasa, onions, and gouda. The smoked herring scramble comes with rye toast and smoked roasted tomatoes, and the Swedish heart-shaped cardamom waffles are topped with whipped cream and lingonberry preserves. Fresh Danish pancake balls or *abelskiver* can only be ordered on the weekend and the scones are only baked and served on Sunday.

Eola, 2020 P St. NW, Washington, DC 20036; (202) 466-4441; www.eoladc.com. Once a month this charming restaurant tucked into a

Dupont Circle town house opens its doors for brunch. Eola's bacon flight is the highlight. Chef Daniel Singhofen presents a progression of three different types of his house-smoked and house-cured bacon and what he creates bears little resemblance to the thin strips you see on most breakfast plates. Singhofen finds thick, expertly crafted bacon that amazes diners, even the skeptical ones who can't imagine why you would pay $12 for three pieces of bacon. But truly this isn't your grandma's bacon. About a dozen other bacon starters can be ordered a la carte. Brunch entrees are a nice mix of expertly prepared breakfast favorites. Singhofen uses fresh and local ingredients and does much of his shopping at the nearby Dupont Circle farmers' market. For a sweet ending to the Eola pork fest, try the house-made doughnuts or the strawberry shortcake.

Founding Farmers, 1924 Pennsylvania Ave. NW, Washington, DC 20006; (202) 822-8783; www.wearefoundingfarmers.com. Built around the farm-to-table concept, Founding Farmers prides itself on its deliberate choice of ingredients. As a continuation of that commitment, Executive Chef Rob Ross and his team also embrace sustainable business practices, including offsetting the restaurant's footprint by purchasing credits so it can operate as carbon neutral. Brunch at Founding Farmers is a good time to admire the pretty yet sustainable design here as light floods the 2-story space through the massive windows. Both downstairs and upstairs have communal tables as well as more intimate ones. Wherever you choose to sit, order the made-to-order beignets. The warm, fresh doughnut holes are a little piece of fried-dough heaven and come with caramel and chocolate dipping sauces. Now that your sweet tooth is awake, try the stuffed french toast made from house-made brioche soaked in brandy crème anglaise or the waffles topped with bananas Foster. For a more savory dish opt for one of the pan scrambles or the Southern-inspired fried chicken, eggs, and waffles. Chef-Mixologist Jon Arroyo has crafted a much-loved brunch cocktail list, including a Bloody Mary made with a house-made pepper-infused vodka. Supports the local food movement. Vegan/vegetarian friendly.

Georgia Brown's, 950 15th St. NW, Washington, DC 20005; (202) 393-4499; www.gbrowns.com; Southern; $$$. Georgia Brown's puts on an insane Sunday brunch done in three acts to the sounds of a live jazz band and busily clinking silverware. Act One features an overflowing buffet filled with mounds of peel-and-eat shrimp, biscuit-battered french toast, applewood smoked bacon, sliced Virginia ham, creamy stone-milled grits, and other Low Country takes on morning dishes. There is also a made-to-order omelet station. I must admit I thought my server was kidding when he came to take our order for our entrees for Act Two. But believe it or not there is a full meal that follows the indulgent buffet. Fortunately, you can order your entree to go and it will be wrapped up and given to you to take home at the end of meal for a time far in the future when you feel hungry again. Southern buttermilk chicken, fried cornmeal catfish, Carolina gumbo, black-eyed pea cakes, and shrimp and grits are some of the entree choices. Sweets define the third and final act, including southern-inspired choices like peach cobbler, red velvet cupcakes, and key lime pie bars. Cocktails can be ordered as a pre-show treat or any time throughout the meal and include choices like a Georgia peach martini, a Low Country Bloody Mary served with spiced jumbo shrimp, and a Dirty Cajun spiced with ground black pepper, hot sauce, and a touch of Old Bay. Cocktails are a la carte while the three acts are priced together around $40 per person.

The Greenhouse, The Jefferson, 1200 16th St. NW, Washington, DC 20036; (202) 448-2300; www.jeffersondc.com; New American; $$$. Breakfast at the iconic Jefferson Hotel has long been known as one of the great morning power plays in town. Just up the street from the White House, the graceful Pennsylvania Avenue boutique hotel caters to the known and the in-the-know. But as the light of day delicately streams through the arched skylight above, you might forget how close you are to the seat of power and begin to think you woke up in an elegant chateau in France. Amid all the white marble and dappled sunlight, brunch is served. The menu offers three choices of eggs Benedict: a classic interpretation, a lobster version, and one made with smoked whitefish. Other selections include lemon ricotta pancakes, a three-egg omelet, and a bagel with lox done with Scottish smoked salmon. There is also a listing of some nice "lighter" fare like steel-cut oatmeal,

CREPES AT THE MARKET

Mitchell Salland is used to crowds. Every Saturday and Sunday morning the masses swell around him for the out-of-this-world crepes he makes to order at Eastern Market. Sometimes the wait can be an hour long for one of Mitch's sweet or savory creations, but few seem to complain or be disappointed once they taste the final product. Mitch uses local ingredients whenever possible and is at the market from 8 a.m. to 4 p.m. on weekends only. During the summer, don't forget to make it a la mode. Visit http://crepesatthemarket.com.

house-made granola, and house-made smoothies in either mango, banana, strawberry, raspberry, papaya, pineapple, or açai.

Juice Joint Cafe, 1025 Vermont Ave. NW, Washington, DC 20005; (202) 347-6783; www.juicejointcafe.com; $. A shout out to Emily of Wild and Crazy Pearl blog fame (www.wildandcrazypearl.com) for clueing me in to the deliciousness of a Juice Joint breakfast. The juice bar and cafe start the morning with a menu of organic wraps, bagels with homemade cream cheese, omelets, whole-grain pancakes, and even vanilla cinnamon french toast. Daily specials are worth eyeing, including Emily's favorite, the Friday spinach tortilla wrap made with potatoes, scrambled eggs, turkey bacon, and cheese. Pair it with a smoothie or a create-your-own juice blend.

Juniper, 2401 M St. NW, Washington, DC 20037; (202) 457-5020; New American; $$$. Modern American food is the theme at the elegant brunch served at the Juniper, housed at The Fairmont. Fresh, sustainable, and locally grown ingredients drive the menu choices. Saturday the chef prepares a prix-fixe 3-course brunch, and on Sunday it's a buffet full of old and new favorites.

Kafe Leopold & Konditorei, 3318 M St. NW, Washington, DC 20007; (202) 965-6005; www.kafeleopolds.com; Austrian; $$. Kafe Leopold & Konditorei serves Austrian creations against the backdrop of its clean, modern European decor. The pastries here at this Cady Alley cafe get rave reviews and include a flaky almond croissant, a raisin danish, and a ham and cheese scone. Belgian waffles and egg dishes round out much of the rest of the breakfast menu, which is served until 4 p.m. The espresso is strong and well made and the lovely outdoor patio is the perfect spot for enjoying it on a pretty day. Kafe Leopold & Konditorei does not take reservations.

The Lafayette, The Hay-Adams Hotel, 800 16th St. NW, Washington, DC 20006; (202) 638-6600; www.hayadams.com; New American; $$$$. In order to have Sunday brunch closer to the White House, you need to have a pretty serious security clearance. Fortunately, you don't need either to partake in Hay-Adams's champagne brunch. The meal is done in 3 courses served in The Lafayette, a lovely light-filled space in the historic hotel. An appetizer buffet of starters and salads makes up the first course. The menu changes each week but you can expect to find a sampling of salads, roasted meats, seafood, smoked salmon, breads, cheese, and fresh fruit. Plated entrees follow. Choices are expertly prepared and include favorites like house-made, slow-braised corned beef hash with poached eggs and

Provençal tomato; cornflake-crusted cranberry focaccia french toast with a warm pear compote and caramel sauce, and pan-seared Maryland crab cakes with English peas, whipped potatoes, long pepper, and lemon sauce. Each Sunday the hotel's pastry chef prepares a new mix of creations for dessert. Diners can sip from their choice of Taittinger Brut Champagne, classic Bloody Marys or Strawberry Orange Mimosas. On special occasions brunch is taken upstairs to the newly renovated Top of the Hay, which offers one of the best views of D.C. in the entire city. Brunch here is not inexpensive and as a result it is often filled with people celebrating happy milestones or occasions. The Lafayette and the Hay-Adams in general are also known for hosting D.C.'s power players for meals and drinks, so keep your eyes open between courses for some familiar famous faces.

Masa 14, 1825 14th St. NW, Washington, DC 20009; (202) 328-1414; www.masa14.com; Fusion; $$$. It's Latin-Asian fusion meets all-you-can-eat-and-drink every Saturday and Sunday at Masa 14. For $35 per person you can order as much and as often as you like from the entire brunch food and cocktail menu. Seating for the prix-fixe meal ends at 2 p.m. but you can sit and order until 3 p.m. The restaurant always showcases its small plates and brunch is no exception. The flatbreads and the breakfast pizza with house bacon, eggs yolks, gruyère, pico de gallo, and arugula are good places to start. Continue with the eggs and omelets, which feature a popular tenderloin Benedict. The feast goes on with a selection of salads and sandwiches, like the *pan dulce,* crunchy shrimp, and bacon fried rice. Bacon-Rye Bloody Mary, Lychee Bellini, and a spiked strawberry lemonade can all be found on the brunch cocktail list.

Peacock Cafe, 3251 Prospect St. NW, Washington, DC 20007; (202) 625-2740; www.peacockcafe.com; $$. Put on your mad scientist hat and let your imagination run wild at the fabulous juice bar here. The rainbow of fruit and vegetables makes the combinations seemingly endless. Apple, banana, grapefruit, lemon, mango, orange, papaya, pineapple, strawberry, carrot, celery, ginger, and wheat grass are some of the regulars you can expect to see behind the bar. And of course, choices also reflect what currently is fresh and in season. The brunch menu, available until 4 p.m., offers a host of egg dishes including an egg-white omelet filled with spinach, roasted peppers, and black bean relish, served with fruit. The Georgetown restaurant's signature tomato bisque is served throughout the day, including breakfast, and several lunch items like the burgers (the curry mint lamb burger, turkey burger, and veggie burger are a few of the restaurant's takes on the original) can also be ordered in the morning. Gluten-free options.

Puro Cafe, 1529 Wisconsin Ave. NW, Washington, DC 20007; (202) 787-1937; www.purobarlounge.com; Cafe $$. Puro Cafe exudes a modern charm with its sleek white furnishing, red chandeliers, and European vibe. The brunch menu is limited but full and offers a selection of omelets, flatbreads, a quiche, and some interesting salads. Coffee is central to the morning experience here and the espresso made with Nutella, steamed milk, and foam works well and finds the delicate balance between sweet and not-too-sweet. Puro also makes an espresso with *dulce de leche,* steamed milk, and foam. The outdoor patio in back is a beautiful piece of restaurant real estate that embraces the same chic style of the interior space with its white cushioned lounge-style seating and crisp white draped fabric panels that gently catch the breeze.

Seasons, Four Seasons Hotel, 2800 Pennsylvania Ave. NW, 20007; (202) 342-0444; www.fourseasons.com/washington/dining/seasons; New American; $$$$. Sunday brunch at Georgetown's Four Seasons Hotel's Seasons restaurant stands as the most elegant and one of the most abundant brunches in the city. Buffet tables artfully adorned with fresh floral arrangements present the seemingly endless choices, which embrace the current time of year, local flavors, and a gourmet edge. Oysters on the half shell, Crab Louie, snapper seviche, caviar, tuna tartare, and seared scallops can be found on the raw bar. Next stop at the cheese and charcuterie station, with roasted lamb, ham, and other meats, before a visit to the made-to-order omelet and waffle stations, but don't forget to save room for dessert. The dessert room is a destination unto itself with its much-loved chocolate fountain. During playoff season you might spy special choices like a chocolate hazelnut hockey puck topped with the Washington Capitals logo. In the winter, indulge with the hot chocolate with toasted marshmallows. The bottomless mimosas and fresh-squeezed orange juice are good choices all year round. The brunch comes with a hefty price tag so come with your appetite intact.

Tabard Inn Restaurant, Hotel Tabard Inn, 1739 N St. NW, Washington, DC 20036; (202) 331-8528; www.tabardinn.com; New American; $$$. Brunch at historic Hotel Tabard Inn is a necessary D.C. rite of passage, to say nothing of a delicious one. Nestled in the back of the eclectically decorated historic inn, the restaurant offers an extensive brunch menu comprised of dishes that start with house-made favorites. The kitchen cures its own meats, smokes its own salmon, and gets many of its fresh ingredients from the farm owned by the hotel. But the best from-scratch creation by far to come out of this kitchen is the soft, warm just-made cinnamon and sugar doughnuts served with the restaurants own fresh vanilla whipped cream. They literally do melt in your mouth. The doughnuts are a hard act to follow, but the rest of the brunch menu holds its own. The scrambled eggs with cream cheese and chives is a fan favorite and is served with house-made Toulouse sausage and home fries, while the chicken schnitzel is a good choice for those feeling more lunch than brunch. The toasted almond waffles topped with a caramel-apple compote and whipped cream are served only on Sunday. The inn's plant-filled patio is almost always in demand  and is a good spot to gaze at the Tabard's amazing green pitched roofs where some of the herbs and even blueberries used by the chefs are grown.

Lunch

For years the country's lawmakers, political trendsetters, and news authorities have sat down together over hearty midday meals to discuss, debate, and decide the issues of the day. While rules about who can actually pick up the check have evolved over the years, the power lunch remains a hallmark of inside-the-Beltway life. And although steak and potatoes still have a prominent place on many a menu, kitchens no longer limit themselves to the red meat meals of days gone by and instead experiment with new choices in addition to putting a modern spin on old favorites. Here we list the power places, followed by some more casual (though perhaps no less powerful) staples.

Power Lunch

You don't have to wear a Congressional ID around your neck or have a recognizable last name to lunch at these institutions, just a reservation. The food is good and the people-watching can't be beat. Keep your eyes open for the same cast of characters who often appear on the Sunday morning news shows, along with the occasional left-coast celebrity in town to lend star appeal to a cause.

Bibiana Osteria-Enoteca, 1100 New York Ave. NW, Washington, DC 20005; (202) 216-9550; www.bibianadc.com; Italian; $$$. Bibiana Osteria-Enoteca serves contemporary Italian food in a chic setting that evokes Paris or New York yet remains distinctly Washington. A varied selection of antipasti, house-made pastas, pesce and carne all find their way on to the lunch menu here.

BistroBis, 15 E St. NW, Washington, DC 20001; (202) 661-2700; www.bistrobis.com; French; $$$$. Members of Congress, senators and TV personalities are a regular part of the lunchtime rush at this modern French bistro on Capitol Hill. Escargot Chablisienne, duck liver pâté and steak tartare Atilla top the starter menu while trout *grenobloise, steak frites,* and a lovely tuna salad niçoise can be found on the entree listings. The Bis Burger on a toasted brioche also shouldn't be overlooked.

Bourbon Steak, 2800 Pennsylvania Ave. NW, Washington, DC 20007; (202) 944-2026; www.bourbonsteakdc.com; Contemporary American; $$$. Housed in the graceful Four Seasons Hotel, Bourbon Steak adds elegance to the steak house concept. The service ranks as some of the best in town and the menu follows suit. Five burgers can be found on the menu, including a veggie one, and can be ordered with duck-fat fries or onion rings. Several cuts of oak-fired beef are cooked on the wood-burning grill, as are the lobster and fish.

The Caucus Room, 401 9th St. NW, Washington, DC 20004; (202) 393-1300; www.thecaucusroom.com; Steak; $$$. Mississippi Governor and Former RNC Chairman Haley Barbour and Democratic power player Tom Boggs joined forces to open The Caucus Room as bipartisan dining experience. Diners from both sides of the aisle still come to the steak house to talk shop or just enjoy a steak. Seven different burgers with names like The Lobbyist, The Diplomat, and The Laissez-Faire are offered on the lunch menu. A favorite with the Hill crowd, the restaurant also offers an extensive wine list.

Central Michel Richard, 1001 Pennsylvania Ave. NW, Washington, DC 20004; (202) 626-0015; www.centralmichelrichard .com; American; $$$. Central's tuna burger is divine. I cannot recommend it enough. If you feel the need for other choices the chef also makes a lobster burger, meatball burger, and a chicken-and-lemon burger. Truly, it's hard to make a bad choice here so follow your heart and taste buds. For dessert, do not pass Go or collect $200 before heading directly to Michel's chocolate bar, the celebrity chef's take on a Kit Kat bar and the restaurant's signature dessert.

Charlie Palmer Steak, 101 Constitution Ave. NW, Washington, DC 20001; (202) 547-8100; www.charliepalmer.com; Steak; $$$. If you dined any closer to the reflecting pool you would, well,

be seeing your reflection. Located at the foot of the Capitol, this swanky steak house oozes red meat and power. The 3-course prix-fixe lunch offers the choice of pan-roasted skate or grilled hanger steak bookended by salad or soup and a dessert. Filet mignon, a rib eye, and several fish choices can be found on the more extensive a la carte lunch listing. Power cocktails boast fun names like The First Congress, Dirty Politics and The Filibuster. *Top Chef* Alert: Brian Voltaggio, now of Volt fame, previously ran the kitchen here.

DC Coast Restaurant, 1401 K St. NW, Washington, DC 20005; (202) 216-5988; http://dccoast.com; New American; $$$. During lunchtime, the buzz of political chatter and business banter rise up toward the sky-high ceilings in DC Coast's massive Art Deco dining room. Fortunately, the giant bronze mermaid statue that watches over the space never betrays a confidence. The menu here boasts the kitchen's take on classic lunch choices like the DC Coast Salad made with applewood bacon, hard-boiled egg, blue cheese, toma-toes, radish, and Lorenzo dressing. The popular DC Coast Burger comes topped with Vermont cheddar cheese, fresh herb aioli, and a house-made pickle. There are also a fair number of seafood-related options. Make your lunch the three-martini kind with DC's Coasts long cocktail list, which includes the delicious K Street Martini, made with white grape juice or, in spring, the Cherry Blossom Martini with its base of cherry-infused Smirnoff Vodka.

Equinox Restaurant, 818 Connecticut Ave. NW, Washington, DC 20006; (202) 331-8118; http://equinoxrestaurantdc.blogspot .com; New American; $$$. The Obamas headed to Equinox on their first night out in D.C. Just a few steps from the White House, the restaurant shares the first lady's commitment to fresh food and locally harvested produce. Chef Todd C. Gray, who runs Equinox with his wife Ellen Kassoff Gray, builds his menus around the sustainable and seasonal food movement. Whenever possible Gray cooks only with community-farmed, organic ingredients that have been grown within 100 miles of the restaurant. Depending on the season, you might experience dishes like gnocchi of wild nettles with spring garlic, loin of thyme-marinated Hawaiian yellow marlin or "pride of the plains" beef ravioli. Supports the local food movement.

Johnny's Half Shell Restaurant, 400 N. Capitol St. NW, Washington, DC 20001; (202) 737-0400; www.johnnyshalfshell.net; Seafood; $$$. The glow of the Capitol building in the background makes it hard to forget where you are when you dine at this Capitol Hill seafood fixture. Chesapeake and Gulf Coast seafood are the focus here and all of it comes from sustainable sources.

The Monocle Restaurant, 107 D St. NE, Washington, DC 20002; (202) 546-4488; www.themonocle.com; Steak; $$$. An institution on the Senate side of the Hill since it opened in 1960, The Monocle falls under the heading of an oldie but a goodie. The restaurant serves old-school business lunch favorites like porterhouse steak, crab cakes, and salmon filet, and does them all well. Pictures of senators and other D.C. notables adorn the walls and the people-watching does not stop with the photographs. Senators, news personalities, and others pop in often. The private dining room upstairs is a popular venue for fundraisers, and the Senate's Women Caucus claims The Monocle as a regular meeting spot.

Old Ebbitt Grill, 675 15th St. NW, Washington, DC 20005; (202) 347-4800; www.ebbitt.com; Seafood; $$$. Steps from the White House, the Old Ebbitt Grill exudes old Washington. Presidents Grant, Cleveland and Harding all dined at Old Ebbitt. And the animal heads on the wall are rumored to have been a gift from Teddy Roosevelt, another presidential customer. Today many well-known Washingtonians still frequent the iconic restaurant housed behind a Beaux-Arts façade. The Oyster Bar with its array of choices remains a big draw throughout the day and the lunch menu features many seafood options, including grilled shrimp skewers, trout Parmesan, and linguini with clams. Try to snag one of the velvet booths in the mahogany-filled main dining room to really feel the pomp and history here.

The Oval Room, 800 Connecticut Ave. NW #110, Washington, DC 20006; (202) 463-8700; www.ovalroom.com; New American; $$$. Washington elites from former presidents to current members of Congress flock to the inside-the-Beltway favorite that serves Mediterranean-influenced American cuisine in its beautiful dining room. The coffee-cured hamachi with blood orange and fennel slaw is one of the more unusual starters while the Oval Room Cobb salad shows a modern kitchen can embrace a classic lunchtime favorite. A balance of seafood, chicken, lamb, and beef round out the entrees and the four sandwiches on the menu are perennial favorites. The outdoor patio is the perfect place for lunch on a pretty day and even puts you one step closer to the nearby Oval Office. *Top Chef* Alert: The Oval Room Sous Chef Tamesha Warren did a stint on the popular reality show.

Palm Restaurant, 1225 19th St. NW, Washington, DC; (202) 293-9091; www.thepalm.com; Steak; $$$. My first week in Washington many years ago, I spied a king and queen walking out of The Palm. It wasn't until a few more years had passed and I had earned my Washington stripes that I learned that it wasn't an unusual occurrence. Heads of state, royalty, and celebrities are often spied coming in and out of the 19th Street power restaurant. Inside you can see some of them immortalized in the caricatures painted on the walls in the dining room. Steaks, chops, lobster, and fish are the order of the day here. And the signature Palm Surf 'n' Turf remains a best seller.

Ristorante Tosca, 1112 F St. NW, Washington, DC 20004; (202) 367-1990; www.toscadc.com; Italian; $$$. The beautiful dining room and exquisite Northern Italian dishes keep summer associates, partners, lobbyists and others in the know coming back time and

TOP DOG

Ben's Chili Bowl, 1213 U St. NW, Washington, DC 20009; (202) 667-0909; www.benschilibowl.com. Half-smokes. $.

Although not a typical power restaurant decked out in crisp linens and crystal barware, everyone from presidents to movie stars have eaten at Ben's Chili Bowl since it first opened in 1958. President Barack Obama even popped by the landmark U Street spot for a half-smoke several days before he took the oath of office in 2009. Bill Cosby has been coming here for so long that the signature half-smoke chili dog now bears his name. Ben's stays open late into the night, closing at 4 a.m. on Fri and Sat, 2 a.m. Mon through Thurs, and 11 a.m. on Sun.

time again. The chef makes the pasta fresh each day and you taste the difference between what is served here and anything that has been sitting around more than a day. The restaurant offers a $35 prix-fixe lunch menu.

701 Restaurant, 701 Pennsylvania Ave. NW, Washington, DC 20004; (202) 393-0701; www.701restaurant.com; American; $$$. Located on Pennsylvania Avenue between the White House and the Capitol, 701 is no stranger to diners who work with both institutions. The fare is New American and includes old/new favorites like a pulled-pork sandwich, a beef burger, and rye-braised lamb ribs. A $15 eat-at-the-bar menu includes a choice of entree and a glass of wine or soft drink. On Thurs nights a jazz pianist tickles the ivories and on Fri and Sat a bass player joins in.

Casual Lunch

Not every lunch in the city changes the course of policy, but it should please the taste buds. These more casual choices stand out as spots worthy of your midday break and lunch money. Besides, the true secret of the city is that as much business is done over turkey sandwiches taken to go as is done over three martini meals served on porcelain plates.

Bread and Brew, 247 20th St. NW, Washington, DC 20036; (202) 466-2676; www.breadandbrew.com; Sandwiches/Soups/Pizza; $$. The chef at Bread and Brew stocks the kitchen with organic milk, farm-fresh eggs, and lots of local produce, all of which go into the soups, salads, quiches, and individual pizzas made here. Soups range from the traditional chicken noodle to the more unusual but still yummy mushroom brie. Quiche flavors change daily and the pizzas have a crisp, thin crust. On sunny days the outdoor patio is a pleasant spot to enjoy your meal. If you decide to dine inside, head downstairs to check out the bar, which serves craft beers, organic wines, and small plates.

Breadline, 1751 Pennsylvania Ave. NW, Washington, DC 20006; (202) 822-8900; www.breadline.com; Sandwiches; $. Don't be scared away by the long lines that crowd the Breadline during the weekday lunch rush. Once you take your first bite of one of the sandwich shop's famous creations, you'll swear you'd go right back and do the wait all over again. Breadline's offerings change daily so check the website for the current week's listing if you don't like surprises. Specials include a fried cod sandwich, a BLT on brioche made with farm-fresh tomatoes and a prosciutto *piadine* made with fontina and greens. The store, which has very limited seating, also sells great soups, empanadas, and pizzas.

Capital Q BBQ, 707 H St. NW, Washington, DC 20001; (202) 347-8396; www.capitalqbbq.com; Barbecue; $$. Chinatown's Capital Q strives to bring a little bit of the Lone Star State to the nation's capital with its overstuffed smoked barbecued brisket and pulled pork sandwiches. Wash it down with fresh lemonade or a glass of sweet tea.

Chinatown Express, 746 6th St. NW, Washington, DC 20001; (202) 638-0424; Chinese; $. Cozy up to the window at Chinatown Express and spend a few minutes watching the chef stretch noodles and fold dumplings at a staggering pace. Inside the cramped, somewhat dingy shop, the tea flows and the noodle dishes make up for the lack of ambience. One of the few businesses in the neighborhood left that remind you that you indeed are in Chinatown.

Perfect Picnic Spots

Build an escape route into your day by planning a lunchtime picnic. Even if you turn into a pumpkin when an hour is up or the BlackBerry goes off, looking at something other than your computer screen even for a short time can help recharge your mind and soul before returning to your office or your day of touring. Washington is rich in hidden and not-so-hidden spots calling for you, an overstuffed sandwich, and your phone's mute button to come visit. Here are a few favorites:

Dupont Circle Fountain (19th St. NW & Connecticut Ave. NW). The Circle that gives the popular downtown neighborhood its name fills up with hipsters, students, and office workers alike during the day. Benches look out onto the fountain at the center of the circle and a small grassy area stretches between the benches and the street. Although the lanes of traffic circle around, it still feels like an escape.

Georgetown Waterfront Park (1000 31st St. NW; www.georgetown waterfrontpark.org). A 10-acre stretch along the waterfront provides a green escape from the hustle and bustle of busy Georgetown. Park yourself on a bench and take in the view of the Kennedy Center, Roosevelt Island, and the Potomac before you venture back to the city's buzz.

Gravelly Point Park. Aviation junkies flock to this Arlington park that sits just 400 feet north of the runway at Ronald Reagan Washington National Airport. Bring a picnic and watch the airplanes take off and land. They are so close it's hard not to believe you can touch them as they make the final descent—and most people try at least once to reach up and touch one. The spot also offers a pretty view of the city from across the Potomac.

Hains Point (1100 Ohio Dr. SW). The expansive park offers picnic tables, benches, and plenty of green space. It's also a great spot for airplane watching.

Kenilworth Park and Aquatic Gardens (1550 Anacostia Ave. NE; www.nps.gov/keaq). Magnificent water lilies, bird watching, and tranquillity define this place of beauty hidden away in the urban jungle. Water lilies bloom in the summer but the gardens always have something pretty to share.

Meridian Hill Park (2500 16th St. NW; www.nps.gov/mehi). Another off-the-beaten-path gem tucked away from the busy city.

Sculpture Garden at the National Gallery of Art (The National Mall at 7th Street and Constitution Avenue NW; www.nga.gov/feature/sculpturegarden/general/index.shtm). Oversize, whimsical art pieces dot the grass-and-tree-filled Sculpture Garden and help make it a prime lunchtime picnic spot. Benches near the fountain at the park's center fill up quickly on sunny days and grassy spots to stretch out always are yours for the taking. In the summer, the park plays host to free jazz concerts from 5 to 8:30 p.m. on Fri.

The Spanish Steps (S Street & 22nd Street NW). Grab a step and daydream. A picturesque old stone staircase in Kalorama that once led to an estate that no longer stands now serves as romantic detour from city life.

DC-3, 423 8th St. SE, Washington, DC 20003; (202) 546-1935; www.eatdc3.com; Half-smokes; $. The vintage air travel themed DC-3 serves up half-smokes and hot dogs in several different ways, each designed to conjure up the flavors of a different region of the country. The Bay Bridge dog is served on a pretzel roll with crab dip and Old Bay while the NYC Street Vendor dog takes it old school with a Nathan's hot dog on a steamed bun with sauerkraut and yellow mustard. Vegetarians can order the California Left Winger, a meatless falafel dog on a deli bun topped with *tzatziki* and avocado. Don't forget to order a side of the addictive fried-pickle-potato-chip hybrid known as Frips.

Good Stuff Cafe, 303 Pennsylvania Ave. SE, Washington, DC 20003; (202) 543-8222; www.goodstuffeatery.com; Burgers; $$. This whole place is a *Top Chef* alert. Spike Mendelsohn started and runs the Capitol Hill cafe with his parents, sister, aunt, and cousin. Together they keep customers content and full with juicy burgers, crispy fries, and thick milk shakes in flavors like toasted marshmallow. Check out the Obama burger that boasts applewood bacon, onion marmalade, Roquefort cheese, and horseradish mayo.

Hill Country BBQ and Market, 410 7th St. NW, Washington, DC 20004; (202) 556-2050; www.hillcountrywdc.com; Barbecue; $$. Slow-cooked smoked beef brisket, done Texas BBQ joint style, is the star of this lunchtime line dance. A dry-rub is used on the meat before it is smoked low and slow with oak wood the restaurant ships in from Texas. The meat is then hand carved. Customers purchase

as much or as little as they want—by the slice, the rib, or link. Leave room for the side dishes like baked beans, cheddar mac and cheese, corn pudding, green bean casserole, and bourbon mashed potatoes.

Java Green, 1020 19th St. NW, Washington, DC 20036; (202) 775-8899; www.javagreen.net; Vegetarian; $$. To borrow a phrase from the classic Levy's ad campaign: You don't have to be a vegetarian to love Java Green. Vegetarian, vegan, raw, and organic dishes make up the menu here with lots of mock meat cooked into the tasty wraps, sandwiches, salads, and soups. Java Green continues its commitment to the planet with eco-friendly business practices and products.

Khan's Bar and Grill, 1125 H St. NE, Washington, DC 20002; (202) 399-6010; www.khansdc.com; Mongolian barbecue; $. The walls on this Mongolian barbecue style spot are lined with oversize TV screens each playing a different game. When you take your eye off the ball, fill up your bowl with all the veggies, meats, and sauces you crave and bring them to the grill to be cooked. Mild, sweet, or spicy wings can be ordered as an appetizer because, really, how can you watch a game without wings?

MGM Roast Beef, 905 Brentwood Rd. NE, Washington, DC 20018; (202) 248-0389; www.mgmroastbeef.com; Sandwiches; $. Killer roast beef and turkey sandwiches made on soft rolls with enough condiment choices to satisfy most tastes—lettuce, tomato, onions, ketchup, deli mustard, mayonnaise, horseradish sauce, honey-mustard, pickles, jalapeños, hot peppers, and cranberry chutney. Wash it down with some authentic sweet tea and then go take a food-coma nap. The Brookland spot also serves a good breakfast.

Mixt Green, Two locations: 1200 19th Ave. NW, Suite 105, Washington, DC 20036; (202) 630-4018; and 1700 K St. NW, Washington, DC 20006; (202) 630-7538; www.mixtgreens.com; Salads; $. Fresh design-your-own salads and a commitment to Mother Earth are the focus of Mixt Green. The shop only uses in-season produce and compostable and biodegradable packaging.

Rasika, 633 D St. NW, Washington, DC 20004; (202) 637-1222; www.rasikarestaurant.com; Indian; $$. Rasika brings a modern flair to the classic favors that define good Indian food. Some of Rasika's takes on Old World favorites include calamari chile garlic, tandoori lamb chops, and *dum ka* duck. The menu has a ton of vegetarian options.

Sticky Rice DC, 1224 H St. NE, Washington, DC 20002; (202) 397-7655; www.sticky ricedc.com; Sushi; $$. I would never in a million years think to pair sushi with Tater Tots, but fortunately the brainpower behind Sticky Rice DC did. Located on the H

Street Corridor, the restaurant offers a menu filled with a variety of fun sashimi, maki, and sushi rolls (traditional and more out-there house combos like a chile roll). A host of noodle dishes, salads, and Asian-inspired sandwiches—with tots on the side—round out the choices. Sticky Rice also offers lunchtime delivery. Gluten-free options and vegan/vegetarian friendly.

Teaism, 401 7th St. NW, Washington, DC 20004; (202) 628-1005; 2009 R St. NW, Washington, DC 20009; (202) 667-3827; and 800 Connecticut Ave. NW, Washington, DC 20006; (202) 835-2233; www .teaism.com; Asian; $$. A personal favorite, Teaism is a lovely spot to sit, sip and eat. The bento box lunches (salmon, veggie, handroll, and chicken) don't disappoint and the udon noodle soup is love in a bowl. Other menu items include dishes with Japanese, Chinese, and Indian influences. Cozy up to a pot of tea on a cold day or an iced glass during the hot, humid D.C. summer. The Moroccan Mint is my favorite. The choices, not surprisingly, are many. Pretty teapots and other tea paraphernalia also may be purchased here. Gluten-free and vegan/vegetarian options.

The Well Dressed Burrito, 1220 19th St. NW, Washington, DC 20036; (202) 293-0515; www.cffolksrestaurant.com; Tex-Mex; $. This hole-in-the-wall is actually the burrito-shop-in-the-alley. For more than 25 years, the in-the-know set has been swearing by the homemade burritos sold from the shop tucked away in the alley between M and N Streets Northwest. Tostada salads, tacos, chimichangas, and fajitas are also sold here. Carry out only.

Pizza, Burgers & Falafel

Although both pizza and falafel have roots that start far beyond our borders, both foods have joined the classic American burger as a quick food staple in this country. The next pages list some of the favorite places to find great examples of the tasty pizza-burger-falafel trifecta.

Pizza

More than statehood, snow removal, and the changing traffic patterns on Connecticut Avenue, Washingtonians have spent years pondering one issue: pizza. The lack of a decent slice hovered over the city like a dark cloud sending hungry residents fleeing to New York or Chicago now and again for a fix. Fortunately, the dark days are over and D.C. can now claim its rightful place among the cities of the world where one does not have to rely on Domino's as the sole source of the gift that is a pizza pie. D.C. has arrived. The city now boasts several good pizza choices, some so good that they could compete in the big sauce-and-cheese leagues.

Comet Ping Pong, 5037 Connecticut Ave. NW, Washington, DC 20008; (202) 364-0404; www.cometpingpong.com; $$. The decision to combine Ping Pong with pizza ranks up there with the decision to top dough with sauce and cheese. Pizza at this fun Northwest D.C. restaurant is made on a light, thin crust with just the right amount of chewiness that ably hold the farm-fresh local ingredients on top. Anything with the smoky mozzarella is worth devouring, including The Smoky, made with the smoked cheese, smoked mushrooms, smoked bacon, melted onions, and garlic. The Yalie boasts fresh clams and The Drive has broccoli rabe, garlic, Whitmore Farm egg, melted onion, and pecorino. Wash it down with a microbrew or glass of wine. Ping Pong tables are in back and the large dining room embraces a whimsical table tennis theme, with its found-wood tables painted to mimic Ping Pong tables. Comet also will make any of its pizzas with gluten-free pizza crusts or soy cheese. Supports the local food movement. Gluten-free options and vegan/vegetarian friendly.

Coppi's Organic Restaurant, 1414 U St. NW, Washington, DC 20009; (202) 319-7773; www.coppisorganic.com; $$. Coppi's is an homage to good wood-fired pizza and the Italian cycling legend Fausto Coppi whose pictures, jerseys, and other memorabilia adorn almost every inch of wall the cozy 14th Street restaurant. Coppi's makes a very good pie by combining flavors like lamb sausage, ricotta, cucumber, onion, rosemary, garlic, and tomato sauce, or greens, green tomato, mozzarella, Romano, and red onion. Coppi's pizza makers have a reputation for being very generous with the toppings and the final product comes out not the least bit greasy. Don't forget about the pasta dishes and other entrees before you delve into a Nutella calzone and house-made gelato for dessert. The kitchen at Coppi's uses only organic ingredients, including sustainable seafood, grass-fed meats, and free-range chicken. Wind-power electricity keeps the cozy restaurant lit up and the woodwork and benches have been repurposed from a nearby church. Coppi's offers curbside pick up. Supports the local food movement.

Ella's Wood Fired Pizza, 901 F St. NW, Washington, DC 20004; (202) 638-3434; www.ellaspizza.com; $$. Located in the heart of the bustling Penn Quarter, Ella's serves Neapolitan-style pizzas made in its blistering-hot, wood-fired pizza oven. The thin-crust pizza is the base for many different combinations including Genovese, *bosco,* and Margherita versions. Ella's also makes a very good gluten-free pizza pie. The double chocolate pudding by itself is worth the trip. Gluten-free options.

Il Canale, 1063 31st St. NW, Washington, DC 20007; (202) 337-4444; www.ilcanaledc.com; Pizza; $$. If you want to find a more authentic interpretation of Neapolitan pizza, you should start looking at transatlantic flights. The owner and executive chef at Il Canale make the traditional thin-crust pies for all to see. The pizza cooks in a wood-fired oven imported from Naples and many of the toppings, including the *bufala* mozzarella, are imported from Italy. The pizza menu is divided up into *rosse* and *bianche,* which are offered in combinations that strictly adhere to the standards of the Verace Pizza Napoletana in Naples, which governs the ingredients and cooking methods can rightfully be used in Neapolitan pizza. The Georgetown restaurant sits just a few steps from the C&O Canal, with the upstairs patio overlooking it.

Italian Pizza Kitchen, 4483 Connecticut Ave. NW, Washington, DC 20008; (202) 364-1010; www.theitalianpizzakitchen.net; Pizza; $. My neighborhood pizza parlor and a solid choice for a good slice of 'za. During the day you can order by the slice at the counter and at dinnertime it's table service or delivery. Italian Pizza Kitchen also makes some great calzones, like its oversize Prima Calzone stuffed with spinach, artichoke hearts, Roma tomatoes, caramelized onions, ricotta cheese, mozzarella cheese, and tomato sauce.

Matchbox, Capitol Hill, 521 8th St. SE, Washington, DC 20003; (202) 548-0369; www.matchboxcaphill.com; $$. Thin-crust pizzas expertly baked in a wood-burning brick oven are the centerpieces of both Matchbox locations. The dough and toppings are all made in-house. Combinations include a white prosciutto pie, an Italian ham and arugula pizza, and a spicy vegetable pie made with chipotle pepper tomato sauce, smoked gouda, Spanish onions, and fresh basil. A second location is at Matchbox Chinatown, 713 H St. NW; (202) 289-4441.

Pete's New Haven Style Apizza, 1400 Irving St. NW, Washington, DC 20010; (202) 332-7383; www.petesapizza.com; $$. A thin crust that is at once chewy on the inside and crispy on the outside defines good New Haven–style pizza, properly known as *apizza*. Pete's apizza crust passes with flying colors on both counts and serves as the basis for some really great pies. Pete's Edge of the Wood is one of my favorite pizzas in town, with sautéed spinach, caramelized onions, ricotta, and some of the thinnest, most delicious fried crisp Italian eggplant slices imaginable. You can order by the slice or by the pie. Pete's also has a store in Columbia Heights and Clarendon and makes gluten-free pizza at all its locations.

Pizza Paradiso, 3282 M St. NW, Washington, DC; (202) 337-1245; www.eatyourpizza.com; $$. In the old days you pretty much couldn't call yourself a Washingtonian until you had waited in line for a table to open up at Pizzeria Paradiso, this town's first real gourmet pizza restaurant. Now with two city locations and lots of competition, Pizza Paradiso's thin-crust pies still remain a crowd pleaser. Fan favorites include the Quattro Formaggi, made with pecorino, fontina, gorgonzola, mozzarella, parsley, and garlic, and the simple-yet-delicious Paradiso, made with tomato and mozzarella. A second location is at 2003 P St. NW; (202) 223-1245. Vegan/vegetarian friendly.

RedRocks, 1036 Park Rd. NW, Washington, DC 20010; (202) 506-1402; www.firebrickpizza.com; $$. From its prime corner location in Columbia Heights, RedRocks cooks up authentic Neapolitan pizza in its wood-fired oven. The thin-crust firebrick pies are topped with locally grown vegetables and herbs, handmade cheeses, and sustainably raised meats, many of which are cured in-house whenever possible. RedRocks also makes its own sausages. The large patio outside the converted Federal townhouse is in-demand real estate during good weather and an ideal place to sip a bottle of craft beer or a glass of the Italian wine.

Radius Pizza, 3155 Mount Pleasant St. NW, Washington, DC 20010; (202) 234-0808; www.radiusdc.com; $$. Radius's husband and wife team here bake up thin-crust New York–style pies with ingredients that come from no farther south than Virginia and no farther north than Pennsylvania. The Mount Pleasant pizzeria's commitment to environmental practices extends to just about every part of the restaurant and even the cooking oil in the kitchen is donated to a group that coverts it into biodiesel fuel. And the best part of this feel-good operation is that it is a tastes-good one, too. Locals rave about the pizza here, especially when taking advantage of the $5 slice and pint special offered every night from 5 p.m. to 7 p.m. Supports the local food movement. Vegan/vegetarian friendly.

Seventh Hill Pizza, 327 Seventh St. SE, Washington, DC 20003; (202) 544-1911; www.montmartredc.com/seventhhill; $$. "Life's too short, have a seat," Pizzaiolo Anthony Pilla playfully calls out to a group of customers as he effortlessly tosses pizza dough into the air behind the counter at Seventh Hill. "My special today is amazing. Try my special. Come on." Today's special pizza is a pie topped with sliced potatoes, arugula, Black Forest mushrooms, and orange oil. And, for the record, it really is amazing. All the thin-crust pizzas he creates in the hickory-fired oven behind the counter at Seventh Hill are amazing. And all come with a healthy side of Pilla's entertaining, dough-throwing ways. Pizzas at this gem of a shop near Eastern Market come in a personal-pan size and a 12-inch size more suitable for sharing. Pilla also uses his handmade pizza dough in the bread for sandwiches. The spicy tuna, with avocados, spinach, and a slight kick, is especially good but whatever you wind up ordering, make sure to save some room for the Nutella calzone for dessert.

2Amys, 3715 Macomb St. NW, Washington, DC 20016; (202) 885-5700; www.2amyspizza.com; $$. I have never passed by this popular Northwest restaurant without seeing a crowd in front waiting for tables inside. 2Amys specializes in Neapolitan pizza baked to perfection in its wood-burning oven with three offerings that meet the Italian government's strict standards for the delicacy. The menu also features other less traditional combinations that don't adhere to the guidelines but are delicious all the same. There are also three stuffed pizzas to choose from. If the noisy buzz of the restaurant's main area gets to you, wait a bit longer for a table in the back near the bar.

The Upper Crust Pizzeria, 1747 Pennsylvania Ave. NW, Washington, DC; (202) 463-0002; www.theuppercrustpizzeria.com; $$. This popular Boston pizzeria recently set up shop on Pennsylvania Avenue and is keeping D.C. slice lovers happy with its thin crunchy crust and long list of toppings. The store even created a few special D.C. combinations in honor of its new location, including a FLOTUS pie, inspired by the First Lady's commitment to fresh food—a pie that comes topped with spinach, broccoli, and feta.

Vace, 3315 Connecticut Ave. NW, Washington, DC 20008; (202) 363-1999; www.vaceitaliandeli.com; $. Vace sold pizza-by-the-slice back in the days when D.C. was a pizza wasteland. Now that this is no longer a one-slice town, Vace slices still holds up. Vace makes its pizza with the homemade sauce on top of the cheese and all of its pizza, by the slice or by the pie, is strictly to go. There are no tables here inside or outside of the Cleveland Park Italian deli. Vace also sells its delicious homemade pastas and sauces. They also have a Bethesda store.

We, the Pizza, 303 Pennsylvania Ave. SE, Washington, DC 20003; (202) 544-4008; www.wethepizza.com; $$. We, the Pizza marks *Top Chef* contestant Spike Mendelsohn's second time opening a restaurant in town. Next door to his popular Good Stuff Eatery,

Mendelsohn's pizzeria serves up New York–style 'za by the slice or by the pie. Either way, they are topped with fresh, local ingredients. He also cooks up Sicilian pies and mixes made-to-order Italian sodas. You can even order an egg cream.

Burgers

Classic, American, and everyone has a different opinion on where to find the best one. Here are a few worth trying:

BGR, The Burger Joint, 1514 Connecticut Ave. NW, Washington, DC; (202) 299-1071; www.bgrtheburgerjoint.com; $. Juicy burgers cooked to order with three kinds of "fries" to choose from—Yukon gold potato fries, sweet potato fries, and asparagus fries. They also serve a very good veggie burger.

Chef Geoff's, 3201 New Mexico Ave. NW, Washington, DC; and 1301 Pennsylvania Ave. NW, Washington, DC; (202) 464-4461; www .chefgeoff.com; $$. Geoff cooks up several kinds of burgers and they are the starring act of the restaurant's happy hour special.

Five Guys Burgers and Fries, Various locations; www.fiveguys .com; $. The name says it all: burgers and fries.

Matchbox: Chinatown, 713 H St. NW, Washington, DC 20001; (202) 289-4441; www.matchboxchinatown.com; $$. The beef sliders have many loyal fans. Order a plate of three, six, or nine, and choose from three cheeses to go on top or just enjoy 'em straight-up.

Palena Cafe, 3529 Connecticut Ave. NW, Washington, DC 20008; (202) 537-9250; www.palenarestaurant.com; $$. Washingtonians from all over the city have been Metroing up to Cleveland Park for years to order The Palena Cheeseburger.

The Reef, 2446 18th St. NW, Washington, DC 20009; (202) 518-3800; www.thereefdc.com; $$. Bite into a bison burger on the rooftop patio at this Adams Morgan's hang out.

Shake Shack, 1216 18th St. NW, Washington, DC 20036; (202) 683-9922; www.shakeshack.com; $. A burger and shake haven in the spirit of Fonzie and the jukebox. Shake Shack also offers a full gluten-free menu.

Sign of the Whale, 1825 M St. NW, Washington, DC 20036; (202) 785-1110; www.signofthewhaledc.com; $. For more than a half century this loud bar/lounge and popular college hangout has been serving its "Famous Whale Burgers."

The Wonderland Ballroom, 1101 Kenyon St. NW, Washington, DC 20010; www.thewonderland ballroom.com; $. Neighborhood hole-in-the-wall with good burgers and cold beer. Wonderland's Monday trivia is an experience every Washingtonian should have at least once.

Falafel

Like pizza, the other hallmark of a city worth living in, in my humble opinion, is good falafel. I am happy to report that Washington has many great sources that stay open late into the night, serving the insomnia and hangover crowds alike. Regulars even come on line to post and search for new tips on how to pack the most salads and sauces into one precious pita.

Amsterdam Falafelshop, 2425 18th St. NW, Washington, DC 20009; (202) 234-1969; www.falafelshop.com. This Adam's Morgan hole-in-the-wall is no-frills but the falafel is all-flavor. Amsterdam Falafel serves some of the best falafel in town. Order a whole or half sandwich and then go to town on the toppings bar, which includes a rainbow of delicious sauces and salads—deep-fried eggplant, pickled cabbage, and *tzatziki* to name just a few. You get one shot at the toppings so pick wisely and heed the advice of "smashing your balls" to fit more yummy stuff into your sandwich. The shop stays open late into the night (on the weekend lots of hungry drunk people filter in from the bars during the wee hours of the night) and also sells brownies, lemonade, and divinely inspired fries that are even better when dunked in the garlic mayo. There are no plates or forks for the wrapped up sandwiches but some diehards have been known to bring their own.

Greek Deli & Catering, 1120 19th St. NW #1, Washington, DC 20036; (202) 296-2111; www.greekdelidc.com; $. There is a huge run on the Greek Deli during lunchtime and once you get your first bite you'll understand why. In addition to some great sandwiches, this Farragut North shop makes good crispy falafel with the added twist of feta as a topping. You'll wonder why more people don't combine the two more often. The baklava here is worth trying, as are the spinach pies.

Lebanese Taverna, 2641 Connecticut Ave. NW, Washington, DC, 20008; (202) 265-8681; www.lebanesetaverna.com; Mediterranean; $$. In addition to its varied Mediterranean menu, Lebanese Taverna makes a good falafel sandwich that can be ordered at any of its locations. The nicely seasoned falafel balls along with salad and tahini are wrapped up in the restaurant's fresh-baked pita bread. Gluten-free options and vegan/vegetarian friendly.

Maoz Vegetarian, 1817 M St. NW, Washington, DC 20036; (202) 290-3117; www.maozusa.com; $. An outpost of the international chain that began in Amsterdam, the D.C. Maoz Vegetarian serves good falafel that can be topped with a host of salads made from fresh, local ingredients. You can order your falafel either on a salad or as a sandwich in pita bread. Then choose from a list of "add-ons" like hummus, eggplant, feta, avocado, and baba ghanoush. There are about a half-dozen sauces you can add to any item. Maoz also sells regular and sweet potato fries. Kosher and vegan/vegetarian friendly.

Old City Cafe, 1773 Columbia Rd. NW, Washington, DC 20009; (202) 232-1322; $. Another Adams Morgan no-frills spot that sells good falafel late into the night. In addition to the falafel, Old City Cafe also serves shawarma and kebabs.

Shawafel, 1322 H St. NE, Washington, DC 20002; (202) 388-7676; $. Hard to say but easy to swallow, Shawafel spit-roasts lamb, chicken, and beef shawarma at its H Street shop. The meat is sourced locally and prepared according to an old family recipe. Falafel sandwiches and platters along with fries and other sides also help keep customers happy. Shawafel stays open until 3 a.m. on Friday and Saturday night. Supports the local food movement and vegan/vegetarian friendly.

vFalafel, 2157 P St. NW, Washington, DC 20037; (202) 296-2333; www.vfalafel.com; Vegan/Vegetarian Friendly; $. vFalafel is a triple threat. It's cheap, delicious, and friendly. The all-vegetarian menu features traditional falafel sandwiches along with a falafel burger and a must-try meatless falafel shawarma. Many of the salads and sauces found on the all-you-can-pile-on toppings bar come from family recipes. vFalafel closes at 4 a.m. on Fri and Sat night and opens again on Sun morning at 10 a.m., the only day of the week the store offers a breakfast platter—a $7 special of falafel, eggs, hummus, feta, tomatoes, olives, pita, and fries.

Dinner

Approaching food with a creative eye and a commitment to local, seasonal flavors links kitchens big or small, and the food created in them is praised with words like "best," "standout," and "authentic." And although the cuisine crafted in these kitchens sometimes could not be more different, it's the experience of the first taste of an artful approach to cooking that connects the posh hot spot with the neighborhood hole-in-the-wall. It's why I've included both Komi and Thai X-ing under the same heading. Chef Johnny Monis prepares a seemingly endless parade of refined artistic food at the wildly popular urban chic **Komi**, while Chef Taw Vigsittaboot re-creates family recipes for the guests who find him cooking in the eclectically furnished restaurant tucked away in the basement of his home.

   I like to think of this chapter as a kind of written tasting menu, providing a sample of what restaurants are doing when the dinner bell rings in D.C. I've included places like the **Blue Duck Tavern, Estadio,** and **BlackSalt,** where an exceptional meal can be considered the norm, and spots like **H Street Country Club, Souk,** and **Star and Shamrock** where what is on the plate is only part of the experience. I've divided the chapter up into Tasting Tables, Hotel Hot Spots, Nights Out, Fun and Funky, Neighborhood Feel, and More Casual Eats. I hope you have as much fun as I had and add your own finds to the list.

Tasting Tables

The chefs at these diverse restaurants go off-menu to embrace their creative side while cooking multicourse meals for guests. Go with a sense of adventure and fun and you might just be surprised by which dish you deem your favorite at the end of the night.

CityZen, 1330 Maryland Ave. SE, Washington, DC 20024; (202) 787-6006; www.mandarinoriental.com/washington/dining/cityzen; Asian; $$$$. Housed in the gracious Mandarin Oriental hotel, Chef de Cuisine Eric Ziebold presents his version of modern American cuisine in three menu variations: a 3-course prix-fixe menu, a 6-course chef's tasting menu, and 6-course vegetarian tasting menu. Seasonal local ingredients drive the dishes Ziebold chooses to highlight in all three of the menus. Expect to try dishes like veal sweetbreads larded with felts country-cured bacon, bigeye tuna confit, and roasted tenderloin of King Richard Leek. Dining at the romantic restaurant always feels like a special occasion, and during cherry blossom season the view of the pink blossoms is nothing short of enchanting.

Komi, 1509 17th St NW #1, Washington, DC 20036; (202) 332-9200; www.komirestaurant.com; Mediterranean/Eclectic; $$$$. The golden ring of D.C. dining experiences, Komi remains the hottest and hardest-to-secure reservation in town. There are no printed menus to hand out at the softly lit 12-table restaurant that cannot accommodate parties larger than four. Wunderkind Owner and Chef Johnny Monis instead crafts an elaborate multicourse meal filled with his original creations, many of which are influenced by the flavors of his Greek heritage. The experience begins with a series of *mezzethakia,* or light small plates, before moving on to heartier flavors of a pasta dish and then a shared entree, often of suckling pig or roasted goat. A series of desserts complete the meal. The menu changes from night to night but the phenomenal mascarpone-stuffed Medjool dates topped with sea salt almost always appear in the lineup, as does a re-imagined half-smoke, which Monis added to his repertoire shortly after the Obamas dined at Komi. An optional wine pairing can be added to the meal for $70. The reservation phone line is open from Tues through Sat from noon until 5 p.m.

Minibar, 405 8th St. NW, Washington, DC 20004; (202) 393-0812; www.cafeatlantico.com/miniBar/miniBar.htm; Molecular Gastronomy; $$$$. Minibar is a six-seat (yes, only six) restaurant that serves a 25-plus course tasting menu twice a night—once at 6 p.m. and again at 8:30 p.m. Chef Jose Andres uses tools from his molecular gastronomy bag of tricks to create dishes like cotton candy eel, chocolate *foie gras* truffles, and a deconstructed glass of white wine that dazzle both the eyes and the palate. Reservations for the in-demand exclusive experience are taken a month out and often fill up in minutes.

Obelisk, 2029 P St. NW, Suite 101, Washington, DC 20036; (202) 872-1180; Italian; Avant-Garde; $$$$. Tucked into a Dupont Circle row house, Obelisk offers the chance to experience an intimate chef-driven dinner for 30 people at a time. A sampling of antipasti starts off the meal followed by excellent house-made pasta, fish, grilled meats, and finally a cheese course and dessert. Although Obelisk has been around since 1987, it flies a bit below the radar. Despite the lack of hype, it belongs on every good foodie's to-do list. There is no large sign in front of the restaurant so don't be afraid to walk in once you find the address.

Rogue 24, 922 N St. NW (rear), Washington, DC 20001; www .rogue24.com; New American; $$$$. When asked why he started a restaurant built around the concept of fine urban dining, Chef RJ Cooper simply replies, "Why not?" The former Vidalia Chef de Cuisine Derek Brown along with his handpicked staff curate a 24-course meal from the kitchen in the center of the modern 52-seat restaurant. Diners can also opt for a 16-course progression. Cooper reimagines many classic foods to create dishes like liquid fried chicken. Mixologist Derek Brown of Columbia Room fame is the force behind the avant-garde cocktail pairings at the restaurant, where everyone sits at a chef's table. "If no one takes risks in this business it gets stale," he shares. "We're taking a jump into being outside the box."

Sushi Taro, 1503 17th St. NW, Washington, DC 20036; (202) 462-8999; www.sushitaro.com; Japanese; $$$. Instead of ordering from a menu, the chef "entertains" guest with a series of surprise dishes that revolve around what are deemed the best and freshest ingredients available that particular day. The style of dining is known in Japan as *kaiseki* and drives the experience at Sushi Taro. Dishes arrive at the table throughout the meal and are done with great care.

Thai X-ing, 515 Florida Ave. NW, Washington, DC 20001; (202) 332-4322; www.thaix-ing.com; Thai; $$$. You are in the right place if you think you have mistakenly walked into someone's living room rather than a restaurant. There are no matching dishes here, and not the slightest bit of fanfare associated with most restaurants that offer multicourse prix-fixe menus. Instead Chef Taw Vigsittaboot cooks traditional Thai dishes in the basement of his home and serves them in a makeshift dining room space filled with a hodgepodge of furniture, knickknacks, and his cats, which you very well may have to move off the chair, sofa, or bench that you will be sitting on that night for dinner. Still you will be hard-pressed to find better or more authentic ethnic food within city

limits. Taw only serves a multicourse chef's-choice menu, one he fills with dishes he learned to cook from his grandmother, mother, and aunt. Expect to be dazzled with creations like mango sticky rice, pumpkin curry, and drunken noodles. You must make a reservation to experience Thai X-ing and the small, atypical space fills up quickly. Reservations are taken by phone only. An answering machine picks up and the message asks you to leave your information including any food restrictions. If there is room on the date you request, you will get a call back. Sunday is vegetarian night, and the cost every night is $30 per person or $40 if you are coming in with a large group.

The Wine Room at Occidental, 1475 Pennsylvania Ave. NW; (202) 783-1475; www.occidentaldc.com; American; $$$$. The dark wood and lush leather sets the tone at this exclusive restaurant within a restaurant. While seated in the wine room, order the chef's tasting menu paired with wines recommended by the sommelier.

Hotel Hot Spots

Forget every bad stereotype you might be carrying around about cookie-cutter hotel food. These fabulous dining establishments are about as far and away as you can get from a roadside HoJo's. Sophisticated, elegant, and innovative, you will be hard pressed to find a finer meal than the ones served at the Blue Duck Tavern in the Park Hyatt or J&G Steakhouse in the mod W Washington, D.C. But consider yourself warned. Once you walk through the door at these upscale and innovative hotels, you might find yourself checking in for the night.

Adour, 923 K St. NW, Washington, DC 20050; (202) 509-8000; www.adour-washingtondc.com; French; $$$$. French-American creations are served against the backdrop of the luxurious St. Regis Washington, D.C., where Adour is housed. Dishes have been designed with wine pairings in mind and are inspired by the southwest region of France, where Chef Alain Ducasse spent his early days. The filet mignon with seared *foie gras* and black truffle sauce stands out amid a well-curated menu that includes other favorites like roasted Maine lobster and braised beef short ribs. The chef will also prepare several tasting menus, including one for vegetarians.

Art and Soul, 415 New Jersey Ave. NW, Washington, DC; (202) 393-7777; http://artandsouldc.com; New American/Soul; $$$. Art Smith first made a name for himself as Oprah Winfrey's personal chef before coming to D.C. to open Art and Soul. New spins on soul food define much of the menu with dishes like dirty rice, shrimp and grits, and stewed sweet pepper hoecake. Try the lamb shank when it makes an appearance on the menu. Art and Soul picks up on the hip urban vibe of the Liaison Capitol Hill boutique hotel that houses it.

BistroBis, 15 E St. NW, Washington, DC 20001; (202) 661-2700; www.bistrobis.com; French; $$$. Hotel George, Washington's first contemporary boutique hotel, houses the seen-and-be-seen D.C. power restaurant BistroBis. Fabulous French cooking and fabulous people-watching define this fine-dining restaurant.

Blue Duck Tavern, 1201 24th St. NW, Washington, DC 20037; (202) 419-6755; www.blueducktavern.com; New American; $$$. Simple American food made simply divine is the focus of the kitchen at this West End restaurant run by Executive Chef Brian McBride and Chef de Cuisine Eric Fleischer. Signature dishes include oven-roasted bone marrow and braised beef ribs in a homemade steak sauce. For dessert the house-made ice cream is a must. Served in a glass ice bucket with a wooden spoon, the creamy dessert in flavors like chocolate cinnamon, honey vanilla, and strawberry is one of the best ice creams in town, if not the best. The milk chocolate and banana s'mores also do not disappoint. The restaurant's decor embraces the clean, contemporary Shaker design that fills the rest of the simple-yet-elegant Park Hyatt Hotel. A 12-seat communal dining table carved from a single piece of wood from a 50,000-year-old slab of an ancient Kauri tree from New Zealand adorns the expanded patio space. Herbs and vegetables used in many of the restaurant's creations are grown in and around the popular outdoor seating area. See the recipe for the Blue Duck Tavern's **Roasted Beet Salad** on p. 305.

Say Cheese

Not long ago Brenton Balika, the pastry chef at Bourbon Steak, began dabbling in cheese making. What began as some playful experimenting quickly turned into a passion for Balika, who now creates cheeses in the kitchen of the posh Georgetown restaurant. The chef makes everything from blue to brie and has reached enough critical mass that it is beginning to appear on the menu regularly. His cheeses, which all start from organic cow and goat milk from Trickling Springs Creamery, can be sampled as a starter or as the finale to the meal and also may be ordered at the bar.

Bourbon Steak, 2800 Pennsylvania Ave. NW, Washington, DC 20007; (202) 944-2026; www.bourbonsteakdc.com; New American; $$$$. The Four Seasons Hotel's Bourbon Steak brings elegance to the steak house concept. The service ranks as some of the best in town and the same holds true for the menu. Adam Sobel recently took over as executive chef.

Firefly, 1310 New Hampshire Ave. NW, Washington, DC 20036; (202) 861-1310; www.firefly-dc.com; American; $$$. Executive Chef

Daniel Bortnick describes his approach to cooking as comfort food reimagined. "I want people to say I ate this when I was a kid but my mom never made it that way," he says. "I want the experience to spark memory." And that is exactly the reaction he gets from customers when they first taste his take on deviled eggs or his mini pot roast cut from short ribs. You may even stumble upon a menu featuring chicken matzoh-ball soup made from his family recipe. The braised lamb shank, mac 'n three cheese, and house burger served with truffle fries and topped with a beer-battered pickle are other standouts at the neighborhood restaurant with the big "firefly"-dotted tree in the middle of the dining room. Bortnick's commitment to the planet can be seen in all aspects of the restaurant, which is attached to Dupont Circle's Hotel Madera, from the rainwater collection barrels to the recycled glassware to the local produce and other ingredients used in the kitchen. Supports the local food movement. Gluten-free options. See the recipe for Firefly's **Grilled Red Wine Braised Octopus with Smoked Avocado, Roasted Olive Gremolata & Olive Aioli** on p. 302.

J&G Steakhouse, 515 15th St. NW, Washington, DC 20004; (202) 661-2440; www.jgsteakhousewashingtondc.com; Steak; $$$$. The glow from the monuments at night lights up the dining-room-with-a-view at the contemporary yet elegant J&G Steakhouse. And the food matches the majesty of the sites that can be seen from the upscale steak house located in the über-modern W Washington,

Put a Cork in it: Wine Cork Recycling.

Firefly recently became an official ReCork recycling drop-off site. Anyone walking by can toss old wine corks into the recycling barrel in Firefly's vestibule. Instead of heading to the landfill, recycled corks can be made into everything from shoes to building insulation. The Portuguese company Amorin, the world's largest producer of natural cork, sponsors ReCork. Other drop off locations around town include **Schneider's of Capitol Hill** (300 Massachusetts Ave. NE, Washington, DC 20002; 202-543-9300; http://cellar.com), **Wide World of Wines** (2201 Wisconsin Ave. NW, Washington, DC 20007; 202-333-7500; http://wideworldofwines.com), and **The Four Seasons Hotel** (2800 Pennsylvania Ave, NW, DC 20007; 202-342-0444; www.fourseasons.com/washington).

D.C. Expert cuts of beef drive the menu, which also offers several wonderful fish choices like the rice-cracker crusted tuna with citrus-chile sauce appetizer and the grilled Sichuan peppercorn–crusted yellowfin tuna. A modern take on creamed spinach with basil goes well with meat or fish selections. For dessert embrace your inner child with one of the seasonal ice cream sundaes, like the strawberry shortcake sundae or the carnival-inspired sundae topped with peanuts, popcorn, and caramel corn. Head upstairs to POV rooftop bar for an after-dinner cocktail and one of the most spectacular views available in the city.

Michel Richard Citronelle, 3000 M St. NW, Washington, DC 20007; (202) 625-2150; www.citronelledc.com; French; $$$$. Chef Michel Richard's artistry touches every dish served at this Georgetown restaurant often frequented for special nights out. Everything from the braised short ribs to the lemon meringue for dessert showcases Richard's exceptional talent. The popular French restaurant is found in the Latham Hotel.

Poste Modern Brasserie, 555 8th St. NW, Washington, DC 20004; (202) 783-6060; www.postebrasserie.com; New American; $$$. The magical garden courtyard behind Poste blooms with strawberries, quince, tomatoes, asparagus, and happy diners toasting the night away while nibbling fresh food. The outdoor area not only serves as in-demand seating but also a stage for an elaborate kitchen garden. Grapes grown on the patio are pickled and often wind up on the cheese boards, and vinegar infusions from the herbs and produce the staff tends to outside are used in the kitchen. The Penn Quarter spot, found in the Hotel Monaco, sponsors a wildly popular happy hour and Poste Roast, where you and a bunch of friends choose from a pig, lamb, or goat that is then roasted whole in front of you before being served intact—head, toe, and all—at a special chef's table in the garden.

Todd Gray's Watershed, 1225 1st St. NW, Washington, DC 20002; (202) 534-1350; www.toddgrayswatershed.com; Seafood; $$$. If it can be eaten uncooked it might just turn up at the raw bar at Todd Gray's Watershed. Crudo, beef tartare, and sashimi are as likely to appear at the self-described modern raw bar as oysters, crab, and shrimp. Found in the Hilton Garden Inn, the hip NoMa restaurant offers a great outdoor space and warm chocolate chip cookies for dessert.

Urbana Restaurant and Wine Bar, 2121 P St. NW, Washington, DC 20037; (202) 956-6650; www.urbanadc.com; Italian; $$$. Executive Chef John Critchley recently came up from Miami to take over the kitchen at this Italian restaurant in the Hotel Palomar. Try the market pizza, which changes every week based on what the chef finds that Sunday at the nearby Dupont Circle farmers' market. His creations have included a pizza topped with bison, lavender béchamel, and pickled ramps as well as a pizza with morel mushrooms, goat cheese, and stinging nettles. The menu also features handmade pastas and grilled fish and meats. Gluten-free options. See the recipe for Urbana Restaurant and Wine Bar's **Shellfish Stew with Coconut & Lime** on p. 307.

Zentan, 1155 14th St. NW, Washington, DC 20005; (202) 379-4366; www.zentanrestaurant.com; Asian; $$$. Many repeat customers come to Zentan in the funky Donovan House hotel just for the amazing Singapore Slaw. Made tableside, the crunchy, slightly sweet slaw is made with 19 ingredients including hazelnuts. Even with all the hype surrounding it, the dish does not disappoint. A long list of sushi and entrees featuring pork belly, duck, chicken, fish, lamb, and steak round out the rest of the varied menu.

Nights Out

A night out is something to celebrate, be it a special occasion, date night, or much-needed respite from the workweek. Consider these choices for your next night out.

Acadiana, 901 New York Ave. NW, Washington, DC 20001; (202) 408-8848; www.acadianarestaurant.com; Creole; $$$. Chef and owner Jeff Tunks re-creates the flavors of his beloved New Orleans at his upscale Creole restaurant, which pays homage to Gulf Coast cuisine. Many a Louisiana native comes by for a taste of home. The most popular dish is the chef's seafood gumbo made with jumbo lump crab, shrimp, crawfish, oysters, redfish, and Mahatma rice. Other authentic eats include the buffalo frog legs, cornmeal-crusted catfish, and the grillades and grits. Order any dish with sides of collard greens with bacon, jalapeño cheese grits or dirty rice. Servers are trained to share the origins of the seafood on the menu. Regular shrimp and crawfish boils are held on the patio. See the recipe for Acadiana's **Louisiana Crawfish Etouffée with Mahatma Rice** on p. 300.

BlackSalt Restaurant, 4883 MacArthur Blvd. NW, Washington, DC 20007, (202) 342-9101; www.blacksaltrestaurant.com; Seafood; $$$. I have yet to have a bad meal at BlackSalt. In fact, they have all been exceptional. The dishes at BlackSalt revolve around fresh sustainable fish cooked with spices, sauces, or rubs that bring out the best flavors possible from each catch. Cornmeal-crusted tilapia, wood-grilled octopus, and lobster ravioli can often be found on the menu at this handsome restaurant. Happy hour dishes are equally tasty and come at great prices. Cocktails always are well crafted. Supports the local food movement.

Corduroy, 1122 9th St. NW, Washington, DC 20001; (202) 589-0699; www.corduroydc.com; New American; $$$. Chef Tom Power lets the tastes of the season and region guide Corduroy's menu. Noteworthy selections are not limited to the red snapper bisque but it's a great place to start. The peppered, rare bigeye tuna and the scallops with Jerusalem artichokes are star entrees. End the meal with the much-loved pistachio bread pudding. Supports the local food movement.

Fiola, 601 Pennsylvania Ave. NW, Ste 125N, Washington, DC 20004; (202) 628-2888; www.fioladc.com; Italian; $$$. Fabio Trabocchi's much-anticipated Penn Quarter restaurant finally opened with much fanfare and it did not disappoint. Trabocchi uses house-made pastas as the base for creations like his 13-layer lasagna packed with veal and lobster ravioli. The elegant restaurant with the sunken dining room embraces the same charming design aesthetics of an Italian villa.

Marcel's, 2401 Pennsylvania Ave. NW, Washington, DC 20037; (202) 296-1166; www.marcelsdc.com; French/Belgian; $$$$. Marcel's is a throwback to a time when dinners weren't rushed and service was impeccable. The exceptional French restaurant continues to be a favorite among those searching for a restaurant experience that feels special. Chef Robert Wiedmaier creates an outstanding menu with dishes like his signature *boudin blanc*. Wiedmaier practices classic butchery using the whole animal to enhance his dishes. Items may be ordered a la carte or you can try a 3-, 4-, 5- or 7-course tasting menu.

Montmartre, 327 7th St. SE, Washington, DC 20003; (202) 544-1244; www.montmartredc.com; French; $$$. A Capitol Hill favorite, Montmartre embraces a modern bistro atmosphere where diners can linger over classic dishes and conversation. Skate, sautéed calf's liver, and braised rabbit are some of the menu staples here.

Palena Restaurant, 3529 Connecticut Ave. NW, Washington, DC 20008; (202) 537-9250; www.palenarestaurant.com; New American; $$$. Palena's restaurant completes the trifecta of restaurant, market, and cafe that make up the Palena experience in Cleveland Park. An elegant setting to sample refined dishes that revolve around the bounty of the season.

Proof, 775 G St. NW, Washington, DC 20001; (202) 737-7663; www.proofdc.com; New American; $$$. The wine-centered restaurant across from the National Portrait Gallery strives to provide the perfect sip with every meal. Proof's wine offerings list several dozen by-the-glass choices as well as sought-after bottles at various price points. Dishes revolve around local, organic, and sustainable ingredients and result in simple yet delicious creations like ahi tuna tartare, crispy pig's head, and sautéed potato gnocchi. Images from the National Portrait Gallery and Smithsonian American Art Museum flash on the four flat-screen TVs above the bar.

Rasika, 633 D St. NW, Washington, DC 20004; (202) 637-1222; www.rasikarestaurant.com; Indian; $$$. Rasika, in Penn Quarter, serves modernity-infused Indian food with style and grace. The service is as distinguished as the menu. The crispy spinach *palak chaat* is wonderful and worth the visit alone. Move on to a host of equally impressive entrees before ending the meal with the apple *jalebi* (beignet) with cardamom ice cream or the date-and-toffee pudding.

RIS, 2275 L St. NW, Washington, DC 20037; (202) 730-2500; www.risdc.com; American; $$$. Chef Ris Lacoste lends her name and her commitment to local food to her upscale neighborhood cafe. Whenever possible she shops at nearby markets and purchases ingredients from regional farms. Her signature scallop margarita wows the crowds with its lime-marinated scallops and tequila ice. A 65-seat patio offers a nice backdrop to enjoy one on a nice night as does the pretty restaurant inside. Pastry Chef Chris Kujala amazes the crowds with his sweet creations such as his butterscotch pudding. Each month RIS posts its daily soup calendar, listing the special combination of the day. Daily specials also bow to local harvest and the current season. Soups are packed to go in either cup, bowl, or quart size. See the recipes for RIS's **Scallop Margarita with Tequila Ice** (p. 314) and **Gluten-Free Pecan Butterscotch Cake** (p. 318).

1789, 1226 36th St. NW, Washington, DC 20007; (202) 965-1789; www.1789restaurant.com; American; $$$. The menu at this tony Georgetown restaurant changes daily and lists the origin of the veal, chicken, flour, lamb, fish, and other crucial ingredients. Each category is listed separately and an asterisk denotes which dishes are intended as starters rather than entrees.

Fun & Funky

Jackets, ties, and stuffy service have no place at these restaurants where fun and funky meet food.

Ardeo + Bardeo, 3311 Connecticut Ave. NW, Washington, DC 20008; (202) 244-6750; www.ardeobardeo.com; New American; $$$. The makeover fairy visited Ardeo in 2010, giving the popular Cleveland Park destination a shiny, new urban glow. The food is as good as ever with the menu leaning toward a modern bistro feel with dishes like an upscale steak and eggs dish, lamb ravioli, and a truly phenomenal side dish of crispy brussels sprouts made with pistachios, apricots, and yogurt. In the spring and summer you can dine on the rooftop, a perfect setting to enjoy your meal and one of the many wines served here.

Birch and Barley, 1337 14th St. NW, Washington, DC 20005; (202) 567-2576; www .birchandbarley.com; New American; $$. The almost 600 beers found here star in this res- taurant's show where all the dishes have been imagined with a brew. Dishes are simple yet flavorful and do not disappoint. Cheeses, charcuterie, flatbreads, pastas, and a brat burger all can be ordered here at this charming and hip spot. A selection of gluten-free bottled beers and gluten-free options are also always available.

El Centro D.F., 1819 14th St. NW, Washington, DC 20009; (202) 328-3131; www.elcentrodf.com; Mexican; $$. El Centro D.F. burst onto the hipster scene with three great spaces rolled into one. A casual taqueria where yummy tacos can be taken to go or eaten in house, a tequileria featuring Latin cocktails mixed from more than 200 tequilas and mezcals and, finally, a stellar rooftop space where two open-air bars serve happy customers late into the night.

Estadio, 1520 14th St. NW, Washington, DC 20005; (202) 319- 1404; www.estadio-dc.com; Spanish/Tapas; $$$. No matter how you order, at Estadio you will likely get one of the best meals in town.

Dishes at this small-plates restaurant embrace the cooking tradition of northern Spain. Stars of the show here include spicy Marcona almonds, the *montaditos* (open-faced sandwiches) with roasted beets and whipped goat cheese, grilled octopus, deviled egg stuffed with *ensaladilla rusa* (Spanish potato salad), and the roasted baby chorizos with potato crisps. Seats at the marble counter overlooking the kitchen offer a meal with a view. Two types of sangria, red and white, are always on tap as are the popular 14th Street spiked slushies. Estadio does not take reservations. See the recipe for Estadio's **Spice-Grilled Chicken** on p. 325.

H Street Country Club, 1335 H St. NE, Washington, DC 20002; (202) 399-4722; www.thehstreetcountryclub.com; Mexican; $$. It's mini-golf all grown up at H Street Country Club. Unlike the putt-putt of your youth, you don't have to sneak cans of warm beer on the indoor course here or put up with whining kids slowing down your game. The bar serves more than 25 different kinds of tequila and the under-21 set is not allowed on the course except on Sunday and Monday. H Street serves up great tacos (think smoked lamb) and other Mexican dishes like brisket enchiladas and duck in mole sauce. You can also play Skee-ball & Xbox Kinect.

Indique, 3512 Connecticut Ave. NW, Washington, DC 20008; (202) 244-6600; http://indique.com; Indian; $$. *Paneer makhani*, garlic nan, saffron *malai* chicken and mini *dosa* are just a few of the flavor-rich choices you'll find at this pretty Cleveland Park Indian restaurant. Curry entrees include fish, shrimp, lamb, and chicken options.

Lincoln, 1110 Vermont Ave. NW, Washington, DC 20005; (202) 386-9200; www.lincolnrestaurant-dc.com; New American; $$$. If thoughts are worth a penny, then this small-plates restaurant has about a million to share. The floor is masterfully tiled with seven figures worth of the copper coins. Signature cocktails are served in mason jars and sport names that pay homage to the 16th president. The menu revolves around fresh, seasonal, and local ingredients and even includes a few of Honest Abe's favorites like oysters, chicken fricassee, and gingerbread.

Lost Society–DC, 2001 14th St. NW, Washington, DC 20009; (202) 618-8868; www.LostSociety-DC.com; Steak; $$$. Purple velvet couches, cordoned off booths, and house music serve as the backdrop for the experience that is Lost Society, the new boutique steak house that opened in the summer of 2011 on 14th Street. Former Smith & Wollensky Chef Joseph Evans serves as the meat master, putting new spins on classic cuts. The massive windows on the second floor provide an engaging view of the U Street Corridor and the rooftop deck offers an even wider look at the city and, on a clear night, the stars. Every evening at 10 p.m. DJs start spinning tunes as diverse as the neighborhood.

Oyamel, 401 7th St NW, Washington, DC 20004; (202) 628-1005; www.oyamel.com; Mexican; $$$. Against the backdrop of its funky dining room, Oyamel serves up creative Mexican small plates under the direction of Chef José Andrés. Try the guacamole made tableside and, if you are feeling daring, the sautéed grasshopper tacos. If that isn't your thing, go for the expertly seasoned wild mushroom version. Every year the restaurant has a Day of the Dead festival celebrated with special creations from José Andrés and Head Chef JohnPaul Damato.

PS 7, 777 I St. NW, Washington, DC 20001; (202) 742-8550; www .ps7restaurant.com; New American; Cocktails; $$$. While the food at PS 7 can stand on its own, it's the drinks that steal the stage. Hand-crafted cocktails like Pimpin Pimm's made with Pimm's, gin, strawberry, tarragon, and rhubarb and Gnome Water (a combination of Hendrick's gin, cucumber water, and lemon-lavender syrup) make other bar menus seem anemic. Live on the edge and order the "Questionable Content," the bartender's choice and see what flavors arrive.

Ristorante Posto, 1515 14th St. NW, Washington, DC 20005; (202) 332-8613; www.postodc.com; Italian; $$$. This modern Italian restaurant won some major cool points when high-level White House officials began hanging out here during the early days of the Obama administration. But even if it didn't have a recognizable clientele, the 14th street haunt would still be worth visiting for its selection of antipasti, pastas, and pizzas. The more than 100-year-old building once had another life as a car dealership.

Star and Shamrock Tavern and Deli, 1341 H St. NE, Washington, DC 20002; (202) 388-3833; www.starandshamrock .com; Irish; Deli; $$. It's a "mixed" marriage of the tastiest sorts. Star and Shamrock blends two strong food cultures to create an Irish-Jewish gastronomic experience where you can order corned beef, latkes with sauerkraut, and individual shepherd's pie all under one roof. Wash it down with a glass of homemade Manischewitz sangria or a cold Guinness while dancing a jig to the sounds of a klezmer band.

Toki Underground, 1234 H St. NE, Washington, DC 20002; (202) 388-3086; www.tokiunderground.com; Asian; $$. Forget everything you know about the college-dorm version of ramen before you walk into the hip shop with graffiti art scribbled on the walls and Taiwanese ramen filling the menu. The 24-seat hot spot features about five different version of the noodles in broth dish. Dumplings, sake, and Asian cocktails round out the offerings. Despite the name, look up to find the popular H Street ramen shop. Toki Underground is on the second floor.

Zaytinya, 701 9th St. NW, Washington, DC 20001; (202) 638-0800; www.zaytinya.com; Middle Eastern; $$$. Zaytinya helped elevate the small-plate concept into popularity in D.C. when it first came onto the scene in 2003. The contemporary Penn Quarter restaurant serves a host of meze that feature modern interpretations of the traditional Greek, Turkish, and Lebanese cuisine. Gluten-free options.

Zengo, 781 7th St. NW, Washington, DC 20001; (202) 393-2929; www.richardsandoval.com; Fusion; $$$. The kitchen at Zengo seamlessly combines Latin and Asian flavors to create dishes like beef tenderloin palomilla, chipotle-miso soup, and Peking duck daikon tacos. The drinks served also embrace these two food styles in Zengo's impressive bar list, which includes extensive sake, tequila, and Latin wine choices. Gluten-free options and vegan/vegetarian friendly.

Neighborhood Feel

Comfortable, consistent, and friendly, local haunts can be found around many a corner in this town, where the urban neighborhood is making a strong comeback.

Acacia Bistro & Wine Bar, 4340 Connecticut Ave. NW, Washington, DC; (202) 537-1040; www.acaciabistro.com; Mediterranean; $$$. The Van Ness neighborhood seems finally to have found a new business it can hang on to—and it's a good one. Acacia serves a delicious mix of small plates and entrees to pair with its extensive wine list. Start with the anchovy toast with lemon aioli or fava bean crostini and move on to a main course that could involve anything from seafood to veal to rabbit. Chef and Owner Lilliana Dumas's desserts delight with creations that combine Mediterranean-inspired flavors like chocolate and hazelnut or nougat and pistachio.

The Atlas Room, 1015 H St. NE, Washington, DC 20002; (202) 388-4020; www.theatlasroom.com; New American; $$$. A worldly menu embraces flavors from around the globe, while at the same time focusing on local flavors, at the elegant and tasty Atlas Room. The menu is organized in a nontraditional way, grouping selections by protein rather than listing appetizers first followed by soups, entrees, and the other courses. Here the menu shows all the chicken options, be it a soup or main course, together under the heading of chicken. Supports the local food movement.

Bar Pilar, 1833 14th St. NW, Washington, DC 20009; (202) 265-1751; www.barpilar.com; American; $$. A good bar with good food, Bar Pilar has built its reputation around tasty small plates, an intimate atmosphere, and extensive bar offerings. The neighborhood favorite also serves a fabulous brunch complete with chocolate chip malt pancakes, steamed mussels, and ginger mimosas. Bar Pilar gets very crowded on the weekend so if that's not your scene try it midweek. No matter which day of the week or weekend you come in you will have to find your own table and seat yourself—the bistro does not have a hostess and does not accept reservations.

Brasserie Beck, 1101 K St. NW, Washington, DC 20005; (202) 408-1717; www.beckdc.com; Belgian; $$$. Mussels, mussels, and more mussels. Chef-Owner Robert Wiedmaier prepares them every which way from a classic take in white wine with roasted garlic and parsley to a spicy red curry to a version with goat cheese and lemon. The light and bright restaurant also offers a pages-long Belgian beer list and a fun chef's table experience in the kitchen.

Cafe Saint-Ex, 1847 14th St. NW, Washington, DC 20009; www .saint-ex.com; Cafe; $$. Saint-Ex is many things at once. A great neighborhood bistro, a weekend dance club, and a bar that serves indie and hard-to-find bottles. On pretty days the patio at the corner restaurant fill with brunch-goers nibbling on brioche french toast or steak and eggs. As the day moves on, inside and out regulars flock to the fried green tomato BLT or burger, and then when the sun goes way down the basement crowds with revelers ready to dance and party.

Granville Moore's Belgiam Beer and Gastropub, 1238 H St. NE, Washington, DC 20002; (202) 399-2546; Belgian; $$. The twice-fried frites have a following all their own and for good reason. The hand-cut fries are insane. Two sauces come with each order—choices include truffle mayo, bacon-chive mayo and Dijonnaise.

Local 16, 1602 U St. NW; Washington, DC 20009; (202) 265-2828; www.localsixteen.com; New American; $$. The folks behind Local 16 put their money where their mouth is. In 2005 the restaurant invested in Whipple Farm, an all-heirloom biodynamic farm in Virginia that now sources the produce, eggs, and many other ingredients used in the kitchen. Words like "organic," "locally sourced," and "farm fresh" are part of the fabric of Local 16. Wood from the farm fires the pizza oven and the ashes get returned to the farm where they help fertilize the ground. The farm-fresh dishes change with the season and can include spinach gnocchi, steak fries, and pizzas topped with the season's best. A special late-night menu is served from 10 p.m. to midnight Sun through Thurs and from 11 p.m. to 1 a.m. Fri and Sat. Supports the local food movement.

Meiwah Restaurant, 1200 New Hampshire Ave. NW, Washington, D.C. 20036; 202-833-2888; www.meiwahrestaurant.com; Chinese; $$. The best Chinese takeout (or eat-in) in town as far as my household is concerned and I have a wad of receipts to prove it. Meiwah is consistently good and fresh and reliable. The tofu curl (deep fried tofu strips wrapped in lettuce leaves), steamed dumplings, and eggplant in garlic sauce have yet to disappoint. The noodle dishes are similarly worth trying. Meiwah also has good sushi. Vegan/ vegetarian friendly.

Meridian Pint, 3400 11th St. NW, Washington, DC 20010; (202) 588-1075; www.MeridianPint.com; Beer; American; $$. American craft beer is the star of the show here at this corner haunt in Columbia Heights. DC Brau's Public Ale flows freely here and is one of the most requested beers on tap. The restaurant's owner holds firm to his commitment to environmental sustainability in a variety of ways, from using sustainable building materials to hiring people who live nearby so they don't leave carbon footprints on the way to work. Every Tuesday the restaurant holds "Bombers for Brewers," where home brewers can take home 750-ml specialty beer bottles to reuse so that the restaurant doesn't have to recycle them. Supports the local food movement. Vegan/vegetarian friendly.

901 Restaurant and Bar, 901 9th St. NW, at I St., Washington, DC 20001; (202) 524-4433; www.901dc.com; Fusion; $$. 901's contemporary clublike look invites diners to experience a menu that borrows flavors from a variety of different places and regions. Dishes are designed to be shared and paired with the extensive offerings from the bar.

The Queen Vic, 1206 H St. NE, Washington, DC 20002; (202) 396-2001; www.thequeenvicdc.com; Pub; $$. Throw back a pint while you discuss Pippa's latest frock at the Queen Vic. Ex-pats and anglophiles alike love the traditional food and drink at this British pub. On tap find favorite ales, stouts, ciders, bitters, and lagers brought in from across the pond. Pub grub like the house-made sausage-of-the-day and fish-and-chips are crowd pleasers. All the bread and mustard are made in-house. Flash the bartender your British passport and receive 10 percent off your tab.

Smoke & Barrel, 2471 18th St. NW Washington, DC; (202) 319-9353; http://smokeandbarreldc.com; Barbecue; $$. Brought to you by the beer-respecting folks at Meridian Pint. Smoke & Barrel's logo pretty much says it all: "Beer. BBQ. Bourbon." Here are a few more things to say: the new Adams Morgan hangout took over the old Asylum space, they do not take reservations, and the restaurant has a full vegan brunch menu (along with a decidedly non-vegan brunch menu).

Souk, 1208 H St. NE, Washington, DC 20002; (202) 658-4224; www .souk-dc.com; Middle Eastern; $$. Hanging lanterns and red walls set the scene for the Moroccan food served here. The chef and owner cooks up dishes like lamb tagine, mixed grill, falafel, shawarma, and all kind of kebabs. Souk does a pretty steady take-out business, but you can also eat in.

Vinoteca, 1940 11th St. NW, Washington, DC 20001; (202) 332-9463; www.vinotecadc.com; Wine Bar; $$. The perfect neighborhood spot that not only caters to those who live near it but also hires its staff from around its 11th and U Street location. The focus here is small plates and cheese flights, paired with the extensive wine list that includes some 80 by-the-glass options.

Choices include a host of flatbreads and grilled meats and veggies. Every Tuesday Vinoteca holds a wine class in its upstairs lounge. Classes are limited to 20 people, cost $35 per person, and focus on five different wines that the chef then pairs with cheeses.

Casual Eats

Etete, 1942 9th St. NW, Washington, DC 20001; (202) 232-7600; Ethiopian; $$. Nestled in the neighborhood often referred to as Little Ethiopia, Etete offers some of the tastiest Ethiopian food in the city. Although lamb, beef, chicken, and other meat can be found throughout the menu, Etete has a long and varied selection of vegetarian choices.

Et Voila!, 5120 MacArthur Blvd. NW (at Dana Pl.); (202) 237-2300; www.etvoiladc.com; Belgian/French; $$. A small and cozy spot in the Palisades that serves traditional Belgian recipes. *Moules* done several ways and *frites* stand as two of the more popular draws.

Julia's Empanadas, Several locations throughout the city, www .juliasempanadas.com; Empanadas; $. Savory and sweet, vegetarian and meat-filled, empanadas here are done every which way. Drop by for an inexpensive yet satisfying way to have dinner or any meal. Soups and salads are also sold.

Pasta Mia, 1790 Columbia Rd. NW, Washington, DC 20009; (202) 328-9114; Italian; $$. Pasta Mia is as much about the chase as it is the catch. Regulars line up early and often to get a coveted spot in the small dining room where the portions are huge and affordable. The Adams Morgan hole-in-the-wall is open from 6:30 to 10 p.m. from Tues through Sun and those in the know swear that getting in line at 6 and 8 p.m. yields the quickest path into the pasta-rich eatery. Cash only.

Surfside, 2444 Wisconsin Ave., Washington, DC 20007; (202) 297-5033; www.surfsidedc.com; Tacos/Beach Cuisine; $. Great tacos, burritos, and salads at great prices keep the crowds coming back for more at Glover Park's Surfside. Handy forms allow you to pick your fillings, toppings, and sides before heading into line, making Surfside an efficient operation. The rooftop deck is great any time of the day or night.

Tackle Box, 3407 Connecticut Ave. NW, Washington, DC 20008; (202) 450-6875; www.tackleboxrestaurant.com; Seafood; $$. Informal dine-in or takeout seafood prepared New England style. Lobster rolls, fried clams, and chowder abound.

Zenebech Injera, 608 T St. NW, Washington, DC 20001; (202) 667-4700; Ethiopian; $. A tiny off-the-beaten-path Ethiopian joint with something of a cult following. The food is yummy and cheap. Carry out or eat in the small, no-frills restaurant.

Oh, Sweetie:
Cupcakes, Chocolate, Ice Cream & More

Sweets in the nation's capital at once reflect the city's local flavors and international flair. Farm fresh ingredients often come from the many farms that dot the Eastern Seaboard region. Southern tastes like mint, lime and, peach make it into everything from cupcakes to custards while the city's diverse culture is evident among the gelato shops and international bakeries. In short, there is something for everyone and when it comes to dessert, that's rarely is a bad thing.

ACKC, 1529C 14th St. NW, Washington, DC 20005; (202) 387-2626; www.thecocoagallery.com. ACKC looks like the kind of place Charlie would open after retiring from the Chocolate Factory. The cocoa bar is slightly whimsical, slightly hodgepodge, and all chocolate. Ironically, the divas are the opening act on the menu. All named for Hollywood starlets, these chocolate drinks can be enjoyed either hot or cold. Some favorites include the Marilyn Monroe, a white chocolate base with crème de menthe; the Lucy, a semi-sweet chocolate infused with chipotle and topped with whipped cream along with a dusting of cinnamon; and the Judy Garland, milk chocolate with a shot of hazelnut finished with whipped cream and rainbow sprinkles. Pair your drink with a variety of sweet seconds like fruit fondue, brownie sundaes, or molten lava cake. The cafe also serves a host of coffee drinks, many of which, no surprise, include chocolate. You can buy gourmet and artisan chocolates from the case and a range of unusual packaged chocolates that combine flavors like bacon and chocolate. ACKC also runs classes, chocolate tastings, serves brunch, and has a wine bar.

Baked & Wired, 1052 Thomas Jefferson St. NW, Washington, DC 20007; (202) 333-2500; www.bakedandwired.com. Hands down the best baked goods in town. The cupcakes at this Georgetown cafe are so good some people cry tears of joy as they take the first bite. Big and fluffy and delicious, the cupcakes come in fabulous flavors like chai tea latte, carrot cake, and Texas sheetcake (a chocolate cake with a hint of cinnamon that is slathered with chocolate-pecan topping while it's still warm so it oozes into the cake and creates a praline-like topping). Seasonal favorites include the Smurfette (fresh blueberries baked into a vanilla cake with lemon buttercream icing), pumpkin spice, cherry blossom, peach, and peppermint patty. But the genius of Baked & Wired only begins with the cupcakes. The cafe also crafts delicious pies, cakes, cookies, quiches, biscotti, muffins, and scones. There is even a muffin/doughnut hybrid on the menu that only makes appearances on Tuesday and Friday morning. Gluten-free options and vegan/vegetarian friendly.

Biagio Fine Chocolate, 1904 18th St. NW, Washington, DC 20009; (202) 328-1506; www.biagio chocolate.com. Biagio showcases an array of Certified Fair Trade and organic chocolate bars, truffles, caramels, bonbons, drinking chocolates, and other cacao delicacies that are the foundation of this Dupont Circle shop. The owner and staff are extremely knowledgeable, helpful, and take great pride in the products they sell. Biagio Fine Chocolate is a must-visit (and then a must-taste) for any self-respecting chocoholic.

BAKERY WITHOUT WALLS

Just like a good sugar rush, you have to embrace **H Street Bakes** when you can. The pop-up bake sale happens about once a month in the Atlas District in Northeast, DC. Four local chefs came together to cook up the idea of the occasional bakery. Moore's Executive Pastry Chef Kim Moffatt, along with bakers-in-arms and H Street locals Faith Sleeper, Amber Yankulov, and Tiffany Coln, are the force behind the concept and the cookies. Follow the sale on Twitter at @HStreetBakes to find out the next time and place where they are selling their goodies, like bacon-cinnamon rolls and chocolate ganache tortes.

Chatman's D'Vine Bakery & Cafe, 1239 9th St. NW, Washington, DC 20001; (202) 290-3681; www.chatmansbakerycafe.com. Key lime plays a very important role at Chatman's D'Vine, which bills itself as a South Carolina–style bakery. Here you can taste key lime pound cake, key lime cheesecake, and key lime cupcakes. The walls are even painted a pale lime green. OK, you had us at key lime. The banana pudding is similarly dreamy.

Co Co Sala, 929 F St. NW, Washington, DC 20004; (202) 347-4265; www.cocosala.com. Co Co Sala could easily be called Club Chocolate. The chocolate-themed bar infuses decadent gourmet chocolate into its brunch, evening, and drink menus. At the bar consider cocktails like the Co Cojito made with chocolate-infused vodka, fresh mint and limes, Caymus Conundrum white wine, and dark chocolate flakes. On a cold day, warm up with a flight of hot chocolates with your choice of three from the list of dark, white, milk, peanut butter, salted caramel, chipotle, and pumpkin spice. Brunch highlights include the s'mores french toast, and the restaurant also offers savory items like a bacon mac and cheese, lamb sliders, and a Creole crab cake. Artisanal and gourmet chocolates can be purchased from the restaurant's boutique.

Dangerously Delicious Pies, 339 H St. NE, Washington, DC 20002; (202) 398-7437; www.dangerouspiesdc.com. All pie, all the time. Dangerously Delicious cooks up sweet and savory choices in

---

PEEP PARADISE

Peeps & Co., (150 National Dr., National Harbor, MD 20745; 301-749-5791; www.justborn.com). The sweetest sign that spring finally has arrived is when the first Peeps hit the shelves after a long, hard Peep-free winter. And, at the first-ever store dedicated to those delicious squishy yellow sugarcoated marshmallow chicks, it's like spring every day. Milk- and dark-chocolate-covered Peeps can be savored at the 3,500-square-foot National Harbor flagship store along with Peep merchandise, from mugs to t-shirts to oversize stuffed-Peep pillows. Peep art even adorns the wall and the Peep brand cousins Mike and Ike, Hot Tamales, and Peanut Chews are also sold here.

---

a dizzying array of combinations. The store with the tag line "we make bad ass pies" recently threw its hat into the food truck game. Follow it @dcpietruck.

Firehook Bakery and Coffee House, 1909 Q St. NW, Washington, DC; (202) 588-9296; www.firehook.com. Seven-layer bars, oatmeal raisin cookies, key lime tart, apricot rugelach, and black-and-white chocolate cake are just a few of the reasons to go to Firehook. The other reasons are alongside these reasons in the display cases and on the bread racks behind the counter. Other D.C. locations include: 215 Pennsylvania Ave. SE, (202) 544-7003; 912 17th St. NW, (202) 429-2253; 3411 Connecticut Ave. NW, (202) 362-2253; 1241 F St. NW, (202) 393-0951; and 441 4th St. NW; (202) 347-1760.

Georgetown Cupcake, 3301 M St. NW, Washington, DC 20007; (202) 333-8448; www.georgetowncupcake.com. Sisters Katherine Kallinis and Sophie LaMontagne brought D.C. into the cupcake age in 2008 when the pair opened the city's first cupcake shop on the corner of 33rd and M Streets. A line still forms in front of that flagship store to order the cupcakes that come in the signature pink box. Flavors change daily and include red velvet, key lime, salted caramel, maple, and lemon blossom. Seasonal choices rotate in throughout the year with special offerings on almost every holiday including Mother's Day, Valentine's Day and Election Day, when you get to choose if you want a donkey or elephant atop your cupcake. You can get a behind-the-scenes peek at the inner workings of the pretty-in-pink bakery and its co-owners on the TLC reality show *DC Cupcakes*. Gluten-free options.

Heller's Bakery, 3221 Mount Pleasant St. NW, #5, Washington, DC 20010; (202) 265-1169; www.hellersbakery.com. A part of D.C. since 1922, Heller's is an old-school tie-the-box-with-a-red-and-white-string bakery. No gourmet mini cupcakes or fancy flavors here. What they do sell is a standard assortment of sheet cakes, cookies, doughnuts, and bagels. They also make good croissants and breakfast sandwiches.

Love Cafe by CakeLove, 1501 U St. NW, Washington, DC 20009; (202) 265-9800; www.cakelove.com/lovecafe; $. CakeLove, started by Warren Brown when he left a promising law career to follow his passion for baking, quickly has become a Washington, D.C. institution. The shop has locations all over town, including the tiny storefront on U Street where it all began. Not far from there sits Love Cafe, where customers can sit and enjoy a slice of strawberry shortcake or a s'mores cupcake. The cafe also serves coffee and espresso drinks, sandwiches, soups, and salads. Gluten-free options and Vegan/Vegetarian friendly.

Pan Lourdes Bakery and Coffee Shop, 3407 14th St. NW, Washington, DC 20010; (202) 332-0002; www.lourdesbakery.com. An array of fresh cookies, pastries, and breads are sold from this off-the-beaten-path Latin bakery. The staff is friendly, the sweets delicious, and the prices are cheap. A triple threat in my book. Pan Lourdes also sells coffee and has free Wi-Fi.

Patisserie Poupon, 1645 Wisconsin Ave. NW, Washington, DC 20007; (202) 342-3248; www.patisserie poupon.net. This pretty little Georgetown bakery has been serving French pastries for more than 25 years. Try the napoleons, brioche, or gourmet macaroons in pastel hues with a cup of Illy espresso. Head toward the back of the store to enjoy your selections on the outdoor patio nestled next to the brick building.

Serendipity 3 DC, 3150 M St. NW, Washington, DC 20007; www .serendipity3dc.com. I can still remember crossing the bridge for frozen hot chocolate at the original Serendipity in Manhattan. And now that cold sweet taste can be had again right here in D.C. Georgetown's new Serendipity 3 serves the same secret recipe that made the iconic original store famous. Served in an oversize goblet, the frozen dessert comes in several flavors like Oreo, white chocolate, strawberry, vanilla, and moccchacino, but for me the original will always be my first love. You can also order the cafe's famous ice cream sundaes, the Golden Opulence Sundae, billed as the world's most expensive sundae that comes with mounds of ice

CUPCAKES COMPOSITE

Taste test a few more of the cute individual cakes that have taken over the town, frosting and all.

Crumbs Bake Shop, 604 11th St. NW, Washington, DC 20001; (202) 737-4001; and Union Station, Train Concourse, 40 Massachusetts Ave. NW, Washington, DC; www.crumbs.com; Kosher.

Hello Cupcake, 1361 Connecticut Ave. NW, Washington, DC 20036; (202) 861-2253; and 705 8th St. SE, Washington, DC 20003; (202) 544-2210; Gluten-free options.

Red Velvet Cupcakery, 501 7th St. NW, Washington, DC; (202) 347-7895; www.redvelvetcupcakery.com; Gluten-free options; Vegan options.

Sprinkles Cupcakes, 3015 M St. NW, Washington, DC; (202) 450-1610; www.sprinkles.com.

cream topped with a 23-carat edible gold leaf, gold sprinkles, and a thousand dollar price tag.

Shake Shack, 1216 18th St. NW, Washington, DC 20036; (202) 683-9922; www.shakeshack.com; Burgers; $. D.C. got bumped up in the food-chain pecking order when with much fanfare Shake Shack recently opened in Dupont Circle. The burger and fries joint serves custard and ice cream and, hence the name, excellent shakes in fabulous flavors like banana bread, honey roasted peanut, and Boston cream pie.

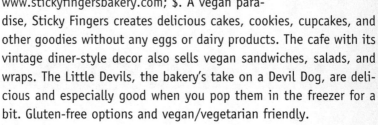

Sticky Fingers, 1370 Park Rd. NW, Washington, DC 20010; (202) 299-9700; www.stickyfingersbakery.com; $. A vegan paradise, Sticky Fingers creates delicious cakes, cookies, cupcakes, and other goodies without any eggs or dairy products. The cafe with its vintage diner-style decor also sells vegan sandwiches, salads, and wraps. The Little Devils, the bakery's take on a Devil Dog, are delicious and especially good when you pop them in the freezer for a bit. Gluten-free options and vegan/vegetarian friendly.

Super Tacos and Bakery, 1762 Columbia Rd. NW, Washington, DC 20009; (202) 232-7121; www.supertacosdc.com; Mexican; $. In addition to selling authentic tacos, tamales and tortillas, this authentic Mexican store offers the chance to try some great sweets. Try the *tres leches* cake, *atol de elote,* or bread pudding to get started.

The Sweet Lobby, 404 8th St. SE, Washington, DC 20003; (202) 544-2404; www.thesweetlobby.com; $$. Sweet, indeed. This lovely little shop nestled along Barracks Row creates Parisian-style pastries that look as pretty as they taste. Beautifully hued macaroons stand as the signature treat here and come in a revolving selection of interesting flavors like rose, passion fruit, green tea, blue lavender, milk chocolate, cappuccino, and the specialty of the house, orange-ginger. The brother-and-sister team behind the bakery also sells shortbread cookies, *mendiants,* madeleines, and rich, European-style hot chocolate. The shop boasts its own line of loose-leaf teas under the label "Steep, by The Sweet Lobby" and runs a cupcake lab where you can custom order just about any flavor cupcake you can dream up.

Frozen Treats

Cone E. Island, 2000 Pennsylvania Ave. NW, Washington, DC 20006; (202) 822-8460. Cone E. Island wins nostalgia points from anyone who has spent time on the GW campus. The store on the edge of the campus also serves an ice cream–deprived part of the city. The lower-fat Skinny Minnie is a popular draw and comes in flavors of the day including: vanilla tart yogurt, chocolate fudge brownie, fresh strawberry, chocolate fudge, French vanilla, peanut butter, mint chocolate chip, cookies 'n cream, angel food cake, and chocolate raspberry torte.

Dickey's Frozen Custard, 1710 I St. NW, Washington, DC 20006; (202) 861-0669. Dickey's takes a traditional approach to its frozen custard. The thick, creamy custard comes in two flavors—vanilla and chocolate—and in two sizes—large and small. You can also order the popular vanilla/chocolate swirl. In addition to the frozen custard, Dickey's makes some fabulous paninis, a favorite lunchtime choice for many who work in the area.

Dolcezza Artisanal Gelato, 1560 Wisconsin Ave. NW, Washington, DC 20007; (202) 333-4646; and 1704 Connecticut Ave. NW, Washington, DC 20009; (202) 299-9116; http://dolcezzagelato .com. Dolcezza Artisanal Gelato can easily bill itself as a triple threat—great coffee, great atmosphere, and perhaps most important, great gelato. The owners moved to Buenos Aires for 2 years to master the art of Argentinean gelato-making. The result of this careful study is a creamy, dense gelato, which they handcraft each morning in small batches using fresh ingredients from local farms and markets. (The website even lists and gives some background on the places and people they buy ingredients from.) Flavors reflect the season and change daily. Some that make the rounds are Sicilian blood orange, pistachio, lemon ricotta cardamom, Mexican coffee, Thai coconut milk, sea salt, and cucumber tarragon. You can almost always also expect a few flavors that revolve around *dulce de leche*. The team also makes cooling fat-free sorbet and sells pints of its cold creations at several local farmers' markets around the city.

The Rules According to Mr. Yogato:
Dignity for Discounts

Have no fear of public embarrassment. At Mr. Yogato's fro-yo shop, all it takes is a little public humiliation to rack up the savings.

10 percent off if you:
Sing along with the Styx song "Mr. Roboto" if it comes on while you are in the store.

Answer a trivia question correctly (but be warned, if you get the answer wrong another 10 percent will be added to your bill).

Allow a server to put a Mr. Yogato stamp on your forehead.

Come into the store wearing a kickball uniform. But before you dig one out of the attic, be warned that you must prove you have played hard in it by showing dirty knees and a bit of sweat.

If you can stump the owner Steve with a trivia question about *Seinfeld* or "The Rock."

20 percent off if you dare to:
Re-enact the entire 47-second-long "Thriller" dance Michael Jackson performs in the "Thriller" video. Single white glove and red-and-black leather jacket optional.

Recite the Stirling battlefield speech from the movie *Braveheart* in a believable Scottish accent.

25 percent off if you dare to:
Dress up like '80s tennis legend Björn Borg. Make that 50 percent off if you then croon "I'm Too Sexy" by Right Said Fred in a Swedish accent.

Seinfeld Challenges:
Show up to the store with an actor who portrayed a minor character from the long-running television series in tow and you will be rewarded with either 10 free yogurts or an all-you-can-eat yogurt week. The actor must be photographed in the store in order to get the discount. Recent photos have been snapped with Jon Voigt, who appeared as himself on the show and bites Kramer; Peter Allas, who played the Paisano's Pizza Man; and Teri "They Are Real and They Are Spectacular" Hatcher.

Create an edible Yogato pasta structure a la Fusilli Jerry and get a discount in percentage points equal to the height, in centimeters, of your creation.

FroZenYo, Various locations; www.frozenyo.com. FroZenYo boasts a bevy of flavors at its self-serve shops. Red velvet, cheesecake, mint chocolate, eggnog, macadamia, Georgia peach, root beer float, snickerdoodle, and pumpkin pie are a few of the 16 flavors, both tart and sweet, available every day. There are also fat-free, 98 percent fat-free, no sugar added, and lactose-free choices.

Gelateria Dolce Vita, 3000 K St. NW, Washington, DC 20007. Right along the Georgetown waterfront, Gelateria Dolce Vita is a popular post-movie and post-dinner destination on warm D.C. nights. Stroll along the water with a cup of tiramisu, blood orange, coconut, pistachio, chocolate hazelnut, or one of the other sweet choices.

Ice Cream Station, 3528 12th St. NE, Washington, DC 20017; (202) 526-7419. A favorite Catholic University diner-style shop that serves double duty as an ice cream parlor. The family-run business also makes delicious homemade waffles, best appreciated a la mode.

Larry's, 1633 Connecticut Ave. NW, Washington, DC 20009; (202) 234-2690. There's a reason Larry has been dubbed the Scoop Nazi. The owner who works behind the counter is known for being temperamental and dropping the f-bomb, but his ice cream keeps many coming back for more. Chocolate chip cookie dough, rum raisin, and Kahlua are fan favorites and the latter two are full proof. The shtick is free but the toppings are extra. Larry also sells baked goods, including some well-loved red velvet cupcakes.

Max's Best Ice Cream, 2416 Wisconsin Ave. NW, Washington, DC 20007; (202) 333-3111. Ice cream at Max's is something of a Glover Park rite of passage. The mom-and-pop shop scoops rich, creamy ice cream in a variety of flavors that are rotated in and out each day. Some, like the worth-trying spicy pumpkin, reflect the season while others like the mint Oreo and the honey graham ice cream are always worth trying. Max's makes particularly good French vanilla, which in my opinion is a good marker of a good ice cream parlor. Anyone can make ice cream taste good when you throw lots of candy in it, but to make great vanilla shows your true ice cream–making abilities. Kudos to Max for his! Cash only.

Mr. Yogato, 1515 17th St. NW, Washington, DC 20036; (202) 629-3531; www.mryogato.com. Fun and games stands as the bold mission behind Mr. Yogato, which quite possibly might be the happiest frozen yogurt shop on the planet. The Dupont Circle fixture is known for its trivia challenges, sing-alongs and the Tetris, Super Mario Bros., and board games found in the back. A long list of contests get customers discounts (see sidebar), most of them having to do with singing, dancing, or *Seinfeld*. But do watch your step or you'll wind up on the dreaded "Banned Customers" list posted on the wall for all to see.

Pitango Gelato, 1451 P St. NW, Washington, DC 20005; (202) 332-8877; 413 7th St. NW, Washington, DC 20004; (202) 885-9607; and

Screamin: Other Great Places Around Town to Find Ice Cream

Avalon Theatre Cafe, 5612 Connecticut Ave. NW, Washington, DC 20015; (202) 966-3464. Locally made Moorenko's ice cream is served at the cafe attached to the historic movie theater. You can eat your ice cream or other treat at the cafe or enjoy it during the movie.

Baskin Robbins Ice Cream, 2604 Connecticut Ave. NW, Washington, DC 20008; (202) 483-4820. 31 flavors for the taking.

Ben & Jerry's, locations in Union Station and the Old Post Office pavilion, 1333 19th St. NW, Washington, DC 20036; (202) 785-4882; and 3135 M St. NW, Washington, DC 20007; (202) 965-2222; www.benjerry.com. Ben and Jerry. A fine pair, indeed.

Broad Branch Market, 5608 Broad Branch Rd. NW, Washington, DC 20015; (202) 249-8551; http://broadbranchmarket .com. The charming, old-fashioned market keeps neighbors young and old happy with its ice cream room.

Häagen-Dazs, 3120 M St. NW, Washington, DC 20007; (202) 333-3443; and 703 7th St. NW, Washington, DC 20001; (202) 783-

660 Pennsylvania Ave. SE, Washington, DC 20003. Organic milk is not enough for the folks behind Pitango Gelato. They like to take it one step further by buying their organic milk from a single herd of grass-fed cows that graze at Pennsylvania's Spring Wood Organic Farm. And, the free-range eggs they use in the gelato are used on the very same day they are laid. The result is fabulously fresh and authentic

4711; and 50 Massachusetts Ave. NE, Washington, DC 20002; (202) 789-0953.

Hershey's Ice Cream Store, 3151 K St. NW, Washington, DC 20007; (202) 339-9004; and 927 15th St. NW #B, Washington, DC 20533; (202) 408-1307.

National Museum of Natural History Ice Cream and Espresso Bar (Ground Floor), 10th Street and Constitution Avenue NW, Washington, DC 20560; (202) 633-1000; www .mnh.si.edu/visit/restaurants.htm.

Palm Court Coffee and Gelato Bar, National Gallery of Art, East Wing Concourse. House-made gelato and pastries.

Potbelly Sandwich Shop. Locations all around town. The sandwich shop even makes to-order ice cream sandwiches using the shop's homemade oatmeal chocolate chip cookies.

Ice cream is everywhere at the **National's Park baseball stadium** including **Dolce Gelati** (Sections 112, 135), **Hawaiian Shaved Ice** (Section 143), and **Capitol Creamery** (Sections 217 and 311).

gelato. The shop only offers 20 flavors, which rely on organic chocolate, premium Italian nuts, and fresh-picked organic fruit as a base. Some favorites include crème fraîche, chocolate hazelnut, Bourbon vanilla, cardamom, and Sicilian almond. Apricot, spicy chocolate, orange dark chocolate, Concord grape, cantaloupe, mojito, quince, white grapefruit, and tangerine are among the other flavors offered.

SweetGreen, 1512 Connecticut Ave. NW, Washington, DC 20036; (202) 387-9338; 3333 M St. NW, Washington, DC 20007; (202) 337-9338; and 1471 P St. NW, Washington, DC 20005; (202) 234-7336; www.sweetgreen.com. At all of its locations, SweetGreen serves its signature nonfat Sweetflow, the store's version of tart frozen yogurt. Three toppings come with each cup and trend toward the healthy with choices like fresh berries, chopped mint, nuts, agave nectar, and shredded coconut.

Tangysweet, 675 E St. NW, Washington, DC 20004; (202) 347-7893; and 2029 P St. NW, Washington, DC 20036; (202) 822-2066; www.tangysweet.com. Tangysweet does tart fro yo in three favors—classic, green tea, and pomegranate—and one wildcard special flavor that changes regularly. The shop, which embraces environmental design ideals, also serves smoothies and has a host of toppings.

Thomas Sweet Ice Cream and Chocolate, 3214 P St. NW, Washington, DC 20007; (202) 337-0616; www.thomassweet.com. Since 1979 the good people behind the counter of Thomas Sweet have been scooping out homemade ice cream. A crowded chalkboard overhead lists the many flavors of the day for cones, cups, milkshakes, and sundaes. The hot fudge is homemade and yummy. For a more figure-conscious treat, try the fat-free frozen yogurt. The Georgetown corner store offers outdoor seating. Cash only.

U-Scream Ice Cream and Treatery, 1301 U St. NW, Washington, DC 20009; (202) 299-0020. A family-run indie ice cream parlor where the service is warm and friendly and the ice cream is cold and sweet. U-Scream has some fun, unexpected flavors like red velvet and carrot cake in addition to the standards like chocolate, caramel, and vanilla. U-Scream will do mix-ins and also recently started making crepes.

Yogen Früz, Various locations; www.yogenfruz.com. Part of a chain that began in Canada, Yogen Früz starts with two basic flavors—vanilla and chocolate—and then mixes in fruit resulting in a light, almost whipped final product. The store also makes smoothies and sells the yogurt with the fruit on top rather than mixed in for those who want it straight up.

Yogiberry, 3515 Connecticut Ave. NW, Washington, DC 20008; (202) 362-9644. Yogiberry recently switched to self-serve and customers young and old could not be happier. The Cleveland Park frozen yogurt shop draws in a steady stream of customers wanting to sample the revolving selection of tart favors (original, berry, and green tea are staples) and its toppings bar with dozens of sweet, crunchy, and fruity choices.

Feeding Your Soul:
Making a Difference with Food

I think it's almost impossible to research a book about food in Washington, D.C. without also thinking about the hundreds of thousands of people who experience hunger on a regular basis here in the nation's capital. According to research done by the Capital Area Food Bank, almost a half a million people in our area go hungry. More than 200,000 of them are children.

I knew the problem was significant, but I have to admit that I was a bit surprised to learn that the numbers were that high. And, sadly, that statistic is growing at an alarming rate. So I decided to use the writing of this book not just as an opportunity to chat with chefs and linger at farmers' markets but also to find out more about the impressive mix of organizations and efforts in town that feed those in need. While I had a pretty good familiarity with many of these groups, the more people I talked to the more I was blown away by the scope, depth, and commitment of those in our community who come together to feed those who would otherwise go without. On any given day in D.C., there is a good chance you might find a volunteer at **Miriam's Kitchen** slicing strawberries that will top handmade ricotta crepes or a **Food & Friends** volunteer delivering healthy groceries to a chemo patient too worn out from a morning of treatment and an afternoon of work to get to the store.

In this chapter I have outlined some of the local groups in town that deal with hunger and that have volunteer opportunities that I thought would especially appeal to those who love food. In almost all cases, you don't need a specific skill set other than a good attitude and desire to pitch in. Some groups require a recurring commitment while others allow you to drop in once or once in a while. Volunteers slice, dice, bake, package, serve, clean, chat, and deliver. And, you can even add pick to the list if you try your hand at gleaning at a farm. No matter what you choose, the end result is more than just a hungry person being fed but a community being built and strengthened.

Capital Area Food Bank, 645 Taylor St. NE, Washington, DC 20017; (202) 526-5344; www.capitalareafoodbank.org. You are not alone if you cannot begin to imagine how one organization collects and distributes 27 million pounds of food a year. This is why the Capital Area Food Bank offers tours of its impressive operation—the guided glimpse is a perfect way to begin learning about the food bank and its programs. Tour dates are listed on the website as are an array of other ways to get involved with the Capital Area Food

Bank, the largest nonprofit hunger and nutrition education resource in the Washington metropolitan area. The food bank has one-time and long-term volunteer opportunities that include packing, sorting, and restocking the shelves of its massive warehouses. If you would rather put your sweat equity in while in the great outdoors, the food bank's program with Clagett Farm in Maryland might be for you. Nestled on 20 beautiful acres in Upper Marlboro, the farm runs several efforts aimed at giving low-income individuals and families access to the fresh produce grown on the farm. During the spring, summer, and fall months, volunteers are needed to help maintain the farm and do everything from weeding to mulching to picking fresh fruits and veggies. A great opportunity to get your hands dirty—and maybe even learn a new gardening skill or two—for a good cause. Check out the food bank's website to find out more about Clagett Farm or any of its other volunteer opportunities.

Fresh Start Catering

You know that old adage about teaching a man to fish—**Fresh Start Catering** (425 2nd St. NW, Washington, DC 20001; 202-234-0707 x150; www.freshstartcatering.com) is doing just that. A program of the DC Central Kitchen, the catering company is made up of graduates of the organization's Culinary Job Training program. Fresh Start embraces local ingredients and flavors, serving up dishes like merlot-braised short ribs with Parmesan baked polenta; golden raisin couscous salad with mint, olive oil, and feta; and layered raspberry, currant, and pecan bars topped with coconut. In addition to providing food for many area schools and universities, the company also specializes in group picnics, meetings, and parties.

DC Central Kitchen, 425 2nd St. NW, Washington, DC 20001; (202) 234-0707; www.dccentralkitchen.org. If you think nothing worthwhile ever comes from leftovers then you likely have never seen DC Central Kitchen in action. Every day the organization takes 3,000 pounds of donated "leftover" food and turns it into 4,500 meals, which it then distributes to homeless and hungry people in our community. An army of volunteers is needed to help collect the surplus food from the various restaurants and other food-service businesses around town as well as distribute it to an array of local shelters, medical clinics, and social-service organizations.

Food & Friends, 219 Riggs Rd. NE, Washington, DC 20011; (202) 269-2277; www.foodandfriends.org. What began as a grassroots effort to provide food for AIDS patients during the early days of the epidemic has grown into a far-reaching organization that now feeds some 3,000 people a day. Today Food & Friends delivers meals and groceries to individuals throughout the area who are suffering from life-challenging illnesses including cancer, Alzheimer's disease, and HIV/AIDS. People qualify for Food & Friends services based on medical needs, not financial ones (although many of the recipients do live below the poverty line), which makes Food & Friends different from many of the hunger-based groups and food banks in town. No one in need is ever turned away. In Food & Friends' state-of-the-art kitchen, meals are prepared according to 11 different diets (diabetic, low-sodium, vegetarian, puree, etc.) by staff members and volunteers who together slice, dice, package, label, clean, pack, and ultimately deliver. Volunteer orientation is held the first Thurs of each month at 6:30 p.m. and the third Sat of each month at 10 a.m. Log on to the Food & Friends website for more details.

Martha's Table, 2114 14th St. NW, Washington, DC 20009; (202) 328-6608; www.marthastable.org. Chances are you have passed by McKenna's Wagon and not even realized it. Martha's Table mobile soup kitchen, McKenna's Wagon downtown has been serving hot meals and sandwiches to the city's homeless community for years. The nonprofit organization, which also provides other services for those in need, has many worthwhile volunteer opportunities seven days a week, including driving the truck in the evenings and preparing food every day from 10 a.m. to 1 p.m. If you want to get involved, go on the Martha's Table website and fill out a volunteer application.

Mid-Atlantic Gleaning Network, PO Box 9871, Alexandria, VA 22304; (703) 541-9052; www.mid atlanticgleaningnetwork.org. After a gleaning you likely will have sweat on your brow, dirt under your fingernails, and a really big smile on your face. During a gleaning, volunteers help harvest fruit and vegetables from local farms. Whatever is picked is then transported to food banks, individuals in need, and organizations. The volunteer labor keeps the cost almost minimal and helps fresh produce get into the hands of worthy recipients who might otherwise not have access to it. The Mid-Atlantic Gleaning Network is responsible for harvesting some 3 million pounds of food a year. Check the group's website to find out more about gleanings in our area and to participate.

Miriam's Kitchen, 2401 Virginia Ave. NW, Washington, DC 20037; (202) 452-8926; www.miriamskitchen.org. Every morning at Miriam's Kitchen is like a mini episode of *Top Chef*. The social service organization's two professional chefs, along with an army of eager volunteers await the delivery of that day's donated produce, dairy products, fish, meat, cheese, and other ingredients, never knowing exactly what will come in. Once the ingredients arrive they

FEEL GOOD FOODIES

What's better than a fabulous meal prepared by one of the most sought-after chefs in town? A fabulous meal prepared by one of the most sought-after chefs in town that benefits a local organization on the front lines of the fight against hunger. As a way to raise much-needed funds, many of the groups mentioned in this chapter hold annual events and parties featuring dishes sure to make even the most seasoned foodie salivate. Here is a list of some of the most beloved ones. You can consult the calendar of events in the front of this book for a more extensive list.

Capital Area Food Bank's Blue Jean Ball (April). Denim and good food. Need I say more?

DC Central Kitchen and Martha's Table Sunday Night Suppers (January). Elaborate and sumptuous meals served in elegant private homes.

Food & Friends, Chef's Best Dinner and Auction (June). Dozens of the region's most esteemed chefs do the cooking at this larger-than-life foodie fest.

are sorted and the group is faced with the challenge of using them to make a healthy, homemade dish that will cost Miriam's Kitchen just 50 cents per meal. The meal is then served for free to the hundreds of homeless people who come to Miriam's Kitchen each week to eat and to receive other services like legal help or free Metro cards. Volunteers do everything from slicing vegetables to serving

Food & Friends, Dining Out for Life (March). Diners at a select group of fabulous restaurants are visited by a team of Food & Friends' equally fabulous drag queens. And proceeds benefit Food & Friends.

Miriam's Kitchen, 100 Bowls of Compassion (May). An elegant evening at the National Building Museum featuring delicious delicacies and a silent auction. The event's name is taken from the Tibetan saying that "compassion is like the moon shining on one hundred bowls of water."

SOME: Empty Bowls (Spring). Talented potters and artists create beautiful one-of-a-kind ceramic bowls for sale. Purchasers can then have their new bowl filled with a gourmet soup, which they can then enjoy in the company of other participants.

food to washing dishes. No kitchen skills are needed to help out, but you are requested to commit to volunteering at least once a month. "It's our way of creating a community, which is important for our guests," says Ashley Lawson, the group's development and volunteer manager. Volunteers also enjoy a sense of community, taking part in activities like the kickball team's regular games or volunteer fishing or crabbing trips—the catch is then cooked up the next day for Miriam's Kitchen. Regular shifts happen every weekday from 6 to 8 a.m. and again at 4 to 6:30 p.m. Help also is needed midday Tues, Wed, and Thurs. See the recipe for Miriam's Kitchen's **Venison Pot Pie** on p. 311.

SOME (So Others Might Eat), 71 0 St. NW, Washington, DC 20001; (202) 797-8806; www.some.org. Over the past 40 years, SOME has grown from a small soup kitchen in a church basement to an interfaith organization that provides an array of services to D.C.'s homeless community. Holding true to its roots, SOME still serves about 1,000 meals a day to those in need, and a core of reliable volunteers help make that happen. About 15 volunteers are needed each day to make sure breakfast and lunch can be served at the organization's O Street dining room. In addition to working at the dining room, you can also sign up with friends, colleagues, or your church, synagogue, mosque, or other group to be a Provide-A-Meal (PAM) volunteer. PAM volunteers cook casseroles and the like at home to bring to O Street, where they are then served. You also have the choice to bring ingredients to the O Street kitchen and cook a meal there or purchase meals from one of the vendors that work with SOME. Call or log on to SOME's website for specifics and to sign up in advance. SOME also sponsors an annual Thanksgiving Day Trot for Hunger race.

Washington Youth Garden, 3501 New York Ave. NE, Washington, DC 20002; (202) 245-2709; www.washington youthgarden.org. For some 40 years the Washington Youth Garden at the US National Arboretum has served as a living classroom, a place where local elementary school kids can learn

about nutrition, cooking, personal responsibility, team building, and healthy living through hands-on gardening. The youth garden has many volunteer opportunities for individuals and families and holds weekly volunteer hours on Tuesday and Saturday mornings.

Cooking Classes

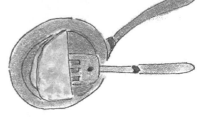

As *Top Chef* and the Food Network have become a part of popular culture, the secrets and politics of professional kitchens have been revealed to the civilian population. Words like braise, foam, glaze, slow-roast, and infuse have crept into the collective culinary consciousness. And with the new kitchen vocabulary has come the rise in recreational cooking schools, where newbies and armchair experts alike can hone and refine their kitchen skills. Some, like L'Academie de Cuisine and CulinAerie, take place in new teaching kitchens that sparkle with stainless steel appliances, while others take place in less formal settings, like Nongkran Daks' restaurant, where she gently shares the kitchen wisdom that she learned in her native Thailand. Classes in this area range from bread baking to sushi rolling, but the across the board most popular class at the majority of local cooking schools is knife skills, where students learn to slice, chop, and dice with expert skill and speed.

Acadiana, 901 New York Ave. NW, Washington, DC 20001; (202) 408-8848; www.acadianarestaurant.com. Several times a year

Acadiana pulls back the curtain and reveals some of the magic of the food and spirits of the Big Easy. Classes include a Father's Day BBQ class, a crawfish/shrimp/crab boil workshop, and bourbon tasting. Sister restaurant **DC Coast** (see p. 133) runs similar occasional classes, including a Scotch tasting.

BLT Steak, 1625 I St. NW, Washington, DC, 20006; (202) 689-8999; www.e2hospitality.com. Executive Chef Victor Albisu leads monthly interactive cooking classes at his D.C. restaurant centered on themes like South American *asado,* Memorial Day BBQ, and The Whole Hog pig-cooking class. He explains and demonstrates cooking techniques from the Argentinean countryside during a 90-minute class, which is then followed by a 4-course lunch featuring all of the demoed dishes.

Cheesetique, 2411 Mount Vernon Ave., Alexandria, VA 22301; (703) 706-5300; www.cheesetique.com. Classes at this part specialty shop, part wine and cheese bar revolve around the Alexandria shop's close to 300 handpicked international and domestic cheeses. Cheesetique owner and founder Jill Erber leads the workshops, which include the sampling of at least ten different cheeses and two matching wines. The store also holds monthly wine classes that usually last an hour and a half and include education, conversation, and the sipping of eight different wines and six matching cheeses.

Cookology, 21100 Dulles Town Circle, Sterling, VA, 20166; (703) 433-1909; www.cookologyonline.com. Cookology offers classes for everyone, from the person who uses the oven for storage to the at-home gourmet who salivates over the latest issue of *Bon Appétit*. Culinary boot camp, where students master the basics, is one of the more popular offerings. Cheese Making, Chicken 101, and Handmade Pastas are some of the other courses at the recreational cooking school located in the Dulles Town Center mall.

CulinAerie, 1131 14th St. NW, Washington, DC 20005; (202) 587-5674; www.culinaerie.com. CulinAerie co-founder Susan Holt knows that being a great chef doesn't necessarily translate into being a great teacher. So she and her partner Susan Watterson make certain that all the instructors at their downtown recreational cooking school are both. Classes at the busy school are designed for all levels, from the students who can barely boil water to the expert-level at-home cooks who register for CulinAerie's intensive master series focusing on a specific skill or food each week. Couples classes tend to fill up quickly and each one looks at a different kind of food. Some of the 3-hour-long date-night classes have included a Heat class devoted to spicy dishes, Italian Food and Wine Pairing, and a New Orleans class that focused on Cajun and Creole cooking. The school even offered a Julia Child tribute class that focused on a menu from the cooking icon's famous book *Mastering the Art of French Cooking*. CulinAerie also does a host of private cooperate events, birthday parties, showers, and other specially crafted cooking parties in its downtown space.

Fancy Cakes by Leslie, 4939 Elm St., Bethesda, MD 20814; (301) 652-9390; www.fancycakesby leslie.com. If you've ever dreamed of becoming your own Cake Boss, then grab your pastry bag and get thee to a Fancy Cakes by Leslie workshop. The cupcake shop runs a series of fun classes that teach you how to wrap a cake in fondant, fashion a butterfly from sugar, and make a cupcake look like a cartoon character, skyscraper, or record album. Classes are limited to 14 students and tend to be held either on Sunday or a weekday night. Choose from such sweet choices as Buttercream Piping, Beginning Fondant, and Sculpting and Modeling. Workshops cost between $75 and $125, depending on the offering, and include all the materials and ingredients. And Buddy Valastro would be so proud.

Hello Cupcake, 1361 Connecticut Ave. NW, Washington, DC 20036; (202) 861-2253; www.hellocupcakeonline.com. Jump on the cupcake bandwagon with a cupcake decorating class at the Connecticut Avenue shop and learn how to make your own edible creations. The store's pastry chef leads you through the ins and outs of crafting artful flowers, curls, swirls, and twirls that decorate the mini cakes. Classes tend to reflect the season, so you can expect a spooky creatures class in October, an Americana workshop in July, and a heart-filled session come February.

Hill's Kitchen, 713 D St. SE, Washington, DC 20003; (202) 543-1997; www.hillskitchen.com. Classes here are as diverse as Introduction to the Pressure Cooker to Pierogi Making and are taught in the upstairs test kitchen at this delightful neighborhood cooking store. Other offerings include Homemade Baby Food, Basic Knife Skills, and Ice Cream Making.

Just Simply . . . Cuisine, 3224 Cathedral Ave. NW, Washington, DC 20008; (202) 487-3316; www.justsimplycuisine.com. The intimate cooking classes Chris Coppola Leibner holds in her Woodley Park home are a bit like small social gatherings that happen to wind up around the kitchen counter. It's this kind of cozy feel that have made Just Simply . . . Cuisine's classes a local favorite that still manage to fly slightly below the radar. Leibner selects recipes to teach based on what she can purchase that week from her local stable of grocers, growers, fishmongers, bakeries, and dairies. She also relies heavily on what she grows in her fertile urban kitchen garden. Sometimes the take from her garden is so rich that all the greens, vegetables, and herbs needed for a particular menu come from her backyard. The self-described lifelong foodie then crafts that week's teaching menu and class around the sum of those ingredients. As she teaches her recipes, she demonstrates techniques and shares stories and pointers from her kitchen experience. Leibner will organize private classes for small groups and will help you craft a special menu for these gatherings.

L'Academie de Cuisine, 5021 Wilson Lane, Bethesda, MD 20814; (301) 986-9490; www.lacademie.com. Founded in 1976 long before *Top Chef* and the Food Network, L'Academie de Cuisine stands as the grande dame of area cooking schools. Still, the hands-on school remains current as it teaches the basics and beyond to the legions of local foodies who pass through its doors. The recreational arm of the school—L'Academie also runs a professional cooking school in Gaithersburg—recently underwent a massive renovation. The inviting Bethesda kitchens now shine with state-of-the-art appliances and equipment. Classes either follow a demonstration or hands-on participation model and are taught by instructors who have graduated from a professional school. An array of the guest chefs and local foodie personalities also step into the instructor lineup on a regular basis. Knife skills holds the title as the most popular course offered by the school and is open, like most of the workshops here, to students at all experience levels. The first 2 hours of the class are devoted to detailed demonstration and are then followed by an hour of practice where students dice an onion, julienne carrots, chop herbs, mince garlic, slice mangoes, and even debone a chicken. Instructors also offer advice and helpful tips on how to sharpen, hone, store, and purchase kitchen knives. Other popular offerings include the advanced technique courses that focus on one type of cooking, like grilling skills or fish techniques. Ethnic cooking classes, baking courses, and couples cooking classes also tend to fill up quickly. Prices vary depending on the offering but tend to be about $65 for a demonstration class and $75 for the hands-on workshops.

Lebanese Taverna, 4400 Old Dominion Dr., Arlington, VA 22207; (703) 841-1562; www .lebanesetaverna.com/cooking_classes. At the Lebanese Taverna cooking classes, you'll learn how to re-create some of the Middle Eastern restaurant's dishes at home. Classes begin with a glass of wine and an appetizer before the chef demonstrates some trade secrets, like how to properly roll a grape leaf. Students get to try their hands during the course of the evening and get to sample the final product. Vegetarian classes are offered on a regular basis. Classes cost about $65 per person.

The Passenger, 1021 7th St. NW, Washington, DC; (202) 393-0220; www.passengerdc.com. A cocktail class at The Passenger might be as close as you get in real life to a potions class at Hogwarts. Mixologist Derek Brown and his talented colleagues step out from behind the bar to share their secrets of the spirits during Passenger's Saturday workshops. Some classes include Make Your Own Vermouth, From Glen to Glen: Scotch and Irish Whisky, and Camellia Sinensis: Tea in Cocktails. Other guest professionals also lead some of the classes. Most of the hour-long workshops are held on Saturday afternoon, cost $65 per person, and include tastings.

Thai Basil, 14511-P Lee Jackson Memorial Hwy., Chantilly, VA 20151; (703) 478-3666; www.thaibasilchantilly.com. The southern Thailand village Nongkran Daks grew up in was so small that her parents sent her to live with her sister-in-law in a bigger town when it came time for her to go to secondary school. Nong's sister-in-law had a catering business and Nong's job was to cook the curries. She has been cooking ever since. Although Nong didn't love it at the time, those early days in the kitchen taught her the intricacies of authentic Thai cooking, a love and art she has been passing on to her students for decades. Nong, the owner of Chantilly's Thai Basil, teaches a 3-day Thai cooking series that is held over three Sundays. Each meeting is devoted to one dish. Chicken with basil, crying tiger flank steak, and sticky mango rice were the dishes learned in one recent course. Another focused on crab fried rice, Thai vegetable soup, and banana in coconut milk with tapioca. She also often teaches how to make her yellow chicken curry, one of the most popular dishes in her restaurant, and, she says, one of the easiest to make. Nong's gentle way and expert hand help guide her students through the process of creating authentic dishes and understanding the story behind the flavors. She also offers tips on where to shop for Thai ingredients and what you can substitute when you simply cannot find coconut sugar or kaffir lime leaf. (For the record, she says you can use brown sugar for the coconut sugar and cilantro stems for the kaffir lime leaf.) At the end of each class you get to eat what you have cooked.

Writing with Spice and Spirit

Monica Bhide's words and recipes dance off the pages of her cookbooks and magazine articles. During her 6-week-long online food-writing class, the locally based food writer shares her insights and wisdom into the art form she has so beautifully mastered. The *Modern Spice* author focuses on turning a passion for food and writing into a marketable skill by focusing on recipe development, article markets, book proposals, restaurant reviews, pitch letters, and more. Assignments range from developing custom recipes to writing essays. Bhide's students come from around the world and with a variety of backgrounds, with everyone from cooks to PR reps signing up for her classes and coaching. For more information or to register, visit www.monicabhide.com.

Seasonal Pantry, 1314½ 9th St. NW, Washington, DC 20001; www.seasonalpantry.com. The small market with an every-changing inventory of handmade food and specialty products, also runs a series of cooking and food-related classes. Sometimes the individuals who create the small batch products the store sells lead the workshops as is the case with the baking sessions taught by the store's house baker or the cheese classes taught by the in-house fromager. Supports the local food movement.

Toscana Cafe and Catering, 601 2nd St. NE, Washington, DC 20002; (202) 525-2693; www.toscanacateringdc.com. Chef Daniele

Catalani shares the secrets of his beloved Italian dishes during his occasional 90-minute-long hands-on cooking classes, held in conjunction with the Casa Italiana Language School. Four recipes are highlighted during the course, which are grouped by theme, like risotto, stuffed pastas, sauces, or Italian desserts. Once the last pot is stirred and the final dish comes out of the oven, the entire class sits down to the feast they have created. Each class costs $50 per person.

Zola Wine & Kitchen, 505 9th St. NW, Washington, DC 20005; (202) 639-9463; www.zolawinekitchen.com. Chef Robert "Robbie" Meltzer and his culinary team share the secrets of his kitchen during the popular weekly classes held at the light and bright Zola Wine & Kitchen. Classes in this beautiful space focus on a single topic like avocados, burgers, chocolate, beets, or soups and the recipes taught tend to reflect the flavors of the current season. The 90-minute-long classes conclude with sharing the meal just cooked along with a glass of wine from a bottle recommended by the shop. See the recipe for Zola's **Strawberry Basil Smash** on p. 317.

Foodie Getaways

The restaurants, markets, and shops within the Washington city limits could keep even the most devoted foodie busy for a good long time, but sometimes the mountains (or the beach, valley, or historic town) call. And when it does, a road trip is the answer.

Washington distinguishes itself as one of the best day-tripping starting points in the country. In addition to being a city packed with its own collection of places to explore, Washington neighbors states with an unbelievable number of parks, historic homes, waterfalls, monuments, farms, beaches, lakes, archeological excavations, mountains, Civil War battlefields, campgrounds, trails, horse stables, wineries, and museums. Along the way there are also world-class inns, restaurants, and performance venues as well as plenty of lesser-known but equally appealing greasy spoons, farm stands, coffeehouses, regional theaters, and artisan cooperatives. The diversity of the sites within driving distance from the city means most everyone can find something that will make them happy. A few favorite ones fill these pages.

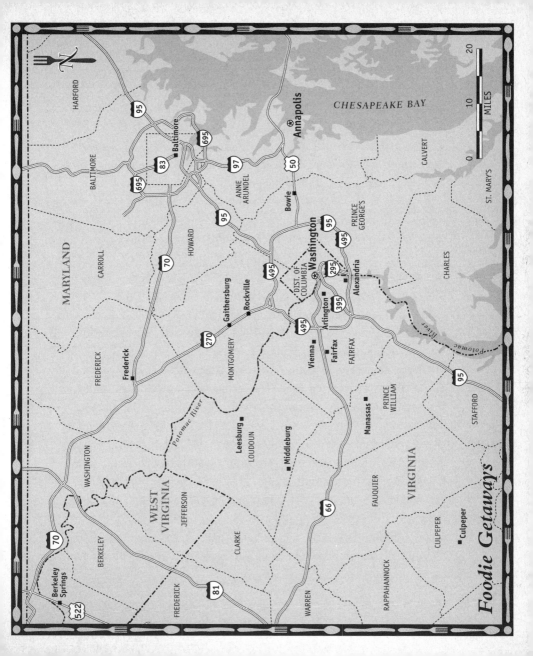

Foodie Getaways

The best part of being a local travel writer and the experience of researching this guide is that there always is a new favorite to be found. (Readers feel free to insert your favorite life metaphor here.) Although I have been berry picking dozens of times in Gaithersburg, it wasn't until a short time ago that I discovered an amazing farm where developmentally delayed adults harvest vegetables for local food banks and staff members live in a cutting edge solar-powered farmhouse. In Poolesville, a Buddhist temple with an aviary for abused and abandoned parrots somehow managed to escape my radar until recently. The same holds true for the mother-daughter-run Seven Oaks Lavender Farm, the Annapolis Ice Cream Company (where the plastic spoon I decorated now joins a collection of thousands), and the Mount Pony movie theater. And I am not sure how I survived this long without Morven Park, the Waterford Historic District, and Peeps and Co. in my life.

If you share my obsession for small picturesque towns, you will be hard pressed to find ones more charming—or smaller than—Waterford, The Plains, Warrenton, or Paris, Virginia. Although each has its own distinct personality, all offer that back-in-time feeling that so many of us crave when we place the city in the rearview mirror. The woman who runs Waterford's authentic general (and only) store often greets guests from behind her spinning wheel and can sometimes be seen out back tending to her sheep. Although Paris and The Plains claim about as many residents as a full trans-atlantic flight, they still play a huge part in creating the allure of Virginia's horse and hunt country. Berkeley Springs, known for its naturally occurring hot springs and the only place I know with the tagline "George Washington bathed here," often gets voted America's best small town and gets props from me, too. You'll likely be similarly persuaded after a soak in the Roman baths or a showing at a 1928 movie theater with a box of butter-topped popcorn made in a vintage Manley hot-oil machine.

Unlike when I first moved to the area years ago, you no longer have to stay within a city's limits to find an outstanding meal. Frederick's Volt and Berkley Spring's Lot 12 Public House have joined the destination-dining revolution and rival most downtown restaurants. The same holds true for many of the boutiques and shops outside of Washington, with the ones in Leesburg, Baltimore, Culpeper, and Annapolis leading the pack.

Whether you prefer urban streets, cobblestone sidewalks, sandy beaches, dirt roads, or historic pathways, the region surrounding the nation's capital holds many tasty destinations where you'll want to leave your footprints over and over again. On these pages you will find a sampling of my favorite day trips and weekend getaways for the times when you don't want to decide between your palate and your wanderlust. Each listing includes suggestions of places to eat, visit, shop, and stay, along with some tips on getting there.

Frederick for Foodies: Frederick, Maryland

For years the lure of treasures hidden in antique shops brought visitors to Frederick, Maryland's historic downtown. While the town is still a fabulous spot for antiquing, now food with a decidedly contemporary twist also tops the list as one the city's biggest draws. Today Frederick counts several "destination restaurants" among its prized attractions with Volt as the brightest star among them. The city now sponsors its own successful annual restaurant week every March instead of solely participating in the D.C. one as it has in the past few years.

While you are in town indulging your palate, consider stopping for a tasting and tour at the city's "urban winery." If you want something more down home, grab a pint of ale at one of the nearby brewpubs. And, who knows, you might just find the perfect vintage stemware for your new favorite vintage while you're in town. Before you embark on your culinary adventure do keep in mind that many of the local restaurants stay dark on Monday.

Getting There

Frederick is an easy 45-minute ride up I-270 North. Get off at Exit 31A and make a left on to Route 355. Follow the signs to the Visitor's Center and park in one of the well-marked parking decks in the downtown area. During the week MARC trains run between Washington and Frederick three times in the evening and come back to D.C. three times in the morning.

Where to Eat

Acacia, 129 North Market St., Frederick, MD 21701; (301) 694-3015; http://acacia129.com; Fusion; $$$. A relatively new player on the Frederick restaurant scene, Acacia offers a range of dishes that stem from the kitchen's focus on fusion. *Jaegerschnitzel,* a breaded pork tenderloin with mushroom–sour cream gravy and bacon-spaetzle braised red cabbage, is one of the more popular entrees. A pretty outdoor patio space is prime seating on sunny days and warm nights. Gluten-free options and vegan/vegetarian friendly.

Angelcakes, 319 East Church St., Frederick, MD 21701; (301) 898-2666; www.angelcakesandcupcakes.com; Bakery; $. Frederick's answer to the cupcake craze, Angelcakes offers eight flavors of the petite cakes every day along with a flavor of the day. Treats are packed in pretty Tiffany-blue boxes.

Black Hog BBQ and Bar, 118 S. Market St., Frederick, MD 21701; (240) 436-6080; www.blackhogbbq.com; Barbecue; $. The Black Hog has the reputation for friendly service and cooking up some of the area's best home style "Q." Order up a beef barbecue sandwich or go hog wild and order the meat-by-the-pound for the table.

Brewer's Alley Restaurant, 124 N. Market St., Frederick, MD 21701; (301) 631-0089; www.brewers-alley.com; American; $$. Many who come to Brewer's Alley wind up not only loving the house brews but also wind up pleasantly surprised by the food. The extensive menu includes wood-fired pizzas, a big selection of burgers including a falafel burger, and lots of bar food favorites like spicy wings, poutine, and fried pickles. Found in a lovely old building that once served as Frederick's city hall, the brewery has several dining areas including outdoor patio seating.

Cacique Restaurant, 26 N. Market St., Frederick, MD 21701; (301) 695-2756; www.caciquefrederick.com; Mexican and Spanish; $$. Cacique offers an extensive menu featuring both Mexican and Spanish dishes. The Mexican side includes seafood fajitas and *tamal de elote* while several different paellas can be found on the Spanish side. The coveted outdoor seating goes fast.

Cafe Anglais, 238 N. Market St., Frederick, MD 21701; (301) 698-1223; Afternoon Tea; $$. Cafe Anglais is a hidden-in-plain-sight find for traditional British tea. The unassuming storefront not far from the center of town won't necessarily call to you, but it's worth stepping inside and then stepping back out again to the lovely little tea garden out back. High tea offers the chance to nibble on finger sandwiches, sweets, and scones with clotted cream while sipping a fresh pot of freshly brewed English tea.

Firestone's Culinary Tavern, 105 N. Market St., Frederick, MD 21701; (301) 663-0330; http://firestonesrestaurant.com; New

American; $$. Seasonal flavors and local produce, some grown on the owner's rooftop, drive the menu here at this pretty restaurant in Frederick's historic district. A Maryland Clam Chowder, the restaurant's signature dish, remains a popular appetizer year round.

Gladchuk Bros. Restaurant, 489 W. Patrick St., Frederick, MD 21701; http://gladchukbros.com; American; $$. Gladchuk Brothers is something of a Frederick institution. The restaurant has been a favorite of locals since it opened more than 20 years ago. Regulars are drawn to the old-school favorites like veal piccata, roast turkey, chicken Cordon Bleu, crab cakes, and pot roast.

Moxie Bakery and Cafe, 629 N. Market St., Frederick, MD 21701; (301) 620-0003; www.moxiedesserts.com; Bakery; $. Moxie serves up yummy treats that pack a feel-good factor into each bite. Housed in a downtown community center, the cafe provides job training and mentoring for local youth who have been in and out of the foster care system. The baked goods are divine with choices like rosemary sugar cookies, cream scones, and hand-rolled croissants. Moxie also serves brunch and lunch featuring in-season creations like a much-loved fried green tomato BLT (a vegan version can also be ordered).

The Orchard, 45 N. Market St., Frederick, MD 21701; (301) 663-4912; http://theorchardrestaurant.com. Another Zagat-rated eatery that stocks its kitchen with seasonal ingredients. The Orchard's menu relies heavily on fresh produce to create its tasty stir-fries, salads, and soups. All the dressings and sauces are made from scratch. The tomato tamari dressing is a house favorite for good reason. Gluten-free options and vegan/vegetarian friendly.

Tasting Room, 101 N. Market St., Frederick, MD 21701; (240) 379-7772; www.tastetr.com; Wine Bar; $$$. Frederick's first wine bar still packs in a crowd for its diverse, pages-long wine list and contemporary fare. The Tasting Room is also known for its seasonal cocktails like the lychee Bellini, agave nectar margarita, and blueberry martini. Situated in a light-filled location at the corner of Church and Market, the Tasting Room gives off a decidedly cosmopolitan vibe and is Zagat-rated.

Volt, 228 N. Market St., Frederick, MD 21701; (301) 696-8658; www.voltrestaurant.com; Modern American; $$$$. Owner Bryan Voltaggio of *Top Chef* fame crafts menus based on the seasonal flavors and the local ingredients available in and around his hometown of Frederick. The restaurant is housed in a spectacular 1890s brick mansion on historic Market Street. Inside the dining spaces embrace a contemporary yet warm style that serves as the perfect backdrop for what will undoubtedly be one of the best meals you can order in this part of the world. Saturday night reservations book far in advance, as does "Table 21," the restaurant's kitchen seating, where patrons dine on a 21-course tasting menu while watching the culinary magic around them. Reservations are not taken for the pretty outdoor patio, which is open in good weather, serves a limited menu, and runs on a first-come first-seated basis. Despite the tremendous amount of hype surrounding Volt, the restaurant does not disappoint. This destination restaurant is well worth the trip. Supports the local food movement. Vegetarian friendly. Closed Mon and Tues.

Where to Go

Candy Kitchen, 52 N Market St., Frederick, MD 21701; (301) 698-0442; Sweets. The corner candy store once again proves that chocolate-covered pretzels, chocolate-covered cookies, and chocolate lollipops never go out of style. But you knew that. For more than a century, the Candy Kitchen has been satisfying the county's sweet tooth with its old-fashioned confections.

Community Bridge Mural and Carroll Creek Park Canal, Between E. Patrick and E. All Saints Streets. The trompe l'oeil mural of an old ivy-covered stone bridge painted on an unremarkable concrete bridge is so convincing that you might have to touch it to believe it. Frederick artist William Cochran's public art marvel stands as the centerpiece to this canal area and promenade, which is lined with restaurants, condo buildings, benches, and a walkway. Free concerts are given here during the summer.

Flying Dog Brewery, 4607 Wedgewood Blvd., Frederick, MD 21701; (301) 694-7899; www.flyingdogales.com; Beer. Flying Dog's craft beers have developed something of a cult following around the country and you can see how the popular brew is made at the Frederick-based brewery. The tours, which the brewery put on hiatus in 2009 to protest some strict state laws that have since been repealed, are free but you do have to don some ugly safety glasses (beer goggles don't count) to participate. Safety regulations also prohibit wearing sandals on the tour. The tour includes samples of some of the 18 different brews made here. Reservations are a must and can be made up to 6 weeks in advance. The 2-hour tours happen every Thurs starting at 4 p.m. and twice on Sat starting at noon and again at 4:30 p.m. Check the website for the most current details and some entertaining copy.

Frederick Cellars, 221 N. East St., Frederick, MD 21701; (301) 668-0311; www.frederickcellars.com; Winery. Learn how the fruit of the vine makes the journey from grape to bottle at Frederick Cellars, a working winery and tasting room right in the middle of the city. For $5 you can sample five different wines (a half ounce of each) in the Tasting Room, and for $8 you can choose to sample as many as you want from that day's selection. Exhibits of the original art that adorns the labels are often held at the winery, which also sponsors concerts. Tours of the winery are given whenever the building, a renovated 1904 icehouse, is open, except during concerts.

The Kitchen Studio, 5301 Buckeystown Pike, Suite 125, Frederick, MD 21701; (301) 663-6442; www.kitchenstudiofrederick .com. Sharpen your knife skills, learn to roll sushi, or figure out how to make fondant at a class at The Kitchen Studio run by Frederick Chef Christine Van Bloem. She also offers classes, camps, and birthday parties for kids and teenagers at her growing recreational cooking school. If you have been hitting the local pick-your-own, consider her canning class. Designed for first-timers and experts, the course focuses on ways to put a new spin on canning with delicacies like Zydeco Green Beans, Maple-Strawberry Smooch, and Indian Pickles that you can enjoy all winter long.

McCutcheon's Factory Store, 13 S. Wisner St., Frederick, MD 21701; (301) 662-326; www.mccutcheons.com. For generations McCutcheon's preserves, jams, jellies, and apple butter have been a favorite of locals, and over the years they have built up a loyal following well outside the city limits.

Molly's Meanderings, 17 N. Market St., Frederick, MD 21701; (301) 668-8075; www.mollysmeanderings.com. Step into Molly's Meanderings for a dose of Victorian charm and a selection of clothing, jewelry, and accessories that take a cue from the store's ladylike theme. Molly's Meandering is a good place to pop in if you want something new to wear for dinner out. Warning: You might suddenly get the urge to reread *Pride and Prejudice* while perusing the old-fashioned hat racks.

A Picnickers Paradise: The Covered Bridges of Frederick County

The image of Meryl Streep and Clint Eastwood falling in love on the big screen against the backdrop of Iowa's covered bridges made an already iconic symbol of the American countryside even more romantic. While the three covered bridges still standing in Frederick County never made it onto the screen during *Bridges of Madison County* or into the novel by Robert James Waller on which it is based, they still are enormously evocative and worth seeing. Covered bridges, like the three in the Frederick area, often spanned across rivers or streams and were covered to keep the wood used to construct them dry. Only a handful remain. Follow this route to take a little covered diversion from urban life. It's about a 30-mile round-trip to catch all three. Pack some favorite cheeses and fresh fruit and make a day of it.

Begin the journey at the junction of Route 15 North and Route 26, which is just north of Frederick, and drive about 4 miles north to Old Frederick Road. Turn right and drive about 1.5 miles and make a left onto Utica Road to the Utica Mills Covered Bridge.

Utica Mills Covered Bridge, Old Frederick Road near Utica. The Utica bridge spans a fishing creek and dates back to about 1850. The

The Muse, 19 N. Market St., Frederick, MD 21701; (301) 663-3632; www.shopthemuse.com. The Muse remembers to keep the fun in functional. The store sells funky jewelry, housewares, baby goodies, kitchenware, and other assorted functional gift items, all made by local artists. Embrace your inner Martha during one of the store's

reddish bridge was rebuilt and moved to its current location circa 1900.

Head back to Old Frederick Road, make a left and drive for about 4 miles to a stop sign where you will turn left onto Route 550. Drive a little less than a half-mile and make a right onto Old Frederick Road. Go about 2 miles and make a left into the Loy's Station Park parking lot.

Loy's Station Covered Bridge, 3600 Old Frederick Rd., Thurmont; Loy's is a favorite among locals not only because it is a scenic structure but also because there is a park next to it. Visitors, particularly young ones, get a kick out of wading in the calm creek, and there are picnic tables and a playground at the park.

From the parking lot of Loy's Station Park, make a left and drive through the bridge. Continue on to a stop sign and make a left onto Rocky Ridge Road. Drive about 3 miles and make a right onto Apples Church Road, which turns into Roddy Road. Go straight on this road for about a mile and half to the bridge. Drive through the Roddy Road Covered Bridge to the parking lot on the left.

Roddy Road Covered Bridge, 14760 Roddy Rd., Thurmont. At only 40 feet long, Roddy Road is the smallest of the county's covered bridges and dates back to the 1850s. The park next to it screams picnic.

weekly Wednesday Wine & Cheese Craft Parties or the monthly Mimosa Make and Take Sundays, where you create a craft while sipping on a cocktail and socializing. Check out the store's blog at www.shopthemuse.blogspot.com for details and other fun tidbits.

Weinberg Center for the Arts, 20 W. Patrick St., Frederick, MD 21701; (301) 600-2828; www.weinbergcenter.org. Pair your perfect dinner with a showing at a perfectly stunning 1926 theater. The Weinberg Center for the Performing Arts—the grand Tivoli movie house from once upon a time—sponsors an array of live performances and sometimes screens old silent films while a musician plays the theater's original Wurlitzer organ.

Zoe's Chocolate Co., 121 N. Market St., Frederick, MD 21701; (301) 694-5882; www.zoeschocolate .com; Sweets. This little upscale chocolate shop is a piece of brown and pink candy heaven. The handmade chocolates blend modern style with good old-fashioned candy-making techniques. Signature chocolates reflect the chocolatiers Mediterranean heritage and include tahini, pomegranate, and baklava truffles. The shop's beautiful hand-crafted "Raw Collection" chocolate bars are worth the trip alone and come in flavors like the sweet-and-salty Sports Bar, with caramel corn and honey-roasted

peanuts mixed into dark chocolate, and the deep, dark Espresso Bar of Swiss chocolate marbled with Italian espresso and white chocolate.

Where to Stay

Hill House Bed and Breakfast, 12 W. Third St., Frederick, MD 21701; (301) 682-4111; www.hillhousefrederick.com. Hill House is a nice choice if you don't want to (or shouldn't) drive back to D.C. after a day of food and drink. The 3-story Victorian inn has four guest rooms and is in the historic district, putting it within walking distance of many of the popular restaurants and shops.

The Inn at Stone Manor Bed and Breakfast, 5820 Carroll Boyer Rd., Frederick, MD 21701; (301) 371-0099; www.stonemanor countryclub.com. The B&B side of the Stone Manor Country Club offers a scenic retreat from the city. Lawns, gardens, and a pond surround the manor, adding a feeling of privacy. The pretty suites have fireplaces, whirlpool tubs, and porches. Breakfast is served in the dining room at 8:30 a.m. and includes homemade muffins and rich casseroles. Stone Manor is a few minutes' drive from downtown.

Eat, Stroll, Shop: Leesburg, Virginia

A great treasure sits beyond the Dulles Toll Road and its name is Leesburg. Rich with elegantly preserved buildings, boutiques, and an assortment of restaurants, the Leesburg Historic District feels like a true getaway. Founded in 1758, the town itself is steeped in history. The Declaration of Independence was read on the steps of the first courthouse here and the city is part of the Civil War

Trail. Stroll along the old red brick sidewalks and admire the historic storefronts now housing antique, craft, and clothing shops. Along the way there are plenty of inviting cafes, restaurants, bakeries, and even a spa or two where sidewalk warriors can refuel and refresh.

After melting some plastic enjoy some nature free of charge at the magnificent Morven Park, which is only about a 5-minute drive from downtown. The rolling hills and manicured gardens will tickle your senses and add another dimension of delight to a delightful day downtown.

Getting There

Getting to and from Leesburg is pretty easy unless you are venturing out or coming home during rush hour, when you will be spending a lot of time staring at brake lights. Otherwise it's less than an hour. Take the Dulles Toll Road until it becomes the Dulles Greenway. Take Exit 1A to merge onto Leesburg Bypass/US-15 S/VA-7 toward Leesburg/Warrenton. Follow the signs for the historic district—it's well marked. Park in one of the public parking structures rather than take a chance with the meters on the street (trust me, I have the tickets to show for it). Bikers can pedal to town on the W&OD Trail.

Where to Eat

Doener Bistro, 202A Harrison St., Leesburg, VA 20178; (703) 779-7880; www.doener-usa.com; German; $$. Brew lovers flock to Doener Bistro for the extensive beer list and the German food with a modern twist. Try the *döner* kebab (*döner* means "turning meat"), a Turkish dish that was altered and became wildly popular in Germany in the 1970s and is still associated with Germany to this day. The meat is stuffed into flatbread, topped with salad and sauce, and folded into a cone.

Eiffel Tower Cafe, 107 Loudoun St. SW, Leesburg, VA 20178; (703) 777-5142; www.eiffeltowercafe.com; French; $$$$. The menu changes every season at this romantic French restaurant. On warm days opt to dine on the outside patio or on the deck upstairs. Eiffel Tower Cafe is open for lunch and dinner Tues through Sat and closed on Mon. Reservations are also taken for an a la carte Sunday brunch.

Leesburg Restaurant, 9 S. King St., Leesburg, VA 20178; (703) 777-3292; $$. Old-school (with old furnishings) diner-style restaurant that looks as though it has served generations of locals.

Lightfoot Restaurant, 11 N. King St., Leesburg, VA 20178; (703) 771-2233; www.lightfootrestaurant.com; New American; $$$$. You might have to remind yourself to look down at the menu your first time here because it's so very tempting to keep gazing upward at the magnificent space, which began life in 1888 as the grand People's National Bank. Details from the Romanesque Revival style have been preserved and the old bank vault has been given new life as a wine cellar. Lightfoot cooks up American fare, which is not as formal as the surroundings. A 4-course meal of the chef's choosing can be enjoyed at a special table in the kitchen.

Lola Cookies and Treats, 109 S. King St., Leesburg, VA 20178; (703) 669-6970; www.lolacookies.com; Sweets; $. The little kitchen in this little pink house cooks up some of the best cookies and cupcakes in town. All the sweets are handmade each day. Try the chocolate ginger cookies. Sounds like an odd combination, but it's good and is the shop's most popular cookie. The chocolate macaroons are gluten-free and available every day. Lola also often bakes a gluten-free cupcake sold in the shop.

Shoes Cup & Cork Club, 17 N. King St., Leesburg, VA 20178; (571) 291-9535; www.shoescupandcorkclub.com; Cafe; $. From the moment you spy the chandelier made of vintage lace-up shoes and the floor-to-ceiling chalkboard (with a ladder so you can scribble on the tippy top) you know you are not in Starbucks anymore. And isn't that nice sometimes. Shoes Cup & Cork brews fair-trade coffee and espresso beans and serves bagels, salads, and sandwiches. The shop has free Wi-Fi and the requisite cool coffee shop mix-and-match furniture. The dinner menu includes a nice wine selection.

Vintage 50, 50 Catoctin Circle, Leesburg, VA 20176; Wine Bar; $$$. An urban pub, Vintage 50 specializes in craft beers, small plates, and a wine list with domestic and international bottles. Local musicians play every Sun starting at 9 p.m.

The Wine Kitchen, 7 S. King St., Leesburg, VA 20175; http://thewinekitchen.com. The wine flights and small plates have been garnering much attention for this standout new player on the Leesburg restaurant scene. Regional farmers keep the kitchen stocked and the philosophy of simple, fresh flavors guides the chefs.

Where to Go

Dodona Manor, 217 Edwards Ferry Rd., Leesburg, VA 20176; (703) 777-1880; www.dodonamanor.org. General George and Katherine Marshall lived in the yellow manor from 1941 to 1959. The manor's interior and exterior have been preserved to reflect the way it looked when they were here, including its *Mad Men*–era kitchen. The general served in many executive branch posts, including secretary of state and is best known as the architect of the Marshall Plan. Tours are given on the hour from 10 a.m. to 5 p.m. on Sat and 1 to 5 p.m. on Sun. A traditional English tea, along with a speaker, is held several times a year either in the manor or on the stone court. There are some summer afternoon tours during the summer. Fee.

Loudoun County Museum, 16 Loudoun St., Leesburg, VA 20175; (703) 777-7427; www.loudounmuseum.org. Housed in two 19th-century buildings, one of which is a log cabin, the museum traces the rich 250-year-long history of the county and the town. Hour-long walking tours are given Mon through Fri by advance reservation. The museum is open Fri and Sat from 10 a.m. to 5 p.m. and on Sun from 1 to 5 p.m.

Morven Park, 17263 Planter Ln., Leesburg, VA 20176; (703) 777-2414; www.morvenpark.org. Morven Park is many things at once—historic estate, equestrian center, garden collection, Civil War encampment site, museum, and expansive park. Set on more than 1,000 acres, it feels like a true oasis of quiet and beauty. The Marguerite G. Davis Boxwood Garden is particularly lovely. Visitors are welcome on foot any time the gate is open, but only in the areas that are open to the public—several sections are clearly marked as not open to the public. Stretch out a favorite tablecloth in the picnic area before exploring the ground. Here are some highlights:

Mansion

The white-columned mansion reopened in 2009 after an extensive preservation effort. Group tours are given—call (703) 777-6034 for scheduling. Many famous individuals have been lucky enough to call the mansion home over the years, including B&O Railroad President Thomas Swann Jr. and famed Virginia Governor Westmoreland Davis.

Winmill Carriage Collection

A collection of more than 100 horse-drawn vehicles from the 19th and early 20th century stand on display here and can be seen from May through November during regular tour hours. Counted among the collection is the carriage owned by Tom Thumb of the Barnum and Bailey Circus.

International Equestrian Center

Site of local, national, and world-class equestrian events with both indoor and outdoor arenas. Check the website for a current calendar of events.

Thomas Balch Library, 208 W. Market St., Leesburg, VA 20176; (703) 737-7195; www.leesburgva.gov. The Thomas Balch Library archives and preserves printed, written, and photographic documents about the history of Leesburg, Loudoun County, and Virginia. Owned by the Town of Leesburg, the Thomas Balch collections specialize in genealogy, the Civil War, and military history. The once segregated library now also serves as a designated Underground Railroad research site.

Where to Shop

On the first Friday of every month, except January, many of the shops and galleries stay open past closing time and entice shoppers with special sales, refreshments, and live music.

The Cottage: Well Loved Furnishings, 105 S. King St., Leesburg, VA 20175; (703) 443-0058; http://cottageatleesburg .com/shop. From the minute I walked through the robin's-egg blue doors of this shop, housed in an old Victorian, I kind of wanted to move in. The store is filled with vintage furniture and whimsical decorative objects the owners have found and spruced up, shabby-chic style. Items are artfully displayed in the home's 12 rooms. Old wooden ladders painted in pretty colors (that are for sale) decorate the front porch. Keep up on the latest finds at the http://the cottagegals.blogspot.com.

Crème de la Crème, 101 S. King St., Leesburg, VA 20175; (703) 737-7702; www.shopcremedelacreme.com. Crème de la Crème sells a collection of exquisite and pricey French country table linens, handmade pottery, and glassware.

Esoterica, 25 S. King St., Leesburg, VA 20175;  (703) 777-4642; www.esotericaofleesburg.com. The aptly named shop bills itself as a New Age superstore. Herbs, crystals, and divination tools are among the items stocked in the 4,000-square-foot space that also offers psychic readings, open Wicca circles, ghost tours, drum circles, and a host of New Age classes.

Leesburg Antique Emporium, 32 S. King St., Leesburg, VA 20175; (703) 777-3553. The corner store houses 2 floors of antiques from more than 50 independent dealers, with items that range from an old wooden bank-teller window to "Viva Kennedy" campaign buttons to an Elvis Presley commemorative pocket knife.

Leesburg Vintner, 29 S. King St., Leesburg, VA 20175; (703) 777-3322; www.leesburg-vintner.com. Wines from around the world and gourmet cheeses are for sale at this shop, which has won many small business and wine retailer awards. The owner also stocks a selection of local wines.

Madisonbelle, 5 Loudoun St. SE, Leesburg, VA 20175; (703) 443-1790; www.madisonbelle.com. Adorable outfits abound at Madisonbelle, which carries designer jeans, tops, and jewelry.

Where to Stay:

Idyll Time Farm, Cottage & Stabling, 43470 Evans Pond Rd., Leesburg, VA 20175; (703) 443-2992; www.bbonline.com/va/idylltime. The log cottage that sits on 50 acres of farmland at Idyll Time sleeps five and can be reserved for a night, a week, or a longer extended stay. Handmade quilts adorn the beds and the pattern of stacked logs in the cabin walls adds warmth and charm. The modern kitchen comes stocked with breakfast staples. The farm is close to seven local wineries.

Lansdowne Resort, 44050 Woodridge Pkwy., Lansdowne, VA 20176; (703) 729-8400; www.lansdowneresort.com. The Lansdowne hotel and spa recently underwent a $50 million renovation that touched all the guest rooms, common areas, and outdoor spaces. A new aquatic complex includes waterfalls, a waterslide, and several different pools. The resort also has a golf course and several restaurants.

The Norris House Inn, 108 Loudoun St., Leesburg, VA 20175; (703) 777-1806; http://norrishouse.com; $$. Innkeepers Carol and Roger Healey make guests feel right at home in their 6-room bed and breakfast. The circa-1760 house has been lovingly restored. All rooms have private baths and one has a whirlpool tub. A home-cooked breakfast is served in the conservatory overlooking the garden. Norris House is within walking distance to most of the historic district's restaurants and shops.

Almost Heaven: Berkeley Springs, West Virginia

George Washington bathed here and so can you. Right over the Maryland border, this small West Virginia town's claims to historic fame are its naturally occurring mineral springs that were a favorite of the first president. All these years later, you can still soak in the warm waters at the recently renovated bathhouses at Berkeley Springs State Park. Other private spas inspired by the healing waters offer an array of treatments. Once you have de-stressed you will be in the perfect frame of mind to soak in the rest of the town, with its quaint main street dotted with independent restaurants, wine bars, and shops.

Places to Eat

Ambrae House at Berkeley Springs, 98 N. Washington St., Berkeley Springs, WV 25411; (304) 258-2333; www.ambraehouse .com or www.wine-with-me.com; Wine Bar; $$. Ambrae House is a wine bar, restaurant, and bed-and-breakfast all rolled into one and housed in a renovated 1907 house. Watch the stars as you sip a glass of wine on the outdoor deck and bar.

Earthdog Cafe, 398 S.  Washington St., Berkeley Springs, WV 25411; (304) 258-0500; www .myspace.com/theearthdogcafe; Barbecue; $. The Earthdog Cafe is known for its all-day breakfast menu, barbecue (diners rave about the pulled pork sandwich), and its hippie vibe. Live-band nights, open-mike nights, and jam nights help keep the late-night crowds happy.

Fairfax Coffee Shop, 23 Fairfax St., Berkeley Springs, WV 25411; (304) 258-8019; www.fairfaxcoffeehouse.com; Cafe; $. The smell of the fresh brewed coffee and cappuccinos lure unsuspecting passersby into this little coffee shop. Across from the town square,

Fairfax uses the famous Berkeley Springs water to brew all of its beloved coffee blends.

La Luna Gallery and Wine Bar, 48 N. Washington St., Berkeley Springs, WV 25411; (304) 258-2522; www.lalunagalleryandwinebar .com; Wine Bar; $$. This casual wine bar and art gallery is a nice spot to unwind after a day in the mountains. Wine tastings are held the second Sat of the month from 3 to 5 p.m. and cost about $15.

Lot 12 Public House, 117 Warren St., Berkeley Springs, WV 25411; (304) 258-6264; http://lot12.com; New American; $$$$. Lot 12 has quickly become the "it" place to dine in Berkeley Springs and is even earning the coveted culinary tourism label of "destination restaurant." Chef Damian Heath's kitchen creates what he likes to call "seasonal upscale comfort cuisine." Heath, a hometown guy, and his wife, who helps him run the restaurant, also embrace the farm-to-table concept, using many local ingredients and flavors. Lot 21 is housed in a lovely old Victorian home. Porch tables are sought-after real estate during the summer months. Supports the local food movement.

Tari's Premier Cafe and Inn, 33 N. Washington St., Berkeley Springs, WV 25411; (304) 258-1196; www.tariscafe.com; American; $$. Tari's three dining areas almost function as three restaurants with one shared menu. The cafe is a cozy spot decorated with West Virginian pottery and crafts while the gallery space is brighter with its long wall of windows and museum-style lighting casting a glow

on the local artwork decorating the space. The tavern, just as the name suggests, offers a pub-like setting with a nice beer list and Thursday night jam sessions with area musicians. No matter where you sit, the food is home-cooked and sometimes homegrown and features burgers, salads, paninis, and stews.

Places to Go

Berkeley Springs State Park, #2 S. Washington St., Berkeley Springs, WV 25411; (304) 258-2711; www.berkeleyspringssp.com. The warm waters of the naturally occurring springs here brought George Washington to this town many times during his life, and the healing waters continue to lure visitors. Soak in the park's large Roman Baths, which were recently renovated. Massage treatments are also offered at the park. Reservations are strongly encouraged and may be booked up to a month in advance.

Ice House, 138 Independence St., Berkeley Springs, WV 25411; (304) 258-2300; www.macicehouse.org. Home to the Morgan Arts Council, the Ice House is a place for people to make and enjoy art of every kind, be it painting, dance, or theater.

Morgan County Observatory, 8989 Winchester Grade Rd. (Rte. 13), Berkeley Springs, WV 25411; (304) 258-1013 or (540) 869-1117; www.nitesky.org. Gaze at the night sky through the observatory's powerful telescopes during regularly scheduled public star parties. Check the schedule for times, dates, and details.

Star Theater, 137 N. Washington St., Berkeley Springs, WV 25411; (304) 258-1404; www.starwv.com. The Star movie theater is the anti-multiplex, and that is exactly its appeal. The brick 1928 movie house sports vintage red vinyl seats, striped silk wall coverings, and a fully functioning Manley hot-oil popcorn machine. The Star is known for its fresh homemade popcorn made in the Manley before each show and topped with real melted butter. The Star shows movies at 8 p.m. on Thurs, Fri, Sat, and Sun nights.

Troubadour Lounge, 25 Troubadour Lane, Berkeley Springs, WV 25411; (304) 258-9381; www.troubadourlounge.com. The Troubadour Lounge provides the opportunity to listen to country music in an authentic venue. Started by Jim McCoy, who has spent a lifetime in the business and helped Patsy Cline get on the airwaves, the Troubadour hosts live music every Saturday night. There is a stage in the club inside and another one outside, along with a tiki bar and a grill in the shape of a six-shooter. Friday night is steak night and the lounge also sponsors karaoke evenings. In March, a special Patsy Cline karaoke night pays tribute to the late singer. Troubadour is open Tues through Sun.

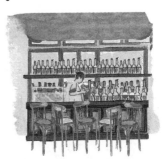

Places to Shop

Heath Studio Gallery, 327 N. Washington St., Berkeley Springs, WV 25411; (304) 258 9840; www.jheath.com. Heath Studio Gallery displays the works of painter Jonathan Heath and printmaker Jan Heath, two Berkeley Springs artists married to one another. The artistic couple are also the parents of Damian Heath, chef and founder of popular local restaurant Lot 21. The gallery is open on Sat and Sun from 11 a.m. to 5 p.m. and by appointment.

Homeopathy Works, 33 Fairfax St., Berkeley Springs, WV 25411; (304) 258-2541; www.homeopathyworks.com/jshop. An authentic homeopathic pharmacy where most of the natural remedies are made by the staff. The larger company, which has an online component, goes by the name Washington Homeopathic Products.

Mountain Laurel Gallery, 1 N. Washington St., Berkeley Springs, WV 25411; (304) 258-1919; (304) 258-1919; http://mtn-laurel .com. The works of hundreds of diverse regional artists are sold at the large gallery.

Pocket Meadow Farms, 116 Peter Yost Rd., Berkeley Springs, WV 25411; (304) 258-5155; www.pocketmeadowfarm.net. Pocket Meadow Farms sells a treasure trove of hand-dyed and hand-spun yarns, wools, and other natural fibers and is a treasured resource for anyone who knits or crochets. The store sells a variety of locally produced yarns, many from its own farm of the same name, which

WATER TASTING

I will never sip water the same way again after spending 2 days as a judge at the Berkeley Springs International Water Tasting. On a cold February weekend I traveled to the historic town to serve as a judge for the final round of the annual competition that showcases water from around the globe. After a few training sessions, the water started pouring. Along with a panel of others, I rated almost a hundred different samples based on clarity, taste, and appearance. And here was the biggest surprise of the weekend: the waters really do taste drastically different from each another. I expected subtle, hard-to-detect distinctions between the glasses and instead tasted bold differences from glass to glass. Both municipal and bottled waters and still and sparkling varieties participate in the competition. The event ends with a much-anticipated "Water Rush" where spectators storm the stage to grab bottles of the entries that have been elaborately set up in front of the judging tables. For more information on this quirky but charming event, click on www.berkeleysprings.com.

is located in the foothills of West Virginia just outside Berkeley Springs.

Recycling Works, 21 N. Washington St., Berkeley Springs, WV 25411; (304) 258-6007; www.recyclingworks1.com. Bibliophiles will feel right at home in this little treasure of a store that stocks an interesting array of new and gently used books. The owners look through hundreds of thousands of volumes each year to find the perfect selection for the store.

Places to Stay

Cacapon Resort State Park, 818 Cacapon Lodge Dr., Berkeley Springs, WV 25411; (304) 258-1022; www.cacaponresort.com. Cacapon reminds me of a summer camp for all ages. If you're a city slicker like me (or anyone else really) who wants a fun, easy, and relatively inexpensive way to hang out in nature without falling off the grid or spending a ton of money on camping equipment, this is the spot for you. The park sits on about 6,000 acres of wooded land in the shadow of Cacapon Mountain and offers visitors the chance to hike, golf, fish, boat, swim, and horseback ride, all while being in the great outdoors. The park has several lodging options for those who want to hang up their hiking boots for the night. Cacapon Lodge, on the east side of the mountain, has 48 simple but clean rooms, each with air-conditioning, private bathrooms, and televisions. The lodge itself has plenty of cozy places to curl up with a good book or admire the mountains, including a living room with a big fireplace and a large porch with rockers. Downstairs is an old-school game room, complete with an air hockey table. Children under 12 stay free and there is a special senior citizen discount. Rooms facing the golf course cost slightly more than those facing the mountains. The restaurant in the lodge serves standard American fare for breakfast, lunch, and dinner.

There are also three different types of cabins available for rent at the park: modern, standard, and bungalows. All three are rustic but vary in degree and size. The modern cabins are built for year-round use and have kitchens, fireplaces, bathrooms with showers, heat, and air conditioning. Standard log cabins are in a more secluded part of the park and can be rented from Mar to Nov, as they only have wall-mounted heat and a/c units. From Apr to Nov small bungalows also are available. Unlike the other cabins, they do not have fireplaces but do have built in double bunks and small screened-in porches.

The Country Inn at Berkeley Springs, 110 S. Washington St., Berkeley Springs, WV 25411; (304) 258-2210; http://thecountryinn atberkeleysprings.com. The Country Inn sits adjacent to the town's famous spring and serves its water and uses it at its Five Senses Spa. The rooms and common areas have a sweet, hometown feel and guests celebrating special occasions or looking for something a bit more private can rent the Inn's Treehouse guesthouse. There are four different dining options on site and the Inn puts guests within walking distance to the downtown eateries and galleries.

Gobblers Knob Guest House, 2442 Creek Rd., Berkeley Springs, WV 25411; (304) 258-3605; http://virtualcities.com/vacation/ wv/p/wvpa8v1.htm. If you want to try something different, consider bedding down in Berkeley Springs in an 1820s log cabin. The 2-story cabin is nestled atop a mountain at the northern end of the Shenendoah Valley and sleeps up to six people. Although the cabins have current-day amenities like a modern kitchen and whirlpool tub for two, its look and charm are authentically 1800s. A large woodburning stone fireplace serves as the centerpiece of the living room and many of the furnishings are antiques from the 20-year period between 1820 and 1840. Activities here include napping in the hammock, picnicking among the pine trees, star-gazing, and watching the deer, turkeys, foxes, rabbits, and other critters make regular appearances.

Highlawn Inn, 171 Market St., Berkeley Springs, WV 25411; (304) 258-5700; www.highlawninn.com. Perched on a hilltop overlooking the town's famed springs, the Highlawn Inn offers a quintessential B&B experience down to the floral bedspreads, wraparound veranda and home-cooked breakfast. Highlawn Inn is housed in a quiet and homey old Victorian and a good spot to get away from it all. Sandra Kauffman could not be a more warm or more attentive host and her breakfast dishes will keep you smiling long after the clock strikes noon.

The Manor Inn Bed and Breakfast, 234 Fairfax St., Berkeley Springs, WV 25411; www.bathmanorinn.com. The last remaining example of a Second Empire Victorian mansard-roof home in Berkeley Springs, the Manor Inn is listed on the National Register of Historic Places. Each of the four cozy rooms has 10-foot ceilings and is individually decorated with items like a vintage marble-top sink and an antique wardrobe. Both smoking and drinking alcohol are not allowed in the inn.

Seaside Capital: Annapolis, Maryland

The sailboat-dotted waters, carefully preserved historic homes, and easy pace make historic downtown Annapolis seem like it's a million miles away from downtown Washington, D.C., instead of the 45-minute drive east it takes to get to here. Founded in 1649, the state capital is home to the United States Naval Academy, Maryland's State House, and a charming brick-paved Main Street, as well as the requisite homemade ice cream and fudge shops.

Two separate circles serve as Annapolis's centerpiece—Church Circle and State Circle—a symbolic design gesture not lost on the early Americans who settled here. The lawn of the State House is a good place to start exploring the city, which sits where the Chesapeake Bay meets the Severn River. From this spot you can shape the rest of your visit, which you can happily fill with museum hopping, eating, shopping, sailing, kayaking, or strolling. Taking it all in at one of the nearby watering holes with a plate of the local catch of the day works well, too. Whatever you choose, you are almost always guaranteed a healthy dose of charm and history when you spend the day in Annapolis.

Getting There

Annapolis is an easy drive from Washington. The two cites are about 35 miles apart and the drive takes approximately 45 minutes. Leave the city via New York Avenue NW, and take US-50E for the majority of the trip. Weekday rush hour traffic can slow you down on either end so your best bet is to leave before or after rush hour. You can also boat over to Annapolis and dock at one of the city's many marinas. Contact the Harbormaster's office at (410) 263-7973 or (410) 263-7974 for details.

Places to Eat

Annapolis Ice Cream Company, 196 Main St., Annapolis, MD 21401; (443) 482-3895; www.annapolisicecream.com. The ice cream here is made on site and very well might ruin you for the supermarket stuff forever. Flavors are displayed on flat-screen monitors and will let you know if the seasonal choices like Cherry Pie or Gingerbread Cookie are available. You can even indulge your creative side while you indulge your sweet tooth by decorating a plastic spoon with the Sharpies kept on the counter. The store has 10,000 and counting art spoons from customers, a display as fun as the cold, creamy stuff that brought you here in the first place.

Aqua Terra, 64 Main St., Annapolis, MD 21401; (410) 263-1985; www.aquaterraofannapolis.com; Seafood; $$. This restaurant serves sushi, steaks, small plates, and seafood and uses local ingredients and flavors in its kitchen. Menus change seasonally to reflect what is in season and fresh.

Boatyard Bar & Grill, Severn Avenue and 4th Street, Eastport, Annapolis, MD 21403; (410) 216-6206; www.boatyardbarandgrill.com; Seafood; $$. The Eastport eatery ranks a favorite with sailors, fisherman, and locals, not to mention anyone looking for a great weekend brunch. The crab cakes and raw bar here turn visitors into repeat customers and are often ordered with a cold pint. *Sail* magazine named the spot "one of the world's top sailing bars." Boatyard Bar & Brill is surprisingly child friendly.

Chick & Ruth's Delly, 165 Main St., Annapolis, MD 21401; (410) 269-6737; www.chickandruths.com; Diner; $. An old-school deli with a personality as big as its multipaged menu. Breakfast is served all day and features the house home fries. The family-run Annapolis institution claims "the largest shakes and sandwiches anywhere," and indeed they are big. Maryland memorabilia and photos of local personalities, politicians, and sports figures cover almost every inch of wall space, and each morning at 8:30 a.m. (9:30 on the weekends) everyone stops, faces the flag over the counter, and recites the Pledge of Allegiance.

Luna Blu, 35 West St., Annapolis, MD 21401; (410) 267-9959; www.lunabluofannapolis.com; Italian; $$. A charming and reasonable little Italian restaurant serving classic Italian flavors. Fresh sauces are made daily and desserts are also made in house. A varied wine and martini list and a nice selection of anti-pasti, including creations like a mozzarella and eggplant napoleon, round off the entree selection.

Mike's Crab House, 3030 Riva Rd, Riva, MD 21140; (410) 956-2784; www.mikescrabhouse.com; Seafood; $$$. Sure, Mike's makes things other than Maryland blue crabs, but many of the diners here simply aren't interested in anything else. Crab cakes, steamed crabs, crab soup, and crab quesadillas are some of the ways Mike's serves up the local delicacy. The large outdoor deck overlooking the South River can't be beat. The restaurant also has a tiki bar and karaoke nights.

Sofi's Crepes, 1 Craig St., Annapolis, MD 21401; (410) 990-0929; www.sofiscrepes.com; Creperie; $. Yummy sweet and savory crepes are made to order at this little eatery across from the Harbormaster and outside the pedestrian entrance to the Naval Academy.

Places to Go

Annapolis City Dock, Bottom of Main Street. Watch the boats come and go and eyeball the ones already docked. Lots of good people- and boat- (and sometimes duck-) watching here at the place locals sometimes refer to as "ego alley." The city dock gets very crowded during the summer. Public restrooms are nearby.

Annapolis Maritime Museum, 723 Second St., Annapolis, MD 21403; (410) 295-0104; www.amaritime.org. The Annapolis Maritime Museum in Eastport recently reopened in the old McNasby Oyster Co. The site, the last remaining oyster-packing plant in the area, suffered severe damage from Hurricane Isabel in 2003. The museum celebrates the city's proud maritime heritage and the museum is starting to use its dock space to sponsor public concerts and events. Boat trips to the Eastern Shore's fabled 19th-century Thomas Point Shoal Lighthouse now run from the museum, require reservations, and cost about $70 a person.

Annapolis Powerboat School and the Annapolis Sailing School, 7001 Bembe Beach Rd., Annapolis, MD 21403; (800) 638-9192; www.annapolispowerboat.com or www.annapolissailing.com. Learn how to take a boat out on the open seas. One of the more popular offerings is "Become a Sailor in One Weekend." Call for prices and course offerings.

The Banneker-Douglass Museum, 84 Franklin St., Annapolis, MD 21401; (410) 216-6180; www.bdmuseum.com. Housed in the former Mount Moriah AME Church, this museum helps tell the story of Maryland's black community from 1633 up until the present. Among the artifacts housed in the museum is the advertisement announcing the slave auction where Kunta Kinte, the hero in the epic book *Roots,* was sold against his will.

Four Centuries Walking Tour, (410) 268-7600; www.watermark journey.com. Tour guides clad in colonial-era garb walk you through the historic highlights of Annapolis. The company also offers a ghost tour, an African-American history tour, and a slew of narrated boat cruises. It's best to call or log on to the website for times, dates, starting locations, and prices before you hit town.

Hammond-Harwood House, 19 Maryland Ave., Annapolis, MD 21401; (410) 263-4683; www.hammondharwoodhouse.org. This beautifully preserved colonial home houses an extensive collection of decorative objects and art from the late 18th and early 19th centuries. The landmark touts itself as having the "most beautiful doorway in America." Hours change during high and low season so your best bet is to call ahead before you show up. Fee for house admission but the boxwood garden and exhibit gallery are free.

The Kunta Kinte–Alex Haley Memorial, Located at the head of City Dock across from the Market House. The life-size statues of author Alex Haley reading to three children helps pay tribute to the waves of enslaved Africans who arrived at this port in shackles and chains. Haley turned one of these individuals, his ancestor Kunta Kinte, into the protagonist in his Pulitzer Prize–winning novel *Roots*. The outdoor memorial also contains a series of plaques and is always open.

Maryland State House, State Circle, Annapolis, MD 21401; (410) 974-3400; www.msa.md.gov/msa/mdstatehouse/html/home .html. Perched atop the hill in State Circle, the Maryland State House stands as the focal point of the Annapolis skyline and possesses a rich history steeped in early American politics. Completed in 1779, the State House holds the distinction of being the oldest state capitol in continuous use and the only state capitol to have served as the United States Capitol. George Washington resigned as Commander-in-Chief of the Continental Congress in the Old Senate Chamber and within these walls Congress ratified the Treaty of Paris that ended the American Revolutionary War. The impressive wooden dome contains no nails (metal was in short supply after the war) and is instead held together with wooden pegs reinforced by iron straps. Today the General Assembly meets in a newer section of the building completed in 1905. When the assembly is in session you can watch the legislative process in action from the visitor galleries. Free tours are given upon request. Stop by the Visitor's Center on the main floor for details. Photo ID is required to enter the building.

United States Naval Academy, 52 King George St., Annapolis, MD 21402; (410) 293-TOUR; www.usna.edu/NAFPRODV/VC/. Each year the best and the brightest high school graduates come to the United States Naval Academy to begin their naval officer training. Guided walking tours of the 338-acre waterfront college campus are given regularly for a fee and begin at the Armel-Leftwich Visitor Center. Highlights include a sample midshipman dorm room, the

Main Chapel adorned by Tiffany stained glass windows and the Naval Academy Museum. If you are on campus at midday, you can watch lunchtime formation when the midshipmen line up for uniform inspection. The "Yard" conducts a special "Tour and Tea" Mon through Wed beginning at 1:30 p.m. and also runs a tour of the Commodore Uriah P. Levy Center and Jewish Chapel. Everyone over 16 must show a valid picture ID. Open daily.

William Paca House and Garden, 186 Prince George St., Annapolis, MD 21401; (410) 990-4543; www.annapolis.org. The Historic Annapolis Foundation carefully restored this lovely historic home that belonged to one of the four signers of the Declaration of Independence who called Annapolis home. The landmark house is considered a wonderful example of classic Georgian architecture and has been restored to portray colonial-era living, giving a glimpse into the lives of the family members and slaves who lived here. Tours of the property are given every hour and visitors are welcome to enjoy the 2 acres of manicured gardens when the house is open. Admission fee. Open daily from 10 a.m. to 5 p.m. and from noon to 5 p.m. on Sun.

Places to Shop

Capital Teas, 6 Cornhill St., Annapolis, MD 21401; (410) 263-8327; www.capitalteas.com. The everything teashop. More than 60 different loose-leaf teas can be found here. They also sell teapots, sandwiches, and drinks.

Casa Nova, 161 Main St., Annapolis, MD 21401; (410) 280-8840; www.casanovajewelry.com. This light, bright, modern store sells exquisite silver jewelry from a select group of cotemporary designers and artists. Also for sale here are whimsical ceramic chickens (narrow your choices down by deciding if you want a chicken with or without a hat) that are displayed beneath the glass and wood cases that line the shop's perimeter. Don't forget to check out the art gallery upstairs.

Lilac Bijoux, 145 Main St., Annapolis, MD 21401; (410) 263-3309; www.lilacbijoux.com. Fun and funky jewelry, bags, and accessories are the name of the game in this little shop. The bead expert at the jewelry bar in the back of the store will help you create your own bauble.

Re-Sails, 42 Randall St., Annapolis, MD 21401; (410) 263-4982; www.resails.com. Just about everything here is crafted from repurposed boat sails. Pick out a one-of-a-kind duffle bag, jacket, or throw pillow. The items here have a distinct nautical look and feel and are no doubt great conversation starters.

Vivo, 6 Fleet St., Annapolis, MD 21401; (410) 268-2258; www.vivo annapolis.com. Fair trade and eco-friendly items fill the shelves here. A nice mix of clothing, accessories, housewares, and spa products. Many of the items—even the sari wrap skirts—are made from repurposed materials.

Places to Stay

The Annapolis Inn, 144 Prince George St., Annapolis, MD 21401; (410) 295-5200; www.annapolisinn.com. Elegance is a permanent guest at The Annapolis Inn. The three suites in this restored 18th century Georgian-style masterpiece exude warmth and charm and are impeccably furnished. Innkeepers pride themselves on personalized service and strive to honor most requests. Lounge over breakfast beneath the Austrian crystal chandeliers in the dining room, take your tea beside the marble fireplace in the parlor, or admire the koi pond in the enclosed garden patio. You may also want to ask about the inn's fabled past. A passageway below the property once served as part of the Underground Railroad and Thomas Jefferson's doctor called 144 Prince George St. home at one time.

Royal Folly, 65 College Ave., Annapolis, MD 21401; (410) 263-3999; www.royalfolly.com. The owners have modernized this charming 19th-century home, adding a slew of upgrades including newly tiled bathrooms in its 14 guest rooms. The house boasts nine fireplaces, an outdoor Jacuzzi tub, and a deck overlooking St. John's College. Each of the royally named rooms and suites features a different decor and list of amenities. Gourmet breakfast is served every day except Sun, when a champagne brunch is the order of the day.

Schooner Woodwind, On the docks of the Annapolis Marriott Waterfront Hotel; (410) 263-7837; www.schoonerwoodwind.com. And now for something entirely different: a boat and breakfast. On Saturday nights from May to September you can spend the night aboard the schooner *Woodwind,* a 74-foot sailing yacht that docks near downtown Annapolis. Arrive around 6 p.m. for a 2-hour sunset cruise, then go get dinner in town and come back between 11 p.m. and midnight to bed down in one of the four double-occupancy rooms in the forward compartments. Rooms are spare but clean and there are two shared heads (bathrooms) for all guests. A continental breakfast is served on deck in the morning.

The State House Inn, 25 State Circle, Annapolis, MD 21401; (410) 990-0024; www.statehouseinn.com. The cheery yellow façade and porch rockers draw guests into this bed and breakfast–style property located across from the state house. Rooms are individually appointed, a few have Jacuzzi tubs, and all have wireless. A European-style continental breakfast is served daily. It's worth checking out the glass-bottom room on the main floor that gives a literal glimpse into the archaeological excavation below. Minimum stay required on some weekends and holidays.

The Westin Annapolis, 100 Westgate Circle, Annapolis, MD 21401; (410) 972-4300; www.Westin.com/Annapolis. Opened in 2009, The Westin Annapolis is one of the newest players on the Annapolis hotel scene. Done in a palette of earth tones and dark-wood accents, the property gives off a Zen vibe from the minute you step inside. The chain's Heavenly Beds, Heavenly Cribs, and Heavenly Dog Beds help keep all travelers sleeping soundly. A heated indoor pool, spa, and the upscale Azure restaurant complete the package. An hourly shuttle runs to downtown—it's otherwise a hike.

Subtly Southern: Culpeper, Virginia

Something happens when you enter Culpeper. The iced tea gets sweeter, the y'alls start flowing freer and the Blue Ridge rises up to greet you in the distance. Before long you might even get a hankerin' for fried okra or maybe even some grits. Don't worry, it's perfectly normal in these here parts. Because when you are in Culpeper, you start to feel like you're in the south.

The town has a long history that dates back to colonial times. During the American Revolution, a group of men from the region banded together to form the Culpeper Minute Men Battalion and carried a version of the now iconic pre-American flag with the motto, "Liberty or Death—Don't Tread on Me." Because of its location, Culpeper was enmeshed in the Civil War. More than a hundred battles and skirmishes took place in the town and just about every house and building was used at some point as either a makeshift hospital or to house soldiers. In the mid-20th century, the town fell into disrepair and in the 1980s a movement began to bring new life to the historic downtown. Today as you walk the charming streets of Culpeper, you can see for yourself that the movement was indeed a success.

Getting There

Culpeper is about an hour and a half from D.C., depending on traffic. Take on I-66 West to Exit 43A (Rte. 29 South toward Warrenton) and continue on Rte. 29 South for approximately 40 miles to the first Culpeper exit. Follow the signs to the historic district.

Places to Eat

Foti's, 219 E. Davis St., Culpeper, VA 22701; (540) 829-8400; www.fotisrestaurant.com; Mediterranean; $$$. Chef Foteos "Frank" Maragos perfected his culinary skills at the acclaimed Inn at Little Washington. And his wife and Foti's co-owner, Sue Maragos, cultivated her restaurant management skills at the famed inn where the two met. Many of the dishes on the menu at the well-reviewed Foti's have a Mediterranean influence. Lunch and dinner served Thurs through Sun and on Tues.

Frost Cafe, 101 E. Davis St., Culpeper, VA 22701; (540) 829-0344; Diner; $. Old-school diner complete with a long counter, red booths, and tabletop jukeboxes. In addition to the regular menu, breakfast is served all day and includes a few distinctly southern options like scrapple omelets, scrapple sandwiches, and fresh grits.

It's About Thyme and Thyme Market, 28 E. Davis St., Culpeper, VA 22701; (540) 825-1011; www.Thymeinfo.com; European; $$$. This pretty European style eatery sells salads, pizzas, and a host of dishes that start out on Thyme Market's wood-fed rotisserie. You can eat in at the restaurant, which also has a sweet little outdoor seating area next to the downtown storefront it occupies. Gourmet goodies and prepared meals can be purchased at the market.

Lucio, 702 S. Main St., Culpeper, VA 22701; (540) 829-9788; Italian; $$. Homemade pastas, antipasto, and seafood are staples at this downtown Italian restaurant.

Places to Go

Belmont Farm Distillery, 13490 Cedar Run Rd., Culpeper, VA 22701; (540) 825-3207; www.virginiamoonshine.com and www.virginiawhiskey.com. You don't need a secret password or a special knock to see how local moonshine is made. You don't even need to come under the cover of darkness. All you need to do is take a tour of the Belmont Farm distillery and see how the facility has been turning out fresh corn whiskey for generations. The moonshine is prepared in a solid copper pot still, which owners claim is the secret ingredient in their twice-distilled Virginia Lightning. Tours are given from Apr to Dec. Call ahead of time for schedules and holiday closures.

The Culpeper County Library, 271 Southgate Shopping Center, Culpeper, VA 22701; (540) 825-8691; http://tlc.library.net/culpeper. Civil War buffs might want to detour over to the Culpeper County Library, which has a large collection of Civil War books, including some rare titles. Open daily but hours vary so check the website before you go.

Culpeper County Court House, 35 W. Cameron St., Culpeper, VA 22701; (540) 727-3438. The current working courthouse is the third to stand in Culpeper (the first was built in 1749 shortly after the county was formed). On the courthouse lawn, two monuments pay tribute to local fallen soldiers—one to those who died in Vietnam and one to Culpeper's Confederate soldiers who were killed during the Civil War.

Culpeper Train Depot and the Culpeper Visitor Center, 109 Commerce St., Culpeper, VA 22701; (540) 727-0611; www .visitculpeperva.com. The Culpeper Train Depot harkens back to a time when the rail was king. In 1998 ownership of the depot was officially transferred from Norfolk Southern to the town of Culpeper and the depot began its new life as the town's visitor's center, the chamber of commerce, and the department of transportation. (It's also a functioning Amtrak station.) The walls of the visitor's center are lined with pamphlets, brochures, and maps for attractions in and around Culpeper and Virginia. In one back corner a display case houses china from the golden days of the railroad, when meals were served in formal dining cars. Outside, visitors can climb on the back of a restored old red caboose.

Museum of Culpeper History, 803 S. Main St., Culpeper, VA 22701; (540) 829-1749; www.culpepermuseum.com. Open daily. The Culpeper museum displays artifacts and items as a way of tracing the Virginia town's history from prehistoric times, with a locally excavated pair of 215-million-year-old dinosaur tracks, to up until the present time. The museum owns a large collection of maps, photos, artifacts, and items from the Civil War era. A working Native American village and a fully restored 18th-century log cabin are also on museum grounds and open to the public. Admission is $3 for adults and free for children under 18 and all Culpeper residents regardless of age.

Old House Vineyards, 18351 Corkys Ln., Culpeper, VA 22701; (540) 423-1032; www.oldhousevineyards.com. When you look at the Old House Vineyards today it's hard to imagine that what is

TOP-SECRET CINEMA

A precious film collection filled with rare treasures gets moved into a former government high-security currency warehouse once owned by the Federal Reserve Board and fortified with lead-lined shutters, walls that are a foot thick, and a steel-reinforced bunker. Sounds like the plot of an obscure old flick. It's not. But if it were ever filmed or recorded it would likely be housed at the Library of Congress Packard Campus of the National Audio-Visual Conservation Center in Culpeper.

A few years back, the audio-visual department of the Library of Congress moved its extensive film and recording collection to Culpeper to a 45-acre campus that once served as an emergency headquarters for the government. Today the building no longer houses top-secret stuff but instead protects the library's collection of more than 1.1 million film, television, and video items and about 3.5 million audio recordings. It takes more than 90 miles of shelving to store the massive collection, which includes a motion picture from the 1890s.

In 2008 the library opened a new 200-seat art deco–style movie theater that regularly holds free screenings of its extensive collection of classic films. Showings tend to be on Fri and Sat evening with a matinee on Sat afternoons. While there is no cost to see the flicks, reservations are required. You can call the reservation line at (540) 827-1079 x79994 or (202) 707-9994 up to a week before a screening to reserve a seat. The line is open Mon through Fri from 9 a.m. to 4 p.m. Mount Pony is one of a handful of theaters in this country that is capable of projecting nitrate film stock, so you never know what might be on the marquee. **Mount Pony Theater,** 19053 Mount Pony Rd., Culpeper, VA 22701; (540) 827-1079 x79994 or (202) 707-9994; www.loc.gov/avconservation/theater.

now a charming Victorian home and lush vineyards was once an abandoned old farmhouse and overgrown alfalfa fields. Regular tours are given of the wine-making process at Old House. Visitors also get to ride through the vineyards and fields, hayride-style. Tastings and tours are held daily for a fee.

Places to Shop

The Cameleer, 125 E. Davis St., Culpeper, VA 22701; (540) 825-8073; www.thecameleer.com. This large light and bright store with the great big camel in the window started out just selling aboriginal art and now sells international giftware and crafts from across the globe. The store is stocked with a nice mix of international clothing, crafts, children's items and housewares.

Clarke Hardware, 201 E. Davis St., Culpeper, VA 22701; (540) 825-9178; www.clarkehardware.com. Clarke Hardware is the anti–box store store. The family-owned old-fashioned hardware store hosts an array of goods from hammers to wooden sleds and specializes in Aladdin mantle lamps, Radio Flyer wagons, and large cast-iron cookware. They also offer professional knife and scissor sharpening.

The Culpeper Downtown Farmers Market, E. Davis Street and Commerce Street Parking Lot, Culpeper, VA 22701; (540) 825-4416; www.culpeperdowntown.com. Every Sat from May to Oct from 7:30 a.m. to 12 p.m. this otherwise unassuming parking lot gets turned

You Can Always Have Paris . . .

The Ashby Inn and Restaurant (692 Federal St., Paris, VA 20130; 540-592-3900; www.ashbyinn.com; $$). Many urban warriors make the hour-plus drive to Paris for a meal at the acclaimed Ashby Inn and Restaurant, so many that the inn is often referred to as a restaurant with rooms. And Ashby's jumbo lump crab cakes have a reputation all their own. Menus revolve around seasonal flavors and many of the herbs and summer vegetables come from the garden at Ashby. The inn dates back to the early 1800s and many of its furnishings come from that time period. Many of the guest rooms in the main house have four-poster beds and antique quilts. There are also four rooms in the schoolhouse located behind the inn.

into an outdoor market, filled with local produce, farm-fresh eggs, and home-baked goods. Local musicians play as shoppers fill their baskets.

The Frenchman's Corner Gourmet and Chocolate Shop, 141 E. Davis St., Culpeper, VA 22701; (540) 825-8025; www .frenchmancorner.com. Decadent gourmet chocolates beckon customers to try them here. The store also has a kitchen

department and sports one of the best doormat quotes a sweet shop can have: "We encourage you to leave your guilt and diet outside."

Gallery, 122 E. David St., Culpeper, VA 22701; (540) 825-0034; http://saraschneidman.com. The bright, vibrant colors of Sara Schneidman's work practically pull you off the streets and into this lovely store showcasing her pottery, paintings, and hand-knotted rugs. Work by other potters and artists also are for sale here.

Places to Stay

Cheesecake Farms Bed, Barn and Breakfast, 4085 Sumerduck Rd., Sumerduck, VA 22742; (540) 439-2188; www.CheesecakeFarms .com. If you are not ready to leave city life behind but want to spend a night or two in a cozy barn suite, this is the place for you. The suite is adjacent to an actual hayloft and has air-conditioning, a private bath, microwave, refrigerator, and a "Sleep Number" bed. You are welcome to explore the grounds and come meet some of the animals that call Cheesecake home. Breakfast is served to all guests as is a substantial afternoon snack that often includes homemade soups, chile, macaroni and cheese, and, of course, cheesecake. Whenever possible, local ingredients, many grown on the farm, are used.

Fountain Hall Bed & Breakfast, 609 S. East St., Culpeper, VA 22701; (540) 825-8300; www.fountainhall.com. This grand old colonial revival home near the historic district boasts the title of Culpeper's first B&B. Inside you will find 10-foot-high ceilings, a sweeping walnut staircase, three parlors, and six guest rooms. Each room has a private bath and air-conditioning and some have private porches and spa tubs. Breakfast is served in the morning from 7 a.m. to 10 p.m. and features fresh croissants.

The Funny Farm Inn, 2437 Funny Farm Rd., Reva, VA 22735; (540) 547-3481; www.bbonline.com/va/funnyfarm; $$. The European-style cottage on this 75-acre horse farm has two levels that can either be rented separately or together as a whole. Each level sleeps six people and comes with a kitchen stocked with dishes, flatware, glassware, and cookware, along with pantry and refrigerator staples. Pets and children are welcome, as are horses that can bunk in the deluxe barn on the farm. And just think of the fun you can have telling your friends the name of where you are going. The Funny Farm Inn is only 10 crazy miles south of Culpeper.

The Hazel River Inn Bed and Breakfast, 11227 Eggbornsville Rd., Culpeper, VA 22701; (540) 937-5854; www.hazelriverinn.com. The Hazel River Inn Bed and Breakfast sits on 5 acres of land on the morning side of the Blue Ridge Mountains. The innkeeper also wears a horticulturalist hat and her gardens also share the property. Guests staying in any of the three rooms at the 19th-century inn can enjoy the heated swimming pool behind the house. The owners also run the Hazel River Inn Restaurant (195 East Davis St.,

Culpeper, VA 22701; 540-825-7148) in downtown Culpeper in a historic corner building thought to be the oldest standing commercial structure in town.

Suites at 249, 249 E. Davis St., Culpeper, VA 22701; (540) 827-1100; www.suitesat249.com; $$. The Suites at 249 combines an urban vibe with small-town charm. Each of the six suites here is individually decorated and the decor incorporates the restored red brick building's lines and angles. Private balconies, gas fireplaces, flat-screen TVs, and king-size feather beds with down comforters and Italian linens are among the many amenities found in every room. The boutique hotel stands near the base of the main street in Culpeper's historic district, putting it steps away from restaurants and shops. Suite 249 does not allow pets, smoking, or children.

Thyme Inn, 128 E. Davis St., Culpeper, VA 22701; (540) 825-4264; www.Thymeinfo.com; $. Three pretty rooms above the downtown Thyme Market can be yours for the night or more. The three rooms—named (what else?) Rosemary, Sage, and Thyme—have fireplaces, balconies, and private baths. A nice, quiet place to spend an evening or to set up a home base while you explore the area.

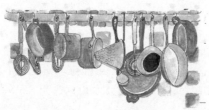

Horse & Hunt Country: *Middleburg, Virginia*

Nestled in the heart of Virginia's horse and hunt country stands the charming town of Middleburg. The affluent colonial town is home to about 600 residents, but since the early 1900s has been welcoming large crowds during fox hunting and steeplechase season. Middleburg counts one street as its downtown and it's perfectly acceptable to trot down the street on horseback.

Getting There

Middleburg is about an hour from Washington and is a pretty easy drive. Take I-495 to 66 West and exit at Route 50 West. Continue about 25 miles west to Middleburg.

Places to Eat

Cuppa Giddy Up, 8 E. Washington St., Middleburg, VA 20117; (540) 687-8122; Cafe; $. Pop into the tiny Cuppa Giddy Up coffee shop for a caffeine fix before the hunt. And, really, what's a latte without one of those delicious-looking pastries?

The French Hound, 101 Madison St., Middleburg, VA 20117; (540) 687-3018; www.thefrenchhound.com; French; $$$. Relaxed French-style bistro with outdoor patio seating. Many of the selections from the restaurant's extensive wine list are sold at The Wine Cellar, the eatery's nearby sister store at 15 S. Madison St.

Hilltoppers at the Goodstone Inn, 36205 Snake Hill Rd., Middleburg, VA 20117; (540) 687-4645; www .goodstone.com; French; $$$$. Hilltoppers is considered one of the best restaurants in the area, so if you plan on dining here, reserve a table at the intimate French restaurant in advance. Hilltoppers serves dinners five nights a week from Thursday through Monday, as well as a Sunday brunch. The estate's own organic herb and vegetable gardens provide many of the ingredients used in the kitchen. No jeans or sneakers.

Mello Out, 2 E. Federal St., Middleburg, VA 20117; (540) 687-8635; www.marshmellos.com; Sandwiches; $$. Mello Out has found a way to make brioche even more indulgent by crafting some fabulous brioche sandwich combinations like apple, peanut butter, bacon, and honey on brioche and peanut butter and marshmallow on brioche. The shop also sells salads, bagels, and cupcakes and has outdoor seating.

Places to Stay

Briar Patch Bed and Breakfast, 23130 Briar Patch Ln., Middleburg, VA 20117; (703) 327-5911; www.briarpatchbandb.com; $$. Guests can choose from eight light-filled guest rooms (some with private baths and some with shared ones) at the Briar Patch B&B. A 1-bedroom cottage with its own kitchen offers even more privacy. Children and pets are welcome and monthly cooking classes are held in their low season from November or December through March or April.

Goodstone Inn and Estate, 36205 Snake Hill Rd., Middleburg, VA 20117; (540) 687-4645; www.goodstone.com. The Goodstone is the closest many of us will get to having a fabulously wealthy uncle with a country estate. Five elegant guesthouses sit on the more than 200 acres of rolling hills, romantic pathways, and babbling brooks. Each building has its own personality, with all the rooms sharing the overall theme of sophistication. In the Manor House, guests will find the inn's formal dining room and a 19th-century mural while the French Farm House boasts two log-burning floor-to-ceiling fireplaces and stone patios. Every afternoon an elegant tea is served at the Carriage House, which once upon a time housed 14 horse stables. A beautiful outdoor pool sits on the property and the inn's world-class restaurant serves dinner in an intimate and romantic setting.

Middleburg Country Inn, 209 E. Washington St., Middleburg, VA 20117; (540) 687-6082; www.middleburgcountryinn.com. From the fireplace in the sitting parlor to the four-poster beds to the complimentary ice cream out back, everything at the Middleburg Country Inn makes guests feel at home. The charming downtown inn has seven antique-filled guest rooms, including at least one suite that can accommodate a family. Apple-spice waffles, eggs

Benedict, and grits are among the inn's breakfast choices. In good weather the pergola in the back makes for a pretty spot to eat breakfast or enjoy a glass of wine.

The Red Fox Inn, 2 E. Washington St., Middleburg, VA 20117; (540) 687-6301; www.redfox.com. The Red Fox Inn and Tavern has been part of the hunt-country landscape since Middleburg's beginning. The original fieldstone section of the inn dates back to 1728 and is listed on the National Register of Historic Places. Inside, the inviting guest rooms reflect the inn's prestigious pedigree with carefully chosen 18th century–style furnishings and art.

Where to Go

Great Meadow, 5089 Old Tavern Rd., The Plains, VA 20198; (540) 253-5000; www.greatmeadow.org. Two-hundred-and-fifty picture-perfect acres make up the field and steeplechase that is Great Meadow. A nonprofit organization owns and maintains the property, which hosts races and events like its annual Fourth of July celebration and the Virginia Scottish Games and Festival. Great Meadow also serves as the permanent home of the Virginia International Cup and the Virginia Gold Cup, the country's oldest steeplechase races.

The National Sporting Library, 102 The Plains Rd., Middleburg, VA 20117; (540) 687-6542; www.nsl.org. Riding devotees come to

Off to the Races

Every year Middleburg hosts two annual steeplechase races. Held the third weekend in April, the **Middleburg Spring Races** started in 1911 and have attracted such dignitaries as President John F. Kennedy. Spectators come with picnic baskets and binoculars to watch the horses and help raise money for the local hospital. The **Virginia Fall Races** also have a long and distinguished past. President Dwight D. Eisenhower watched the first running of the annual races in 1955. Both races require tickets and are held at Glenwood Park, 36800 Glenwood Park Ln., Middleburg, VA 20117. Online you can find more information at www.middleburgspringraces.com for the spring races and www.vafallraces.com for the fall races.

the National Sporting Library to get lost in its extensive collections, which deal with everything from fox-hunting to polo to thoroughbred racing to dressage. Books about fishing and shooting are also catalogued at the research library. A rare-book room includes thousands of old and unusual works, some from as far back as the 16th century. The non-lending library is free and open to the public. The National Sporting Library also sponsors exhibits and readings.

Serene Acres, 19312 Walsh Farm Ln., Bluemont, VA 20135; (540) 554-8618; www.SereneAcres.com. Touring the horse country does not need to be a spectator sport. Hour-long trail rides are offered at

Serene Acres. The farm also gives pony rides and horse boarding and training services. You can even buy the pony your parents would never get you when you were a kid—the farm generally has several for sale. Rides must be reserved in advance and start at around $65.

Where to Shop

Clothes Minded, 8 E. Washington St., Middleburg, VA 20117; (540) 687-4774. Trendy, hip fashions and accessories fill this cute downtown boutique.

Duchessa, 100 E. Washington St., Middleburg, VA 20117; (540) 687-8898; www.middleburgonline.com/duchessa/duchessa.html. Look your finest at the races with an outfit from this downtown women's clothing boutique.

The Fun Shop, 117 W. Washington St., Middleburg, VA 20117; (540) 687-3861; www.thefunshop.com. With its rocking horse sign outside greeting shoppers, The Fun Shop is a lovely little department store with home goods and items to fill the elegant homes found in horse and  hunt country. A family owned business since 1956, this store sells everything from copper kettles to Egyptian cotton towels and was a favorite of First Lady Jackie O.

Hastening Antiques, 7 E. Washington St., Middleburg, VA 20117; (540) 687-5664; www.hasteningantiques.com. Exquisite 18th- and 19th-century Italian, French, and English furniture and accessories fill the Hastening's showroom. The owner began Hastening in the Cotswolds and moved it to Virginia about 10 years ago. Delicate antique restoration work is also performed here.

Middleburg Tack Exchange, 103 W. Federal St., Middleburg, VA 20117; (540) 687-6608; www.middleburgtack.com. This is a consignment store like no other. Middleburg Tack Exchange sells previously owned English hunting tack apparel. The large store has an entire floor dedicated to used saddles, boots, and blankets and it's not uncommon to find items like glass hunting flasks, handmade leather sandwich boxes, and frock coats in the rest of the ever-changing inventory. Closed Sun.

WhiteBench, 100 E. Washington St., Middleburg, VA 20117; (540) 687-8555; www.whitebench.com. The slipcovered furniture and country-chic, repurposed wood accent pieces sold here create inviting, calming interiors and that reflect Middleburg's quaint charm.

Recipes

The recipes in this chapter represent a cross-section of the food scene here in D.C. Each one gives detailed instructions on how to create a dish important to the chef that authored it. Although each recipe stands strong on its own, taken together they speak to the diversely delicious flavors found in the kitchens around town. I hope the next time you feel the need to whisk, braise, or sauté you will consider trying your hand at one of these dishes.

Grassroots Gourmet's
Peanut Butter Buttercream

The activists-turned-bakers at Grassroots Gourmet can organize a get out the vote drive almost as fast as they can frost a counter full of cupcakes. Luckily for my sweet tooth, the pair now spend their professional time on the latter. And the many times that they do ice baked goods it's often with this yummy peanut butter buttercream. Use this delicious buttercream with a rich chocolate cake to achieve the perfect combination of flavors.

"It's light and fluffy, smooth and creamy and rich with delicious peanut butter," tells Grassroots Gourmet Co-Owner Sara Fatell, who suggests using the sweet stuff atop cakes and cupcakes.

Yield: About 4 cups, or enough to frost a 6-layer cake or 4 dozen cupcakes. Recipe can be halved.

1½ pounds of unsalted butter, room temperature	**2 teaspoons vanilla extract**
1 pound confectioners' sugar (1 box)	**3 tablespoons heavy cream**
	1 cup smooth peanut butter

In the bowl of an electric mixer with a paddle attachment beat the butter on a medium speed until smooth and creamy, about a minute.

Reduce mixer speed to low, add the confectioners' sugar, and beat for another minute or so.

Scrape down the sides of the bowl. Then add the vanilla and cream. Beat on medium until light and fluffy, about 2 to 3 minutes.

Add the peanut butter and mix until combined.

Use the frosting immediately. Any leftovers can be stored in an airtight container in the refrigerator for a few days. When ready to reuse, let the frosting come to room temperature and beat again in the mixer to make it fluffy. Additional heavy cream may be added if needed to loosen it up.

Courtesy of Sara Fatell and Jamilyah Smith-Kanze of Grassroots Gourmet (p. 44).

Empanada de Pollos Ensapados (Chicken Empanada with Bacon, Caramelized Onion, Raisins & Lemon)

Chef José Andrés crafted this recipe as part of a menu he created for the National Gallery of Art 2009 special exhibit The Art of Power: Royal Armor and Portraits from Imperial Spain. *Andrés used the museum images and his collection of antique cookbooks as inspiration, and it comes through in each morsel of this artful dish. He adapted several recipes from* Arte de Cocina *by Francisco Martínez Montiño, Chef of Philip II, first published in 1611, which was perfect since Phillip II was featured with both portraits and armor in the exhibition.*

Yields 6 servings.

- **3 chicken legs (thighs and drumsticks), about 2 pounds**
- **⅓ cup (5 tablespoons) extra virgin olive oil**
- **Salt to taste**
- **Freshly ground black pepper to taste**
- **12 slices bacon**
- **½ cup raisins**

- **2 lemons**
- **2 large onions, peeled and thinly sliced**
- **1 bay leaf**
- **1 sprig fresh thyme**
- **1 sprig fresh rosemary**
- **1 package frozen puff pastry (2 sheets), thawed**
- **1 large egg**
- **3 tablespoons sugar**

Preheat oven to 375 degrees.

Put chicken pieces in a roasting pan. Drizzle with 1 tablespoon of the olive oil and season to taste with salt and pepper. Lay half a slice of bacon on top of each chicken thigh. Roast chicken in the oven until golden brown and meat reaches 165 degrees on a meat thermometer, about 40 minutes. Remove from oven and set aside to cool. Once the chicken thighs are cool enough to handle, peel off skin with bacon and finely chop. Remove the meat from the bones and shred with your fingers. Set meat and skin aside and discard remaining solids.

Bring a small pot of water to a boil. Put the raisins in a small bowl and pour in just enough hot water to cover the raisins. Set aside to allow the raisins to plump. Meanwhile, remove the zest from the lemons and finely chop. Juice the lemons into a small bowl and discard the remaining fruit.

Heat 3 tablespoons of olive oil in a 12-inch sauté pan over medium-low heat. Add the onions, bay leaf, thyme, and rosemary and season with salt. Sauté the onions until golden brown, about 20 minutes. (Note: if the onions begin to brown too much, stir in a few tablespoons of water.) Continue to cook the onions slowly until they reach a deep brown color, about 20 minutes more. Add the raisins and continue to cook until any water has evaporated. Add the lemon juice and cook until the liquid evaporates. Transfer the onion mixture to a large bowl and set aside.

Add the reserved chopped chicken to the onions. Stir in the lemon zest until well combined. Season to taste with salt and pepper, and refrigerate until the mixture is cool.

To make the empanada: Preheat the oven to 350 degrees. On a lightly floured work surface, roll each sheet of puff pastry into an 11 x 9-inch rectangle. Lightly brush a baking sheet with 1 tablespoon of the olive oil and carefully transfer one sheet of the puff pastry to a baking sheet. Lay 5 slices of bacon across the pastry, leaving a 1" border around the edges. Spoon the cooled chicken-onion filling across the bacon, evenly spreading out the filling. Lay the remaining 5 slices of bacon across the filling. Beat the egg in a small bowl with a little water and brush the egg wash along the edge of the dough. Carefully place the second rectangle of puff pastry on top of the filling. Fold the dough over and, using your fingers or the tines of a fork, crimp the edges of the dough to seal. Brush the top of the pastry with the remaining egg wash and prick with a fork or sharp knife to allow steam to escape. Sprinkle with sugar and bake until golden brown, about 30 minutes. Allow empanada to cool for at least 15 minutes before slicing and serving.

Adapted by Chef José Andrés for the National Gallery of Art (Garden Cafe, p. 82) from *Arte de Cocina* by Francisco Martínez Montiño, Chef of Philip II, first published in 1611.

Louisiana Crawfish Etouffée with Mahatma Rice

Acadiana Jeff Tunks evokes the spirit of his beloved New Orleans every time he seasons a dish or stirs a pot. This version of etouffée does just that and stands out as one of the restaurant's most popular offerings, both with customers and with the chef himself. Chef Tunks also proudly states it is one of the most authentic items served at Acadiana.

Yields 6 to 8 servings.

- ¼ pound butter
- 1 cup chopped yellow or Spanish onion
- ½ cup chopped celery
- ½ cup chopped green bell pepper
- ½ cup chopped red bell pepper
- ½ cup diced tomato
- 2 tablespoons diced garlic
- 2 bay leaves
- 2 pounds Louisiana crawfish tail meat
- ½ cup tomato sauce
- 1 cup flour
- 2 quarts crab or crawfish stock
- 1 ounce sherry
- 1 cup chopped green onions
- ½ cup chopped parsley
- Salt and Creole seasoning, to taste
- 2 cups steamed Louisiana Mahatma rice
- Tabasco, to taste

In a large sauce pan over medium heat, melt butter.

Add yellow onion, celery, bell peppers, tomato, garlic, and bay leaves. Sauté until vegetables are soft.

Add crawfish meat and tomato sauce and combine well. Dust with flour and whisk to form a roux.

Add stock and cook until mixture achieves consistency of a sauce. Simmer over medium or low-medium heat. (After adding the stock, cook about 30 to 45 minutes to achieve proper consistency and ensure flour has been combined with other flavors.)

Add sherry, green onions, parsley, and season to taste. Serve immediately over steamed rice with Tabasco on the side.

Courtesy of Acadiana Chef de Cuisine Chris Clime and Executive Chef Jeff Tunks (p. 172).

Grilled Red Wine Braised Octopus with Smoked Avocado, Roasted Olive Gremolata & Olive Aioli

When I asked Daniel Bortnick, the executive chef and general manager of Firefly, to share one of his favorite recipes he choose this tasty one. This dish pairs nicely with a Rhone red or other similar red wine.

For the Red Wine Braised Octopus

Yields 4 servings.

- **4 Spanish rock octopi, rinsed**
- **2 cups red wine**
- **1 cup clam juice**
- **¼ cup celery, chopped**
- **¼ cup carrot, chopped**
- **¼ cup onion, chopped**
- **2 garlic cloves**
- **1 bay leaf**
- **3 sprigs thyme**
- **3 sprigs parsley**

Place all ingredients in a pot and add enough water to cover octopi. Place a plate on top of the octopi to keep them under the liquid. Bring to a boil and immediately reduce to a simmer. Cook until tender, approximately 45 minutes. Allow octopi to rest in their own liquid.

For the Smoked Avocado

Yields 2 servings.

- **2 avocados, firm but ripe**
- **1 tablespoon cherrywood chips**

- **1 smoking gun (available from JB Prince, www.jbprince .com)**

Cut avocados in half and place in a closed container. Fill the smoking gun with the wood chips and feed the tube into the container. Smoke for 20 minutes.

(Alternatively, sliced raw avocado may be used.)

For the Olive Gremolata

Yields 1 cup.

- **1½ cups mixed pitted olives**
- **1 tablespoon parsley, chopped fine**

- **1 tablespoon lemon zest**

Rinse olives and place on a baking sheet. Roast at 350 degrees for 10 minutes. Reduce temperature to 200 degrees and continue to cook for an hour. Chop olives and mix with parsley and lemon zest.

For the Olive Aioli

Yields 1 cup.

- **½ cup Niçoise olives, pitted and rinsed**
- **1 garlic clove**
- **1 egg yolk**

- **1 teaspoon lemon juice**
- **½ cup virgin olive oil**
- **Salt and pepper to taste**

Puree olives and garlic in food processor. Add the egg yolk and lemon juice. Puree well. While processor is running, slowly drizzle in the oil to emulsify. Season to taste and pass through a chinois.

Grilling and Assembly

Braised octopi (see recipe above)
Salt and pepper to taste
Olive oil

Remove head and beak from octopi. Season with salt, pepper, and olive oil. Place on very hot grill until hot and slightly charred. Meanwhile, cut avocado into quarters. Slice quarters into thin slices and fan across plate. Using squeeze bottle, place aioli on plate in a zig-zag pattern. Remove octopi from grill and place atop aioli. Finish with a sprinkling of the gremolata.

Courtesy of Daniel Bortnick, Executive Chef and General Manager of Firefly (p. 167).

Roasted Beet Salad

The roasted beets, toasted pumpkin seeds, and red onion work together to create the perfect first course (often ordered at the Blue Duck Tavern).

Yields 4 servings.

20 baby beets (mixed colors)
1 cup California olive oil
Salt and pepper to taste
1 red onion
½ cup balsamic vinegar
2 shallots

¼ cup red wine vinegar
4 tablespoons toasted pumpkin seeds
2 heads Belgian endive
8-ounce piece of goat cheese roulade

Preheat oven to 350 degrees. Toss beets with 2 tablespoons olive oil, salt, and pepper, place in roasting pan and place in the oven until fork tender (approximately 45 minutes to an hour). Remove from the oven and allow to cool at room temperature. Peel red onion and slice into ½-inch rings, place the onion rings in a sauté pan with the balsamic vinegar and cook over medium heat, occasionally stirring until the liquid is reduced to 2 tablespoons and the onions are well cooked. Remove from the pan and allow to cool. Remove the skin from the beets, discard skins and cut the beets in half. Peel and finely dice the shallots, place in a stainless steel or glass bowl with red wine vinegar, olive oil, and season with salt and pepper. Toss the beets, red onion, and pumpkin seeds with some of the vinaigrette, season with salt and pepper, and divide among 4 salad bowls. Dress the endive leaves with vinaigrette and arrange over the beets, cut the goat cheese roulade into eight 1-ounce pieces and place on the salads. Serve.

Courtesy of Blue Duck Tavern Executive Chef Brian McBride
and Chef de Cuisine Eric Fleischer (p. 166).

Geeta's Chai

Geeta of Hush explains that most families she knew growing up in India had their own chai recipe. Each family's recipe is a bit different from the next. This chai recipe is the one she grew up with in Gujarat. Geeta is quick to say that her mother's chai is much better than her own (and with a laugh adds that her mother is quick to mention that, too) but that doesn't stop many a Hush Supper Club member from raving about it.

Yields 2 servings.

- 2 cups water
- ¼ teaspoon freshly grated ginger root
- ½ teaspoon tea masala (spice blend)
- 1 tablespoon loose Assam tea
- 6 to 8 fresh mint leaves
- 1½ cups whole or low-fat milk (do not use nonfat, as it will scald)
- 1 tablespoon sugar (or to taste)

Combine the water, ginger, tea masala, loose tea, and mint leaves in a medium saucepan over high heat. Bring to a rolling boil, then add the milk. Let the mixture return to a boil and almost boil over without stirring. Stir after first boil with milk, then reduce the heat to medium-low and cook for 30 seconds, undisturbed, then increase the heat to high and let it come to a full boil again, being careful not to let the mixture boil over.

Reduce the heat to low; cook, covered, for 2 minutes, then uncover and stir in the sugar to taste.

Pour through a fine-mesh strainer into a large mug. Serve piping hot.

Make sure you use at least a medium-size saucepan with high walls to avoid a stovetop mess. The chai needs to boil up twice.

Courtesy of Chef Geeta of the Hush Supper Club (p. 107).

Shellfish Stew with Coconut & Lime

Sustainable seafood stands as one of the cornerstones of Chef John Critchley's cooking philosophy and one he brought to Urbana when he took over the kitchen there. His shellfish stew is one of his dishes that showcases his passion for these kind of ingredients as well as his talent for working with them.

Yields 4 servings.

For the sauce

1 cup dry white wine
2 shallots, peeled and chopped
1 garlic clove, peeled and
    chopped

1 tablespoon kosher salt
4 limes, juiced
1 12-ounce can coconut milk
½ cup heavy cream

In a small saucepan over medium high heat add white wine, shallots, garlic, and salt and reduce.

When almost dry, add the lime juice and reduce by half.

Add the coconut milk and heavy cream and simmer over medium heat until reduced by half.

Adjust seasoning with salt and reserve for the shellfish.

For the stew

8 littleneck clams, scrubbed
    and free of sand
Water, as needed
2 tablespoons butter, unsalted,
    room temperature

16 mussels, cleaned
½ pound calamari tubes and
    tentacles (cut tubes in half-
    inch rings)

8 jumbo fresh shrimp, peeled and deveined, tail off if you prefer

½ cup scallions, sliced (or spring onion, garlic, ramps, etc.)

Pinch chile threads (found in most Asian markets)

In a clean saucepot with a lid, place the clams with 3 tablespoons of water and 1 tablespoon butter over medium heat. Simmer covered until clams just open (about 3 to 5 minutes). Add mussels and simmer another 2 minutes until opened.

Remove shellfish from pan and add the sauce from recipe above and bring to just barely a simmer. Add calamari and shrimp and cook slowly for 4 minutes (cooking the shrimp for 2 minutes on each side). Add the shellfish back to the pan with the last tablespoon of butter.

Warm thoroughly without boiling (boiling will make your calamari as tender as a rubber band).

Arrange in a large bowl and garnish with the scallions and chile threads.

Courtesy of John Critchley, Executive Chef at Urbana Restaurant and Wine Bar (p. 171).

Wild Rice Salad from the National Museum of the American Indian's Mitsitam Cafe

The Ojibwe people traditionally harvested wild rice, like the kind called for in this recipe, by canoeing through rice fields and gently knocking the kernels off the tops of plants. The kernels would then fall and collect on the bottom of the boat. Ojibwe families on the White Earth Reservation in Minnesota still harvest wild rice this way.

Yields 4 to 6 servings.

- ½ cup pine nuts
- ¼ cup pumpkin seeds
- 6 cups low-sodium chicken broth or vegetable stock
- 1½ cups wild rice

- 1 carrot, cut into 2-inch-long matchsticks
- 3 tablespoons dried cranberries
- 1 Roma tomato, finely diced
- 4 to 5 scallions, finely chopped
- 3 bunches watercress

Preheat the oven to 350 degrees. Spread the pine nuts and pumpkin seeds in a small baking pan, and toast them in the oven for about 10 minutes, until they are golden brown. Let cool.

Combine the chicken stock and wild rice in a stockpot. Bring to a boil, reduce heat to low, and simmer, covered, for about 45 to 55 minutes, until the grains are just opened up and tender. Spread the hot rice on a baking sheet and let cool.

When rice is cool, scrape it into a large bowl and add carrots, dried cranberries, diced tomato, toasted pine nut/pumpkin seed mixture, and scallions.

Toss all ingredients together with the vinaigrette (below), refrigerate for at least 1 hour, and serve over watercress.

For the Vinaigrette

3 tablespoons apple cider vinegar

¼ cup plus 2 tablespoons canola oil

2 tablespoons honey

In a small bowl, combine all the ingredients and whisk to blend. Cover and refrigerate for at least one hour or up to 10 days.

Courtesy of Smithsonian's National Museum of the American Indian, Restaurant Associates, and Fulcrum Books (see Mitsitam Cafe, p. 87)

Miriam's Kitchen Venison Pot Pie

Each year Miriam's Kitchen serves thousands of healthy, made-from scratch meals to people who would otherwise not be able to find a warm, nutritious food in the city. Most of the ingredients used in the kitchen are donated from a variety of sources including individuals who hunt, farm, and fish. The volunteers, along with the staff, create recipes like this one, around the donated meat, fish, vegetables, and other foods, creating filling, tasty, and healthy meals that cost only a dollar for the organization and are free to the recipients.

For the crust

1¼ cups all-purpose flour

½ teaspoon salt

½ teaspoon sugar

¼ pound cold unsalted butter cut into ½ inch cubes

1 tablespoon chopped rosemary

2 to 4 tablespoons cold water

1 egg

Vegetable oil

Place the flour, salt, sugar, butter, and rosemary in a medium bowl and whisk to combine them. Rub the mixture between your fingers to blend the cubes of butter into the flour until it resembles coarse meal.

Sprinkle the ice water onto the mixture, tossing it lightly with a rubber spatula.

Knead the dough with the heels of your hands until the mixture holds together in one piece and feels slightly stretchy when pulled. Be careful not to over-knead it.

Wrap the dough with plastic wrap, flatten it into a disk, and refrigerate for at least 45 minutes, preferably overnight, before you start to roll it out with a rolling pin.

For the filling

1 pound of ground venison

1 pound of ground beef

2 large carrots, cut into medium dice

2 medium white potatoes, cut into medium dice

2 large onions, cut into medium dice

1 cup of chopped fresh herbs such as parsley or chives

2 tablespoons chopped garlic

2 cups chicken stock

2 tablespoons butter (for roux)

1 tablespoon flour (for roux)

Salt and pepper to taste

Cook the meats in a cast-iron pan or sauté pan with salt. Remove the meat from the pan and set aside.

In the same pan as the meat was cooked, sauté the vegetables with the salt, pepper, and garlic. Be careful not to overcook or burn the vegetables—leave some nice texture.

After the vegetables have been allowed to cook sufficiently, add the meat and the herbs back to the pan and deglaze with the stock.

To make your roux, melt butter in a saucepan and allow to brown slightly (it should smell nutty). Whisk in flour and cook for about 1 minute to allow the flour and butter to come together.

Cook the meat and vegetables until the meat is tender and half the stock has cooked off. Add the roux and stir and simmer for 5 minutes until thickened.

Preheat oven to 375 degrees. Transfer the mixture to a baking pan (or if using a cast-iron pan, leave it in for a nice presentation) and cover with the crust. Brush with egg wash (whipped egg with a of touch oil).

Bake for 15 to 20 minutes or until the crust is golden brown.

Courtesy of Miriam's Kitchen (p. 215).

"Cream" of Asparagus Soup

You don't have to tell Sara Polon that soup is good food. She's living proof of it. After all, she's Soupergirl. Polon's soup delivery service, and now her brick-and-mortar store in Takoma Park, D.C., provides a wide range of delicious broths, bisques, consumes, and chowders to her adoring customers. This asparagus soup is a fan favorite and, like everything she makes, is vegan.

Yields approximately 2 quarts.

- 3 tablespoons olive oil
- 1 large bunch of asparagus, ends trimmed, cut into 2-inch pieces
- 2 stalks celery, chopped
- 1 large onion, chopped
- 2 quarts stock
- 1 bay leaf
- 1 cup thick cashew cream (below)
- Sea salt and pepper to taste
- 2 cups fresh baby spinach

Heat the olive oil. Add the asparagus, celery, and onion. Cook for about 5 minutes, until the celery and onion are soft. Add the stock and bay leaf. Simmer 30 minutes. Add cashew cream and simmer for another 10 minutes. Add spinach and puree in a blender. Add salt and pepper to taste. Garnish with an extra dollop of cashew cream, if desired.

For the Cashew Cream

Soak 2 to 3 cups of raw cashews overnight in water. Puree the nuts in batches with a small amount of the soaking water until you get a nice, thick cream. Add water depending on desired consistency.

For this soup, I recommend a thicker cream (blend with only a bit of water).

Courtesy of Sara Polon of Soupergirl (p. 47).

Scallop Margarita with Tequila Ice

Chef Ris Lacoste's Scallop Margarita with Tequila Ice stands as one of her signature dishes and one of the most ordered appetizers at her restaurant. Served in a margarita glass, the layered dish combines many commonly found ingredients for the home cook while at the same time using some sophisticated techniques. The chef recommends preparing the tequila ice the day before so you have it at the ready.

This scallop seviche is very easy to make. There are only two small projects to complete the day before.

Yields 6 servings.

- 1 **cup sugar**
- 1 **cup water**
- ½ **cup freshly squeezed lime juice**
- 1 **tablespoon lime zest**
- ½ **ounce tequila**

For the Tequila Ice

Combine sugar and water in a small heavy-based saucepan. Bring to a boil. Remove from the heat and add the lime juice, zest, and tequila. Stir well and pour into a flat container large enough to create a layer of liquid about ¾-inch thick. Put into the freezer and allow at least 6 hours for it to be well iced. Pass a fork throughout the ice about every hour to loosen the mixture and help create ice flakes.

For the Marinated Orange Sections

Ancho Chile Paste

2 ancho chiles

1 cup orange juice

2 seedless oranges, sectioned

4 tablespoons olive oil

Kosher salt

Freshly ground black pepper

Remove the stem and seeds from the ancho chiles, place in a small saucepan, and cover them with orange juice. Heat gently until the chiles are soft. Set aside until cool enough to handle. Puree all in a blender and pass through a sieve. Mix the orange sections with 1 tablespoon of the ancho puree, the olive oil, salt, and pepper. Keep covered in the refrigerator. The extra ancho puree can be frozen in small packets for later use.

For the Scallops

1 pound fresh, dry scallops, cut into ½-inch chunks

1 small red onion, julienned

½ bunch cilantro, leaves picked and kept covered with a damp cloth

1 jalapeño chile, seeds removed and finely julienned

1 cup freshly squeezed lime juice

1 poblano chile, roasted, peeled, seeds removed, and julienned

2 scallions, chopped

1 avocado, cut into cubes

1 cup of the best extra virgin olive oil you have (I use Tuscan Laudemio)

1 cup sour cream

3 limes, 2 cut into 6 slit rounds, the rest for squeezing

Tortilla chips

6 martini or margarita glasses

Mise en place is the key to the rest of this quick dish. One hour before serving, mix the diced scallops, half of the red onion, a few sprigs of cilantro, and a few slivers of jalapeño together and cover with 1 cup of the lime juice. Cover and keep in the refrigerator. Toss the scallops every twenty minutes to make sure they are being evenly marinated with the lime juice.

During that hour, prepare all of your ingredients as listed above. Also, prepare your margarita glasses by rubbing the edge of each glass with lime juice and then placing each glass upside down into a plate of kosher salt.

After 45 to 60 minutes, check your scallops for doneness by tasting a piece and seeing if it is to your liking. Keep them in the lime juice longer if they are under-done or marinate them less the next time if they are overdone. When ready, drain the lime juice from the scallops and pick out the onion, cilantro, and jalapeño. Place the scallops into a large bowl and add the poblano chile, jalapeño, red onion, scallion, cilantro, avocado, salt, and pepper. Add a good drizzle of the olive oil and the juice of the remaining lime. Mix gently and taste for acid/fat balance and adjust with more oil or lime juice or salt and pepper, if necessary.

To Arrange: *Separate the scallop mixture into six even portions. Place half of each portion in the bottom of each glass, spread a tablespoonful of sour cream over the scallops, followed by some marinated orange sections and then the rest of the portion of scallops. Top with a small scoop of tequila ice and place a lime round on the edge of each glass.*

Serve with tortilla chips on the side.

DEEEEEELICIOUS.

Courtesy of Ris Lacoste of RIS (p. 175).

Zola Strawberry Basil Smash

The cooling combination of the strawberry and basil in this cocktail takes the edge off a humid Washington day—and the smash helps take the edge off a stressful one. The pretty pink-hued cocktail is perfect for parties large or small and is a fun way to end a daytrip from one of the nearby pick-your-own farms.

Yields one drink.

5 purple basil leaves
2 lime segments
¹⁄₁₀ ounce Leonardi Saba vinegar
¼ ounce Rothman & Winter
    crème de violette

1½ ounces Tito's Handmade
    Vodka
2½ ounces Strawberry Nectar
    (recipe below)
Strawberry for garnish

In a mason jar, muddle basil leaves with lime segments, Saba vinegar, and crème de violette. Add ice, Tito's vodka, and strawberry nectar. Screw the cap on and shake vigorously. Unscrew the cap add a straw and garnish with a freshly cut strawberry. Enjoy!

Strawberry Nectar

⅓ pound strawberries
10 liters distilled water

920 grams sugar in the raw
    (turbinado)
2 teaspoons citric acid

Blend whole strawberries and place in a large pot, add water, and sugar and simmer for 45 minutes. Turn off the heat and stir in the citric acid. Strain the nectar with a chinois, and place in an ice bath. When cool, place in a container, date, and refrigerate. Will last 10 days (or about 15 days if citric acid is not used).

Courtesy of Zola (p. 90).

Gluten-Free Pecan Butterscotch Cake

RIS Pastry Chef Chris Kujala works with flour all day long but the white fluffy stuff remains strictly off limits to him when it comes time to eat. Kujala has celiac disease, an autoimmune disorder that requires a strict gluten-free diet, and a fact you would never guess when you taste his amazing creations made both with and without ingredients containing gluten. And when you take a bite of his delicious Gluten-Free Pecan Butterscotch Cake he created in honor of the Phillips Collection's 90th anniversary, you will undoubtedly focus on what is in it instead of what is not.

"I developed this cake in honor of the Phillips Collection's 90th anniversary because I wanted to create something that represents one of the many 'truths' that exist in both art and food," Kujala explains. "Like many great artists, my work in the kitchen requires talent, skill, and precision . . . but we're all still a bit nutty."

Yields one 3-layer cake.

For the Cake

20 ounces toasted pecans	**12 eggs (separated)**
2 cups sugar	**½ teaspoon salt**
4 tablespoons potato flour	**¼ teaspoon cream of tartar**
2 teaspoons baking powder	**1 teaspoon vanilla extract**

Preheat oven to 350 degrees. Spray a 10-inch cake pan and line with parchment paper. Grind pecans fine with 1 cup of the sugar. Place in a large bowl and mix in the potato flour and baking powder. Whip the yolks with ½ cup of sugar to triple in volume. Fold the dry ingredients into the whipped yolks until smooth. Whip the whites with ½ cup of sugar, salt, and cream of tartar. Whip to stiff peaks (do not over whip). Fold the whites into the yolk and nut mixture. Place the batter into the prepared cake pan. Bake for about 20 minutes or until a toothpick placed in the center comes out clean. Remove from oven and let cool.

For the Butterscotch Sauce

3¾ cup dark corn syrup
¾ teaspoon salt
1½ cups + ⅓ cup sugar
1½ cups + ⅓ cup heavy cream

1½ cups + ⅓ cup light brown sugar
3¾ ounces whole butter (unsalted)
1 tablespoon vanilla extract

Combine all ingredients, except the vanilla, in a large saucepot. Place over medium heat and stir until all the ingredients have become smooth. Simmer for about 5 minutes. Strain and add the vanilla extract. Cool and reserve.

For the Butterscotch Marscapone Filling

1 pound mascarpone cheese
Heavy cream, as needed

Butterscotch sauce to taste

In a mixing bowl whip the mascarpone cheese and a little heavy cream until you have a mousse like texture with stiff peaks. Add butterscotch sauce to taste and use for filling between cake layers. To avoid a grainy texture, do not over mix. If mixture becomes too stiff, add more cream and whip to consistency.

For the Butterscotch Buttercream Icing

5 egg whites
7 ounces sugar

1 pound 4 ounces whole butter
(unsalted, room temp.)
Butterscotch sauce to taste

Take a medium saucepot and fill ⅓ full with water. Place over medium heat and bring to a boil. Place the egg whites in a medium bowl and whisk in the sugar. Place the bowl on top of the pot, turn down the heat, and continue to whisk the whites over the simmering water (the bottom of the bowl should not touch the water). Whisk until the whites are hot to the touch. Add the whites to a mixing bowl and whip until the whites are cool and tripled in volume. Slowly whip in the butter until all incorporated. Whip in the butterscotch sauce to taste being mindful not to add too much or the buttercream will be too sweet and soft.

To Assemble the Cake

Cut the cake in thirds horizontally. Fill the layers with the butterscotch mascarpone. Decorate the sides and top of the composed layer cake with the butterscotch buttercream icing. Garnish the sides of the cake with chopped pecans. Use remaining butterscotch sauce to drizzle serving plate.

Courtesy of Chris Kujala, Executive Pastry Chef at RIS (p. 175)
in honor of the 90th anniversary of the Phillips Collection.

CapMac Bolognese

I didn't think I liked macaroni and cheese or food trucks before CapMac so I was thrilled when Chef Brian Arnoff agreed to share one of his recipes for this book. His CapMac Bolognese puts a twist on classic comfort dish and can stand as a meal on its own—although you might not feel like standing on your own after you've had a few helpings.

Yield: About 1 quart

- 1 small or ½ large yellow onion, diced
- 1 carrot, peeled and diced
- 1 stalk celery, diced
- 2 tablespoons extra-virgin olive oil
- ¼ cup tomato paste
- 2 pounds ground beef (brisket is amazing for this if available, also try replacing half the beef with ground lamb)
- 5 sprigs fresh thyme
- 1 stalk fresh rosemary
- 2 sprigs fresh sage
- 2 bay leaves
- 3 cups good quality, full-bodied red wine
- 1 28-ounce can whole peeled tomatoes (the best quality you can find, makes all the difference)
- Parmesan rinds (if you have them)
- 3 ounces chicken liver, finely chopped (optional)
- ½ cup cream (optional)
- Grated Parmesan cheese to taste
- Pasta of your choice

Sauté the onion, carrot, and celery (mirepoix) in olive oil over medium heat until almost caramelized, 10 to 15 minutes. Add the tomato paste to the pan and continue cooking 5 to 7 minutes more until the tomato paste has darkened and begun to stick to the bottom of the pot.

Add the ground beef to the vegetable mixture and cook another 5 minutes, stir-ring often to prevent burning. Add all your herbs, carefully tied together with some butcher's twine for easy retrieval later.

Deglaze the pan with the red wine, scraping all the brown bits (or fonde) off the bottom and reduce over medium-high heat until the pan is nearly dry. Hand-crush your tomatoes and add to the pan. If available, add Parmesan rinds. Reduce the heat and simmer for about 45 minutes. Remove herb bunch and Parmesan rinds, discard.

If using chicken livers, chop finely until almost a paste, add to sauce and simmer for 2 to 3 minutes more. Finish the Bolognese with cream and grated Parmesan to taste and desired consistency.

Boil your pasta of choice until slightly undercooked and finish in the pan with the sauce, using the pasta cooking water to adjust the consistency of your sauce.

Courtesy of Chef Brian Arnoff of the CapMac food truck (p. 27).

Grandma Goodell's Famous Chocolate Chip Cookies (Or, The "Be Well and Happy" Cookie)

As I was writing this book my family was forced to say goodbye to Grandma Goodell, my husband's grandmother, my children's great-grandmother, and my dear friend. Roz died two months shy of her 104th birthday and was always the first to say she had a wonderful life. She volunteered regularly until her late 90s, had a great sense of humor, and smiled at everyone right up until the end. I am fairly convinced that some of her secrets to a good life are found in her cookie recipe, which is her version of a Toll House cookie with raisins. She always did every step by hand, but it also works with electric mixers—although it always tastes better when you cream the butter and sugar by hand with a wooden spoon. Grandma ended every conversation with the sign-off "be well and happy," hence the name for these cookies.

Yield: About 3 dozen.

- 2¼ cups flour
- 1 teaspoon baking soda
- 1 teaspoon salt
- 1 cup (2 sticks) butter or margarine
- ¾ cup sugar
- ¾ cup firmly packed brown sugar
- 2 eggs
- 1 teaspoon vanilla
- 1 12-ounce package chocolate chips
- 1 cup raisins (soak in water and drain well)

Preheat oven to 375 degrees.

Mix first three ingredients together in a bowl. In a separate bowl, cream butter with sugars, add eggs and vanilla, and beat well while gradually adding flour mixture. Stir in chocolate chips and raisins. Drop by teaspoons on ungreased cookie sheet. Bake for 9 to 11 minutes.

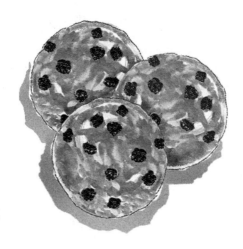

Estadio Spice-Grilled Chicken

The secret to elevating this recipe from good to great is to leave enough time for the chicken to marinate. If you give it a day to soak up the flavors you will see why it is one of the most popular dishes on the menu at Estadio. Try serving the spice-grilled chicken with a fluffy rice dish to turn it into a meal.

Yield: 4 servings.

Marinade for chicken

1 cup plain yogurt
1 shallot, sliced
1 clove garlic
1 tablespoon sambal

2 tablespoons Madras curry powder
1 tablespoon salt
3 pounds boneless chicken thighs

Combine the yogurt, shallot, garlic, sambal, curry powder, and salt in a blender and puree until smooth.

Pour over the chicken thighs and refrigerate 12 to 24 hours.

Salsa Loca

1 cup labneh, or any strained Greek yogurt
1 jalapeño

1 garlic clove
1 bunch cilantro

Combine all the ingredients in a blender and puree until smooth.

Slaw

1 head napa cabbage, thinly
  sliced
1 carrot, thinly sliced
½ red onion, thinly sliced
10 mint leaves, chopped

¼ cup cilantro leaves, chopped
1 lemon, juiced
2 tablespoons olive oil
Salt and pepper to taste

Mix the cabbage, carrot, red onion, mint, and cilantro in a large bowl. In a separate bowl, combine the lemon juice with the olive oil. Toss with the vegetables and season to taste with salt and pepper.

Assembly

2 teaspoons olive oil
Salt to taste

Remove the chicken from the marinade and wipe away any excess. Season the chicken with salt and drizzle with the olive oil. Grill over medium heat for about 6 minutes per side.

If you don't have a grill, place a nonstick skillet over medium-high heat and brown chicken on both sides for 4 minutes per side in 2 tablespoons of olive oil. After browning, finish cooking the chicken in a 400-degree preheated oven for about 8 minutes.

To plate, spoon a couple of tablespoons of salsa loca on a plate. Top with the chicken and slaw.

Courtesy of Estadio Executive Chef Haidar Karoum (p. 177).

Appendices

Appendix A: Eateries by Type

Breakfast & Brunch

Brasserie Beck, 118

Brookland Grill, 113

Chesapeake Room, The, 119

Diner, The, 114

Domku, 119

Eola, 119

Founding Farmers, 120

Georgia Brown's, 121

Greenhouse, The, 122

Highlands Cafe, 114

Juice Joint Cafe, 123

Juniper, 124

Kafe Leopold & Konditorei, 124

Lafayette, The, 124

Lincoln's Waffle Shop, 115

Luna Grill and Diner, 115

Masa 14, 125

Open City, 115

Osman and Joe's Steak and Egg Kitchen, 116

Peacock Cafe, 126

Pete's Diner, 116

Puro Cafe, 127

Seasons, 127

Tabard Inn Restaurant, 128

Ted's Bulletin, 116

Torrie's at Wilson, 117

Tunnicliff's Tavern, 117

Casual Eats

Belgian/French

Et Voila!, 188

Empanadas

Julia's Empanadas, 188

Ethiopian
Etete, 188
Zenebech Injera, 189

Italian
Pasta Mia, 189

Seafood
Tackle Box, 189

Tacos/Beach Cuisine
Surfside, 189

Coffee, Tea & Cafes
Azi's Cafe, 93
Baked & Wired, 93
Big Bear Cafe, 94
Busboys and Poets, 95
Chinatown Coffee Co., 95
Filter Coffeehouse and Espresso
 Bar, 96
Mid City Caffé, 96
Modern Times Coffeehouse at
 Politics & Prose Bookstore, 97
Peregrine Espresso, 98
Pound, 99
Qualia Coffee, 99
SOVA, 100
Tryst, 100

Cupcakes, Chocolate, Ice Cream & More
ACKC, 191
Avalon Theatre Cafe, 206
Baked & Wired, 93
Baskin Robbins Ice Cream, 206
Ben & Jerry's, 206
Biagio Fine Chocolate, 57
Broad Branch Market, 58
Capitol Creamery, 207
Chatman's D'Vine Bakery & Cafe, 193
Co Co Sala, 193
Cone E. Island, 200
Crumbs Bake Shop, 198
Dangerously Delicious Pies, 194
Dickey's Frozen Custard, 200
Dolce Gelati, 207
Dolcezza Artisanal Gelato, 201
Firehook Bakery and Coffee
 House, 195
FroZenYo, 204
Gelateria Dolce Vita, 204
Georgetown Cupcake, 195
Häagen-Dazs, 206
Hawaiian Shaved Ice, 207
Heller's Bakery, 196
Hello Cupcake, 198, 223

Hershey's Ice Cream Store, 207
Ice Cream Station, 204
Larry's, 204
Love Cafe by CakeLove, 196
Max's Best Ice Cream, 205
Mr. Yogato, 205
National Museum of Natural
   History Ice Cream and Espresso
   Bar, 207
Palm Court Coffee and Gelato
   Bar, 207
Pan Lourdes Bakery and Coffee
   Shop, 197
Patisserie Poupon, 197
Pitango Gelato, 205
Potbelly Sandwich Shop, 207
Red Velvet Cupcakery, 198
Serendipity 3 DC, 197
Shake Shack, 155, 198
Sprinkles Cupcakes, 198
Sticky Fingers, 199
Super Tacos and Bakery, 199
SweetGreen, 208
Sweet Lobby, The, 199
Tangysweet, 208
Thomas Sweet Ice Cream and
   Chocolate, 208

U-Scream Ice Cream and
   Treatery, 209
Yogen Fruz, 209
Yogiberry, 209

**Dining in Cultural
Institutions**
Bohemian Caverns, 82
Garden Cafe and the Cascade Cafe,
   The, 82
Hillwood Estate, Museum and
   Gardens, 84
Mezzanine Cafe, The, 85
Mitsitam Native Foods Cafe, 87
Roof Top Restaurant and KC
   Cafe, 88
Source by Wolfgang Puck, The, 88
Tour and Tea at the Washington
   National Cathedral, 89
Zola, 90

Foodie Getaways

Annapolis, Maryland
Annapolis Ice Cream
   Company, 265
Aqua Terra, 266
Boatyard Bar & Grill, 266

Capital Teas, 271
Chick & Ruth's Delly, 266
Luna Blu, 267
Mike's Crab House, 267
Sofi's Crepes, 267

Berkeley Springs, West Virginia
Ambrae House at Berkeley
     Springs, 255
Earthdog Cafe, 255
Fairfax Coffee Shop, 255
La Luna Gallery and Wine Bar, 256
Lot 12 Public House, 256
Tari's Premier Cafe and Inn, 256
Troubadour Lounge, 258

Culpeper, Virginia
Belmont Farm Distillery, 277
Culpeper Downtown Farmers
     Market, The, 281
Foti's, 276
Frenchman's Corner Gourmet and
     Chocolate Shop, The, 282
Frost Cafe, 277
It's About Thyme and Thyme
     Market, 277
Lucio, 277
Old House Vineyards, 279

Frederick, Maryland
Acacia, 235
Angelcakes, 235
Black Hog BBQ and Bar, 235
Brewer's Alley Restaurant, 235
Cacique Restaurant, 236
Cafe Anglais, 236
Candy Kitchen, 239
Firestone's Culinary Tavern, 236
Flying Dog Brewery, 240
Frederick Cellars, 240
Gladchuk Bros. Restaurant, 237
Moxie Bakery and Cafe, 237
Orchard, The, 237
Tasting Room, 238
Volt, 238
Zoe's Chocolate Co., 244

Leesburg, Virginia
Doener Bistro, 247
Eiffel Tower Cafe, 247
Leesburg Restaurant, 247
Leesburg Vintner, 253
Lightfoot Restaurant, 247
Lola Cookies and Treats, 248
Shoes Cup & Cork Club, 248
Vintage 50, 249
Wine Kitchen, The, 249

Middleburg, Virginia
Cuppa Giddy Up, 286
French Hound, The, 286
Hilltoppers at the Goodstone
  Inn, 287
Mello Out, 287

Food Trucks
Big Cheese, 26
CapMac, 27
Carnivore BBQ, 27
Cupcake Buggy, 28
Curbside Cupcakes, 29
DC Empanadas, 29
DC Pie Truck from Dangerously
  Delicious Pies, 31
DC Slices, 30
District of Pi's Pi on Wheels, 31
Eat Wonky, 30
Fojol Brothers of Merlindia, 31
Halal Gyro Plus, 32
Hula Girl Truck, 33
Pleasant Pops, 33
PORC, 34
Red Hook Lobster Pound, 34
Sixth & Rye, 35
Stix, 36

Sweetbites Mobile Cafe, 37
Sweetgreen's Sweetflow
  Mobile, 31
TaKorean, 37

Fun & Funky

Asian
Toki Underground, 181

Deli
Star and Shamrock Tavern and
  Deli, 181

Fusion
Zengo, 182

Indian
Indique, 178

Irish
Star and Shamrock Tavern and
  Deli, 181

Italian
Ristorante Posto, 180

Mexican
El Centro D.F, 177
H Street Country Club, 178
Oyamel, 180

Middle Eastern
Zaytinya, 181

New American
Ardeo + Bardeo, 176
Birch and Barley, 177
Lincoln, 179
PS 7, 180

Spanish Tapas
Estadio, 177

Steak
Lost Society–DC, 179

Gluten-Free Options
Acacia, 234
Baked & Wired, 93, 191
Birch and Barley, 177
Comet Ping Pong, 147
Cupcake Buggy, 28
District of Pi's Pi on Wheels, 31
Ella's Wood Fired Pizza, 148
Firefly, 167
Hello Cupcake, 198, 223
Lebanese Taverna, 157, 226
Lola Cookies and Treats, 247
Love Cafe by Cakelove, 196

Mitsitam Native Foods Cafe, 87
Open City, 115
Peacock Cafe, 126
Pete's New Haven Style Apizza, 150
Red Velvet Cupcakery, 198
Shake Shack, 155, 198
Sticky Fingers, 199
Sticky Rice DC, 144
Sweetbites Mobile Cafe, 37
Teaism, 145
Urbana Restaurant and Wine Bar,
    171, 307, 308
Zaytinya, 181
Zengo, 182

Hotel Hot Spots

American
Bourbon Steak, 131, 167
Firefly, 167

Asian
CityZen, 160
Zentan, 171

French
Adour, 165
BistroBis, 131, 166
Michel Richard Citronelle, 170

Italian
Urbana Restaurant and Wine
   Bar, 171

New American
Art and Soul, 165
Blue Duck Tavern, 166
Bourbon Steak, 131, 167
Greenhouse, The, 122
Juniper, 124
Lafayette, The, 124
Poste Modern Brasserie, 170
Seasons, 127
Tabard Inn Restaurant, 128

Seafood
Todd Gray's Watershed, 171

Steak
J&G Steakhouse, 168

Kosher
Crumbs Bake Shop, 198
Maoz Vegetarian, 157
Sixth & Rye, 35
Souper Girl, 47
Sunflower Bakery, 49

Lunch (Casual)

Asian
Chinatown Express (Chinese), 139
Sticky Rice DC (sushi), 144
Teaism, 145

Barbecue
Capital Q BBQ, 139
Hill Country BBQ and Market, 142
Khan's Bar and Grill
   (Mongolian), 143

Burgers
Good Stuff Cafe (burgers), 142

Half-Smokes
DC-3 (half-smokes), 142

Indian
Rasika, 144, 175

Sandwiches/Salads
Bread and Brew, 138
Breadline, 139
MGM Roast Beef, 143
Mixt Green (salads), 144

Tex-Mex
Well Dressed Burrito, The, 145

Vegetarian
Java Green, 143

Lunch (Power)

American
Central Michel Richard, 132
701 Restaurant, 137

French
BistroBis, 133, 166

Italian
Bibiana Osteria-Enoteca, 131
Ristorante Tosca, 136

New American
Bourbon Steak, 131, 167
DC Coast Restaurant, 133
Equinox Restaurant, 134
Oval Room, The, 135

Seafood
Johnny's Half Shell Restaurant, 134
Old Ebbitt Grill, 135

Steak
Caucus Room, The, 132
Charlie Palmer Steak, 132
Monocle Restaurant, The, 134
Palm Restaurant, 136

Neighborhood Feel

American
Bar Pilar, 183
Meridian Pint, 186

Barbecue
Smoke & Barrel, 187

Beer
Meridian Pint, 186
Queen Vic, The (Pub), 186
Smoke & Barrel, 186

Belgian
Brasserie Beck, 118, 184
Granville Moore's Belgium Beer
    and Gastropub, 184

Cafe
Cafe Saint-Ex, 184

Chinese
Meiwah Restaurant, 185

Fusion
901 Restaurant and Bar, 186

Mediterranean
Acacia Bistro & Wine Bar, 182

Middle Eastern
Souk, 187

New American
Atlas Room, The, 183
Local 16, 185

Wine Bar
Vinoteca, 187

Nights Out

American
RIS, 175
1789, 176

Creole
Acadiana, 172, 220

French
Marcel's, 174
Montmartre, 174

Indian
Rasika, 144, 175

Italian
Fiola, 167

New American
Corduroy, 173
Palena Restaurant, 174
Proof, 174

Seafood
BlackSalt Restaurant, 173

Pizza, Burgers & Falafel

Burgers
BGR, The Burger Joint, 154
Chef Geoff's, 154
Five Guys Burgers and Fries, 154
Matchbox: Chinatown, 154
Palena Cafe, 155
Reef, The, 155
Shake Shack, 155, 198
Sign of the Whale, 155
Wonderland Ballroom, The, 155

Falafel
Amsterdam Falafelshop, 156
Greek Deli & Catering, 157
Lebanese Taverna, 157, 226
Maoz Vegetarian, 157
Old City Cafe, 158
Shawafel, 158
vFalafel, 158

Pizza

Comet Ping Pong, 147
Coppi's Organic Restaurant, 147
Ella's Wood Fired Pizza, 148
Il Canale, 149
Italian Pizza Kitchen, 149
Matchbox, 149
Pete's New Haven Style
    Apizza, 150
Pizza Paradiso, 150
Radius Pizza, 151
RedRocks, 151
Seventh Hill Pizza, 152
2Amys, 152
Upper Crust Pizzeria, The, 153
Vace, 153
We, the Pizza, 153

Tasting Tables

American

Wine Room at Occidental,
    The, 164

Asian

CityZen, 160

Italian

Obelisk, 162

Japanese

Sushi Taro, 163

Mediterranean/Eclectic

Komi, 161

Molecular Gastronomy

Minibar, 161

New American

Rogue 24, 162

Thai

Thai X-ing, 163

Underground Restaurants & Speakeasies

Columbia Room, 104
DC Grey Farmers' Market, 104
Dining Under the Table, 105
Gibson, The, 106
Hush Supper Club, 107
Outstanding in the Field, 109
Patrón Social Club's Patrón Secret
    Dining Society, 109
PX, 110
Wok+Wine, 111

Appendix B: Cooking Classes, Shopping, Food-Related Services, and Agriculture

Community-supported Agriculture (CSAs)
Claggett Farm, 46
Great County Farms, 46
Lamb's Quarter, The, 46
Norman's Farm Market, 46
Sligo Creek Farm, 46

Composting
Compost Cab, 51

Compost Crew, The, 51
Envirelation, 51
Fat Worm Compost, 51

Cooking Classes
Acadiana, 220
BLT Steak, 221
Cheesetique, 221
Cookology, 222
CulinAerie, 222

Fancy Cakes by Leslie, 223
Hello Cupcake, 223
Hill's Kitchen, 224
Just Simply . . . Cuisine, 224
L'Academie de Cuisine, 225
Lebanese Taverna, 226
Passenger, The, 226
Seasonal Pantry, 228
Thai Basil, 227
Toscana Cafe and Catering, 228
Zola Wine & Kitchen, 229

**Food-Related Nonprofit
Organizations**
Capital Area Food Bank, 211
DC Central Kitchen, 213
Food & Friends, 214
Martha's Table, 214
Mid-Atlantic Gleaning
    Network, 215
Miriam's Kitchen, 215
SOME (So Others Might Eat), 218
Washington Youth Garden, 219

Home Delivery Services
Arganica Farm Club, 41
Bon Vivant, 42

Field to City, 43
First Vine, 43
Grassroots Gourmet, 44
Harvest Delivered, 45
Milk Moo-vers, 45
Soupergirl, 47
South Mountain Creamery, 49
Urban Tastes, 50
Washington's Green Grocer, 51
White House Meats, 53

Shopping
A Litteri, Inc., 56
All African Food Store, 57
A Mano, 56
And Beige, 57
Biagio Fine Chocolate, 57
BlackSalt Fish Market, 58
Broad Branch Market, 58
Butler's Orchard, 74
Calvert Woodley Wines &
    Spirits, 59
Canon's Fish Market, 59
Capital City Market/Florida Avenue
    Market, 67
Chez Hareg Gourmet Bakery, 60
Comus Market, 77

Cork Market and Tasting Room, 60

Cowgirl Creamery, 60

Dupont Circle FRESHFARM
  Market, 68

Eastern Market, 69

FarmAtHome Produce, 76

14th and U Farmers Market, 69

FRESHFARM Market by the White
  House, 70

Frog Eye Farm, 76

Glover Park—Burleith Farmers'
  Market, 71

Hana Japanese Market, 61

Hill's Kitchen, 61

Home Rule, 62

Homestead Farm, 78

Kingsbury's Orchard, 79

Le Petit Corner Store, 62

Lewis Orchard Fresh Farm
  Produce, 80

Maine Avenue Fish Market, 71

Mt. Pleasant Farmers Market, 72

New Morning Farm Market, 72

Palena Market, 63

P&C Market, 62

Periwinkle, 63

Petworth Community Market, 73

Rodman's Discount Gourmet, 64

Schneider's of Capitol Hill, 64

Seasonal Pantry, 64

Seven Oaks Lavender Farm, 80

Shemali's, 65

Tabletop, 65

Taylor Gourmet, 66

Tea and Spice Exchange, The, 66

Trohv, 66

Wagshal's, 67

Index

Acacia, 235

Acacia Bistro & Wine Bar, 182

Acadiana, 172, 220, 300, 301

ACKC, 191

Adams Morgan Day Festival, 17

Adour, 165

A Litteri, Inc., 56

All African Food Store, 57

A Mano, 56

Ambrae House at Berkeley
    Springs, 255

Amsterdam Falafelshop, 156

And Beige, 57

Angelcakes, 235

Annapolis City Dock, 267

Annapolis Ice Cream Company, 265

Annapolis Inn, The, 273

Annapolis Maritime Museum, 268

Annapolis Powerboat School
    and the Annapolis Sailing
    School, 268

Annual Seed Exchange at Brookside
    Gardens, 8

Aqua Terra, 266

Ardeo + Bardeo, 176

Arganica Farm Club, 41

Art and Soul, 165

ARTINI Cocktail Celebration, 10

Arugula Files (blog), 8

Ashby Inn and Restaurant,
    The, 282

Asia Festival, 15

Atlas Room, The, 183

Avalon Theatre Cafe, 206

Azi's Cafe, 93

Baked & Wired, 93, 191

Banneker-Douglass Museum,
    The, 268

Bar Pilar, 183

Barrack's Row Festival, 17

Baskin Robbins Ice Cream, 206

Belmont Farm Distillery, 277
Ben & Jerry's, 206
Ben's Chili Bowl, 137
Berkeley Springs Apple Butter
    Festival, 19
Berkeley Springs International
    Water Tasting and
    Competition, 9
Berkeley Springs State Park, 257
Best Bites (blog), 8
BGR, The Burger Joint, 154
Biagio Fine Chocolate, 57, 192
Bibiana Osteria-Enoteca, 131
Big Bear Cafe, 94
Big Cheese, 26
Birch and Barley, 177
BistroBis, 131, 166
Black Hog BBQ and Bar, 235
BlackSalt Fish Market, 58
BlackSalt Restaurant, 173
BLT Steak, 221
Blue Duck Tavern, 166, 305
Boatyard Bar & Grill, 266
Bohemian Caverns, 82
Bon Vivant, 42
Bourbon Steak, 131, 167
Bowie International Festival, 19

Brainfood Grill-Off, 17
Brasserie Beck, 118, 184
Bread and Brew, 138
Breadline, 139
Brew at the Zoo, 15
Brewer's Alley Restaurant, 235
Briar Patch Bed and Breakfast, 287
Broad Branch Market, 58, 206
Brookland Grill, 113
Busboys and Poets, 95
Butler's Orchard, 74
Butler's Orchard Annual Pumpkin
    Festival, 19
Butler's Orchard Holiday Open
    House, 22

Cacapon Resort State Park, 261
Cacique Restaurant, 236
Cafe Anglais, 236
Cafe Saint-Ex, 184
Calvert Woodley Wines & Spirits, 59
Cameleer, The, 281
Candy Kitchen, 239
Canon's Fish Market, 59
Capital Area Food Bank, 211
Capital Area Food Bank's Blue Jean
    Ball, 216

Capital City Market/Florida Avenue
   Market, 67
Capital Q BBQ, 139
Capital Spice (blog), 8
Capital Teas, 271
Capital Wine Festival, 8
Capitol Creamery, 207
CapMac, 27, 321, 322
CapMac Bolognese, 321
Carnivore BBQ, 27
Casa Nova, 272
Caucus Room, The, 132
Central Michel Richard, 132
Charlie Palmer Steak, 132
Chatman's D'Vine Bakery
   & Cafe, 193
Cheese, 167
Cheesecake Farms Bed, Barn and
   Breakfast, 283
Cheesetique, 221
Chef Geoff's, 154
Chesapeake Room, The, 119
Chez Hareg Gourmet Bakery, 60
Chick & Ruth's Delly, 266
Child, Julia, 86
Chinatown Coffee Co., 95
Chinatown Express, 139

Chocolate Lovers Festival, 10
CityZen, 160
Claggett Farm, 46
Clarke Hardware, 281
Clothes Minded, 291
Co Co Sala, 193
Columbia Room, 104
Comet Ping Pong, 147
Community Bridge Mural and
   Carroll Creek Park Canal, 239
Compost Cab, 51
Compost Crew, The, 51
Comus Market, 77
Cone E. Island, 200
Cookology, 222
Coppi's Organic Restaurant, 147
Corduroy, 173
Cork Market and Tasting Room, 60
Cork Recycling, 169
Cottage: Well Loved Furnishings,
   The, 252
Country Inn at Berkeley Springs,
   The, 262
Covered bridges, 242
Cowgirl Creamery, 60
"Cream" of Asparagus Soup, 313
Crème de la Crème, 252

Crepes at the Market, 123
Crumbs Bake Shop, 198
CulinAerie, 222
Culpeper County Court House, 278
Culpeper County Library,
    The, 278
Culpeper Downtown Farmers
    Market, The, 281
Culpeper Train Depot and the
    Culpeper Visitor Center, 278
Cunningham Falls State
    Park Annual Maple Syrup
    Demonstration, 10
Cupcake Buggy, 28
Cuppa Giddy Up, 286
Curbside Cupcakes, 29

Daily Candy (blog), 7
Dangerously Delicious Pies, 194
DC-3, 142
DC Central Kitchen, 213
DC Central Kitchen and Martha's
    Table Sunday Night Suppers, 216
DC Coast Restaurant, 133
DC Empanadas, 29
D.C. Foodies (blog), 8
DC Grey Farmers' Market, 104

DC Pie Truck from Dangerously
    Delicious Pies, 31
DC Slices, 30
DC VegFest, 17
Delaplane Strawberry Festival, 12
Destination DC (blog), 7
Dickey's Frozen Custard, 200
Dine Out for Farms, 20
Diner, The, 114
Dining Under the Table, 105
District Domestic, The (blog), 8
District of Pi's Pi on Wheels, 31
Dodona Manor, 249
Doener Bistro, 247
Dolce Gelati, 207
Dolcezza Artisanal Gelato, 201
Domku, 119
Duchessa, 291
Dupont Circle Fountain, 140
Dupont Circle FRESHFARM
    Market, 68

Earthdog Cafe, 255
Eastern Market, 69
Eat Washington (blog), 8
Eat Wonky, 30
Eiffel Tower Cafe, 247

El Centro D.F., 177
Ella's Wood Fired Pizza, 148
Empanada de Pollos
    Ensapados, 297
Envirelation, 51
Eola, 119
Equinox Restaurant, 134
Esoterica, 252
Estadio, 177, 325, 326
Estadio Spice-Grilled Chicken, 325
Etete, 188
Et Voila!, 188

Fairfax Coffee Shop, 255
Fancy Cakes by Leslie, 223
FarmAtHome Produce, 76
Fat Worm Compost, 51
Fauquier County Fair, 15
Field to City, 43
Fiesta Washington, DC, 17
Filter Coffeehouse and Espresso
    Bar, 96
Fiola, 173
Firefly, 167, 302, 304
Firehook Bakery and Coffee
    House, 195
Firestone's Culinary Tavern, 236

First Vine, 43
Five Guys Burgers and Fries, 154
Flying Dog Brewery, 240
Fojol Brothers of Merlindia, 31
Food and Wine Festival at National
    Harbor, The, 12
Food Festival of the Americas, 12
Food & Friends, 214, 216
Food & Friends, Dining Out for
    Life, 217
Food Safety Summit Conference
    and Exhibition, The, 11
Foti's, 276
Founding Farmers, 120
Fountain Hall Bed & Breakfast, 283
Four Centuries Walking Tour, 269
Four Seasons Hotel, The, 169
14th and U Farmers Market, 69
Frederick Beer Week, 12
Frederick Cellars, 240
French Hound, The, 286
Frenchman's Corner Gourmet and
    Chocolate Shop, The, 282
FreshFarm Farmland Feast, 21
FRESHFARM Market by the White
    House, 70
Fresh Start Catering, 213

Frog Eye Farm, 76
Frost Cafe, 277
FroZenYo, 204
Funny Farm Inn, The, 284
Fun Shop, The, 291

Gallery, 283
Garden Cafe, 299
Garden Cafe and the Cascade Cafe, The, 82
Geeta's Chai, 306
Gelateria Dolce Vita, 204
Georgetown Cupcake, 195
Georgetown Waterfront Park, 140
Georgia Brown's, 121
Germantown Oktoberfest, 17
Gibson, The, 106
Gladchuk Bros. Restaurant, 237
Glover Park—Burleith Farmers' Market, 71
Gluten-Free Pecan Butterscotch Cake, 318
Gobblers Knob Guest House, 262
Goodstone Inn and Estate, 288
Good Stuff Cafe, 142
Grandma Goodell's Famous Chocolate Chip Cookies, 323

Granville Moore's Belgium Beer and Gastropub, 184
Grapes with the Apes, 17
Grassroots Gourmet, 44, 295, 296
Grassroots Gourmet's Peanut Butter Buttercream, 295
Gravelly Point Park, 140
Great County Farms, 46
Great Latke vs. Hamentasch Debate, The, 10
Great Meadow, 289
Greek Deli & Catering, 157
Greenhouse, The, 122
Grilled Red Wine Braised Octopus with Smoked Avocado, Roasted Olive Gremolata & Olive Aioli, 302

Häagen-Dazs, 206
Hains Point, 141
Halal Gyro Plus, 32
Hammond-Harwood House, 269
Hana Japanese Market, 61
Harvest Delivered, 45
Hastening Antiques, 292
Hawaiian Shaved Ice, 207

Hazel River Inn Bed and Breakfast, The, 284

Heart of America Foundation's Sweet Charity, The, 11

Hearts Delight Wine Tasting and Auction, 13

Heath Studio Gallery, 259

Heller's Bakery, 196

Hello Cupcake, 198, 223

Hershey's Ice Cream Store, 207

Highlands Cafe, 114

Highlawn Inn, 263

Hill Country BBQ and Market, 142

Hill House Bed and Breakfast, 245

Hill's Kitchen, 61, 224

Hilltoppers at the Goodstone Inn, 287

Hillwood Estate, Museum, and Gardens, 84

Homeopathy Works, 259

Home Rule, 62

Homestead Farm, 78

Homestead Farm Corn Roast, 16

H Street Bakes, 193

H Street Country Club, 178

H Street Festival, 18

Hula Girl Truck, 33

Hush Supper Club, 107, 306

Ice Cream Station, 204

Ice House, 257

Idyll Time Farm, Cottage & Stabling, 253

Il Canale, 149

Indique, 178

Inn at Stone Manor Bed and Breakfast, The, 245

International Wine and Food Festival, 9

Italian Pizza Kitchen, 149

It's About Thyme and Thyme Market, 277

Java Green, 143

J&G Steakhouse, 168

Johnny's Half Shell Restaurant, 134

Juice Joint Cafe, 123

Julia's Empanadas, 188

Juniper, 124

Just Simply . . . Cuisine, 224

Kafe Leopold & Konditorei, 124

Kenilworth Park and Aquatic Gardens, 141

Khan's Bar and Grill, 143
Kingsbury's Orchard, 79
Kitchen Studio, The, 241
Komi, 161
Kunta Kinte–Alex Haley Memorial,
    The, 269

L'Academie de Cuisine, 225
Lafayette, The, 124
La Festa Italiana, 20
La Luna Gallery and Wine Bar, 256
Lamb Jam, 13
Lamb's Quarter, The, 46
Lansdowne Resort, 253
Larry's, 204
Lavender Farm Festival, 14
Lebanese Taverna, 157, 226, 333
Leesburg Antique Emporium, 252
Leesburg Flower and Garden
    Festival, 11
Leesburg Kiwanis Halloween
    Parade, 20
Leesburg Restaurant, 247
Leesburg Vintner, 253
Le Petit Corner Store, 62
Lewis Orchard Fresh Farm
    Produce, 80

Lightfoot Restaurant, 247
Lilac Bijoux, 272
Lincoln, 179
Lincoln's Waffle Shop, 115
Local 16, 185
Lola Cookies and Treats, 248
Lost Society–DC, 179
Lot 12 Public House, 256
Loudoun County Museum, 250
Louisiana Crawfish Etouffée with
    Mahatma Rice, 300
Love Cafe by CakeLove, 196
Lucio, 277
Luna Blu, 267
Luna Grill and Diner, 115

Madisonbelle, 253
Maine Avenue Fish Market, 71
Manassas Wine and Jazz
    Festival, 14
Manor Inn Bed and Breakfast,
    The, 264
Maoz Vegetarian, 157
Marcel's, 174
Martha's Table, 214
Maryland Irish Festival, 18
Maryland Renaissance Festival, 18

Maryland Seafood Festival, 18

Maryland State Fair at the
  Timonium Fairground, 16

Maryland State House, 270

Maryland Wine Festival, 18

Masa 14, 125

Matchbox, 149

Matchbox: Chinatown, 154

Max's Best Ice Cream, 205

McCutcheon's Factory Store, 241

Meiwah Restaurant, 185

Mello Out, 287

Meridian Hill Park, 141

Meridian Pint, 186

Metrocurean (blog), 8

Metropolitan Cooking and
  Entertaining Show, The, 21

Mezzanine Cafe, The, 85

MGM Roast Beef, 143

Michel Richard Citronelle, 170

Mid-Atlantic Gleaning
  Network, 215

Mid-Atlantic Red Fruit Festival,
  The, 18

Mid City Caffé, 96

Middleburg Country Inn, 288

Middleburg Spring Races, 290

Middleburg Tack Exchange, 292

Mike's Crab House, 267

Milk Moo-vers, 45

Minibar, 161

Miriam's Kitchen, 215, 217,
  311, 312

Miriam's Kitchen Venison Pot
  Pie, 311

Mitsitam Cafe, 309, 310

Mitsitam Native Foods Cafe, 87

Mixt Green, 144

Modern Times Coffeehouse at
  Politics & Prose Bookstore, 97

Molly's Meanderings, 241

Monocle Restaurant, The, 134

Montgomery County Farm Tour and
  Harvest Sale, 15

Montmartre, 174

Morgan County Observatory, 257

Morven Park, 250

Mountain Laurel Gallery, 259

Mount Pony Theater, 280

Mount Vernon's Spring Wine
  Festival and Sunset Tour, 13

Mount Vernon Wine Festival, 20

Moxie Bakery and Cafe, 237

Mr. Yogato, 205

Mt. Pleasant Farmers Market, 72
Muse, The, 242
Museum of Culpeper History, 279

National Asian Heritage Festival, 13
National Building Museum
    Gingerbread Workshop, The, 22
National Gallery of Art, 297
National Harbor Outdoor Holiday
    Market, 22
National Museum of Natural History
    Ice Cream and Espresso Bar, 207
National's Park baseball
    stadium, 207
National Sporting Library,
    The, 289
New Morning Farm Market, 72
901 Restaurant and Bar, 186
Norman's Farm Market, 46
Norris House Inn, The, 254

Obelisk, 162
Old City Cafe, 158
Old Ebbitt Grill, 135
Old House Vineyards, 279
Open-Air French Market, 11
Open City, 115

Orchard, The, 237
Osman and Joe's Steak and Egg
    Kitchen, 116
Outstanding in the Field, 109
Oval Room, The, 135
Oyamel, 180
Oyamel Annual Day of the Dead
    "Dia de los Muertos" Festival, 21

Palena Cafe, 155
Palena Market, 63
Palena Restaurant, 174
Palm Court Coffee and Gelato
    Bar, 207
Palm Restaurant, 136
Pan Lourdes Bakery and Coffee
    Shop, 197
Park Hyatt Masters of Food & Wine
    Tour of the World, 14
Passenger, The, 226
Pasta Mia, 189
Patisserie Poupon, 197
Patrón Social Club's Patrón Secret
    Dining Society, 109
P&C Market, 62
Peacock Cafe, 126
Peeps & Co., 194

Peregrine Espresso, 98
Periwinkle, 63
Pete's Diner, 116
Pete's New Haven Style Apizza, 150
Petworth Community Market, 73
Phillips Collection's Annual Gala,
    The, 13
Pitango Gelato, 205
Pizza Paradiso, 150
Pleasant Pops, 33
Pocket Meadow Farms, 259
PORC, 34
Poste Modern Brasserie, 170
Potbelly Sandwich Shop, 207
Pound, 99
Proof, 174
PS 7, 180
Puro Cafe, 127
PX, 110

Qualia Coffee, 99
Queen Vic, The, 186

Radius Pizza, 151
Rasika, 144, 175
Recycling Works, 260
Red Fox Inn, The, 289

Red Hook Lobster Pound, 34
RedRocks, 151
Red Velvet Cupcakery, 198
Reef, The, 155
Reggae Festival, 15
Re-Sails, 272
Richmond Greek Festival, 13
RIS, 175, 316, 318, 320
Ristorante Posto, 180
Ristorante Tosca, 136
Roasted Beet Salad, 305
Rodman's Discount Gourmet, 64
Rogue 24, 162
Roof Top Restaurant and KC
    Cafe, 88
Royal Folly, 273

Safeway National Capital Barbecue
    Battle, 14
SAVOR: An American Craft Beer &
    Food Experience, 14
Scallop Margarita with Tequila
    Ice, 314
Schneider's of Capitol Hill, 64, 169
Schooner Woodwind, 274
Sculpture Garden at the National
    Gallery of Art, 141

Seasonal Pantry, 64, 228

Seasons, 127

Serendipity 3 DC, 197

Serene Acres, 290

Seven Oaks Lavender Farm, 80

701 Restaurant, 137

1789, 176

Seventh Hill Pizza, 152

Shake Shack, 155, 198

Share Our Strength's Taste of the
  Nation, 11

Shawafel, 158

Shellfish Stew with Coconut &
  Lime, 307

Shemali's, 65

Shoes Cup & Cork Club, 248

Sign of the Whale, 155

Sixth & Rye, 35

Sligo Creek Farm, 46

Smithsonian Folklife Festival, 16

Smoke & Barrel, 187

Sofi's Crepes, 267

SOME: Empty Bowls, 217

SOME (So Others Might Eat), 218

Songkran Festival, 12

Souk, 187

Soupergirl, 47, 313

Source by Wolfgang Puck, The, 88

Southern Maryland Celtic Festival
  and Highland Gathering, 12

South Mountain Creamery, 49

SOVA, 100

Spanish Steps, The, 141

Sprinkles Cupcakes, 198

Star and Shamrock Tavern and
  Deli, 181

Star Theater, 258

State House Inn, The, 274

Sticky Fingers, 199

Sticky Rice DC, 144

Stix, 36

St. Jude Gourmet Gala, 9

Sugar & Champagne Affair, 8

Suites at 249, 285

Summer Fancy Food Show, 16

Summer Restaurant Week, 16

Sunflower Bakery, 49

Super Tacos and Bakery, 199

Surfside, 189

Sushi Taro, 163

Sweetbites Mobile Cafe, 37

SweetGreen, 208

Sweetgreen's Sweetflow Mobile, 31

Sweet Lobby, The, 199

Tabard Inn Restaurant, 128

Tabletop, 65

Tackle Box, 189

TaKorean, 37

Tangysweet, 208

Tari's Premier Cafe and Inn, 256

Taste of Bethesda, 20

Taste of Georgetown, 20

Taste of Success, 20

Tasting Room, 238

Tasting Table (blog), 7

Taylor Gourmet, 66

Tea and Spice Exchange, The, 66

Teaism, 145

Ted's Bulletin, 116

Thai Basil, 227

Thai X-ing, 163

Thomas Balch Library, 251

Thomas Sweet Ice Cream and
    Chocolate, 208

Thyme Inn, 285

Tilghman Island Seafood
    Festival, 15

Todd Gray's Watershed, 171

Toki Underground, 181

Torrie's at Wilson, 117

Toscana Cafe and Catering, 228

Tour and Tea at the Washington
    National Cathedral, 89

Trohv, 66

Troubadour Lounge, 258

Tryst, 100

Tunnicliff's Tavern, 117

Turkish Festival, 20

2Amys, 152

United States Naval Academy, 270

Upper Crust Pizzeria, The, 153

Urbana Restaurant and Wine Bar,
    171, 307, 308

Urban Tastes, 50

U-Scream Ice Cream and
    Treatery, 209

Vace, 153

vFalafel, 158

Vinoteca, 187

Vintage 50, 249

Virginia Fall Races, 290

Virginia Wine Month, 21

Vivo, 272

Volt, 238

Wagshal's, 67

Washington's Green Grocer, 51
Washington Ukrainian Festival, 19
Washington Youth Garden, 219
Waterford Homes Tour and Crafts
    Exhibit, 21
Water tasting, 260
Weinberg Center for the Arts, 244
Well Dressed Burrito, The, 145
Westin Annapolis, The, 275
We, the Pizza, 153
WhiteBench, 292
White House Meats, 53
Wide World of Wines, 169
Wild and Crazy Pearl (blog), 8
Wild Rice Salad from the National
    Museum of the American
    Indian's Mitsitam Cafe, 309
William Paca House and
    Garden, 271
Wine Entrepreneur Conference, 19
Wine Kitchen, The, 249

Wine Room at Occidental, The, 164
Winter Restaurant Week, 9
Wok+Wine, 111
Wonderland Ballroom, The, 155
World Fare: A Street Food
    Festival, 21

Yogen Früz, 209
Yogiberry, 209
Young and Hungry (blog), 8

Zaytinya, 181
Zenebech Injera, 189
Zengo, 182
Zentan, 171
Zoe's Chocolate Co., 244
Zola, 90, 317
Zola Strawberry Basil Smash, 317
Zola Wine & Kitchen, 229
ZooFari, 14